PELICAN BOOKS

THE INNOCENT EYE

Arthur Calder-Marshall was born on August 19, 1908. He was educated at St. Paul's School and Hertford College, Oxford. Although he is best known for his novels, his many books also include biographies, works for children, and travel accounts, as well as an autobiography, *THE MAGIC OF MY YOUTH*. He has written for films, and for several years worked closely with the British Documentary Film Movement, although he was not "a member of the inner circle." He based *THE INNOCENT EYE*, as he described in the book, on a manuscript written by Paul Rotha and Basil Wright, the two well-known documentary film-makers, which is now lodged with The Museum of Modern Art Film Library in New York.

THE INNOCENT EYE

The life of ROBERT J. FLAHERTY

ARTHUR CALDER-MARSHALL

Based on research material by
PAUL ROTHA *and* BASIL WRIGHT

PENGUIN BOOKS INC

Penguin Books Inc.
7110 Ambassador Road
Baltimore, Maryland 21207

First published in Great Britain by W. H. Allen & Co. 1963
First published in the U.S.A. by
Harcourt, Brace & World, Inc. 1966
Published in Pelican Books 1970

SBN 14 021143 8

Printed in the United States of America by
Kingsport Press, Inc.
Set in Bembo

CONTENTS

APPENDICES

ILLUSTRATIONS

Foreword

When Robert Flaherty died in 1951, Paul Rotha and Basil Wright were asked by an English publisher to write a book in tribute to the man who was the 'founder of the Documentary Movement'. Richard Griffith's *The World of Robert Flaherty*, though published after Flaherty's death, had been written almost completely during Flaherty's lifetime. Although planned as an exhaustive study, Flaherty's death hastened publication and through no fault of the author the book was more in the nature of a sketch. Something fuller was needed.

Mrs. Flaherty agreed that something much fuller was needed. But she proposed that someone else should write a definite and monumental work, which could only be undertaken with a grant from one of the great American foundations.

The grant failed to materialize. In 1951 Rotha and Wright were approached by another English publisher. This time Mrs. Flaherty did not oppose the suggestion. She generously made available Flaherty's published work for quotation and also threw open the archives of the Robert J. Flaherty Foundation in Brattleboro. She did not, however, in view of her many commitments, feel that it would be possible to collaborate to the extent of giving her personal recollections, except in so far as they had already been recorded in her book *Elephant Dance* and her lecture notes.

Rotha and Wright intended to produce the book as a combined operation, making it a sort of biographical film history. But being active film-makers, they found that their periods of leisure did not coincide. Together they screened all the Flaherty pictures and made the digests which are printed in Appendices 1–5. But from then on the brunt of the work fell upon Rotha.

Even for him, it was a part-time occupation, filling in gaps between his own films. He went to New York, interviewing people who had known Flaherty. In August, 1957, he visited Frances and David Flaherty at Brattleboro. He wrote innumerable letters and collected reams of reminiscences, especially from David Flaherty, Newton Rowe, John Goldman, John Grierson, Helen van Dongen, J. P. R. Golightly, E. Hayter Preston and Irving Lerner.[1] He consulted innumerable film books and periodicals for contemporary views of Flaherty's work. He collated these materials, submitted them to a number of people and collated their comments on them. At the same time, he collected a larger number of magnificent still pictures which he arranged with the careful skill for which he is renowned.

The result was an encyclopaedic assembly of research material of great value to students of the film. The typescript of this work is now lodged with The Museum of Modern Art Film Library, New York, so that students may consult it.

The publisher who had commissioned the book felt that the interest of this work would be confined to too small and scholarly a public and he suggested that a book about a character as colourful and adventurous as Robert Flaherty could be designed to meet a far wider public. After all, the research had been done.

When Rotha told me of his difficulty in meeting the publisher's request, I was able to sympathize. If one takes great pains to produce one sort of book, it is psychologically almost impossible to unscramble it and make an entirely different type of book.

At the same time, when reading the comments of the publisher (who by then had rejected the typescript) I could understand what he

[1] A full list of acknowledgements will be found on p. 292.

had been driving at. Flaherty's life and personality were interesting to a far larger public than that for which Rotha had written.

Two other publishers, Messrs. W. H. Allen in London and Doubleday in New York, professed an interest in the book, provided that it was rewritten on the lines advocated by the first publishers; and Rotha asked me if I would do, what he considered to be, a work of editing his material.

I knew that this could not be done. The book had to be entirely recast, if it was to be turned from a biographical film history into an exploration of the life and art of Robert Flaherty and a study of his films. If it was so recast, the material accumulated by Rotha and Wright would inevitably be worked over by my mind and would become something different from what either of them had intended.

Though for several years I worked closely with the British Documentary Film Movement, I am not and never was a member of the inner circle. I am not primarily a writer for films and I foresaw that if I tried merely to edit the Rotha-Wright typescript, I would fail to give it what the publishers wanted. So I insisted that if I undertook the work, I should be at liberty to take the typescript and make of it whatever I could, submitting my final draft to Rotha and Wright for their comments, but taking the responsibility for all judgements in any case where I might deviate from them.

I confess that there have been several deviations, because I have followed a different discipline. Rotha set out to record in detail the reception of each film. I have concentrated on the values the films seem to me to have in 1963. Rotha looked back on Flaherty's completed career. I have tried imperfectly to live it forward with Flaherty himself. The reader may consider that I have made assumptions which I cannot prove. I admit it. I have had to use intuition alone, where normally I would use my own sort of cross-checking with research. On the other hand I have benefited from a type of research I might have neglected.

Those who scan these pages for the classic stories of the Flaherty saga will be disappointed. Pearls of anecdotage they may be, but when cast before this swine, they appeared to contain grains of truth too minute to be worth the labour of a shattering examination. They belong rather to the biographies of the men who tell these stories than to that of the man who was their subject.

I want to thank Basil Wright and Paul Rotha, the latter especially, considering the enormous amount of work he had already put in, for making over this material for a book with every conclusion of which they may not necessarily agree. And even more I want to thank my wife, not merely for the arduous working of typing and re-typing, but also for her sharp, critical challenging of loose phrasing and judgements passed without due consideration, even when this meant entire recasting of sections or chapters.

A. C-M.

NOTE

We are indeed grateful to our old friend Arthur Calder-Marshall for writing this biography based on our earlier MS. We should record, however, as he himself states above, that there are divergences in assessment. These occur almost wholly in Chapter 19, *The Epilogue*.

In particular we do not accept the theory that Flaherty, whom we knew so well, needed those periods of enforced idleness between his films in order to prepare himself for the next task. If allowed, we believe he could have been active filmwise all along the years from *Nanook*.

P.R. B.W.

NOTE FROM JOHN GRIERSON

As Arthur Calder-Marshall suggests, we have all been somewhat fanciful in our more personal accounts of Flaherty. This came partly from the conversational respite he gave us when he blew into town. It was not the least of his gifts that he engaged us richly in that Canadian tradition of story telling which insists that Paul Bunyan, Holy Old Mackinaw and all Enchanted Wanderers are not the less real for being improbable. But Arthur Calder-Marshall is now right to say that we have done him less than justice. He was never really the roistering character our legend suggested; and if the film business was a Nessus shirt for him, be sure it was because he was in the fact something of a *grand seigneur* whose more gracious habit was bound to be hurt by it. I am glad of this more objective picture: even if, at times, some of us seem hardly worthy of him. No matter: this is Flaherty's book, not ours.

J. G.

PART ONE

I THE MINERS AND THE MOCCASINS

Robert Joseph Flaherty was born in Iron Mountain, Michigan on 16th February, 1884.

His father, Robert Henry Flaherty, was the son of an Irish Protestant who had left Ireland in the middle of the nineteenth century for Quebec. Flahertys had spread across southern Canada and the northern United States in search of the fortunes which were to be made so much easier than in the land of potato famines. Just north and south of the 42nd parallel there were more opportunities than people and at first sight it was just a question of choosing from what one should get rich. Optimism was as enormous as the unexploited resources.

Robert Henry Flaherty opted for mining. In Minnesota and Michigan iron and copper mines were being opened up right and left. Fortunes were amassed in a few years, sometimes even in months. It was the American dream come true.

Robert Henry Flaherty, well on the way to making a fortune, married Susan Klöckner, a girl from a Roman Catholic family that came from Coblenz, Germany. She was a devout woman. Her confession and attendance at Mass were regular, though she did not convert her husband to the faith.

There were to be seven children of this marriage. Of these Robert Joseph (Bob) Flaherty, the concern of this book, was the eldest. It would be interesting if we had details of his early life. That we haven't indicates that in his early years, he had a sense of security. The incidents of happy childhood are as hidden as the bricks in the foundation of a good building.

Jack London, who was eight years older than Bob Flaherty and in some ways similar in his responses to the urges of time, remembered the horrors of personal insecurity at the age of five, when he got paralytically drunk.

But Bob Flaherty's first memory dated only from 1893, when he was aged nine. His father was owner-manager of an iron-ore mine. He was in Bob's eyes a great man, and Bob as the boss's son was a specially privileged person, born with an iron-ore spoon in his mouth.

In 1893 a panic slump swept the United States. The mine had to be closed down. The miners were locked out. The Flahertys, who had their life savings invested in the mine, were suddenly faced with the obverse side of the land of opportunity. In the United States you were free, not merely to make a fortune, but also to go to the wall, bankrupt because of economic conditions outside your control.

Nine-year-old Bob Flaherty must have heard talk about this during the lock-out, have known that the security on which he as the boss's son depended was suddenly ebbing away. The buoyancy of his world was dropping.

This was a gradual thing, the pruning away of unnecessary household expenses, a dull retrenchment. The Flahertys were still comparatively privileged. Robert Henry Flaherty after all was still the boss. The miners themselves were far worse off.

> For months the mine in which my father had his all-in-all had been closed down. The miners were starving. One day they banded together hundreds strong and marched towards the office where my father was. I watched them gathering round it. Some bombarded the little building with stones; others with axes began chopping the veranda, until suddenly a throng rushed in and

> began tearing it away. The sound of splintering wood always brings back that terrifying day.[1]

This is clearly what psycho-analysts would call a 'traumatic', but I would say rather a character-forming, experience. The nine-year-old boy was afraid his father would be murdered. His father wasn't; but the savage violence was typical of industrial unrest at that time: one year fortune, the next ruin and maybe death.

Bob's father went North to what was then the little-known Canadian northern frontier of Lake of the Woods, leaving his family in the poverty-stricken mining town of which he had been boss. Susan Flaherty kept her children's spirits up, saying that their father had gone to search not for iron and copper but for gold.

This was a different version of the American dream, more distant but richer. When Robert H. Flaherty came back after a year, 'if ever there was a happy reunion it was ours. For he brought with him amazing tales of gold, and out of a great bag, like a genii [*sic*] in *The Arabian Nights*, he drew forth pieces of white, pink and yellow quartz, speckled and strung with yellow gold.'

Though Robert Henry Flaherty may have discovered gold, it was not a rich enough strike to be commercial.

> But, boy that I was, he brought me something that was still more wonderful – Indian moccasins, real Indian moccasins, he said. I never wore them. I carried them to school. My particular friends, as a great favour, I let smell them – a smell which is like no other in the world – the Indian smell of smoked buckskin. I slept with them under my pillow at night and dreamed of Indians in a land of gold.[2]

In 1896 Robert H. Flaherty went back to Canada, this time as manager of the Golden Star Mine in the area of Rainy Lake, Ontario. He took young Bob with him, partly perhaps for company, partly in the belief that it would teach him more than he was learning in school. It was assumed that he would follow in his father's footsteps. Susan Flaherty remained in the house in the dead Michigan mining town with the rest of her growing family.

[1] Quoted from unacknowledged source by Richard Griffith, *The World of Robert Flaherty*, Duell, Sloan & Pearce, 1953.

[2] Op. cit.

The period of almost two years which young Bob spent at Rainy Lake was the most formative in the shaping of his bent. Bob and his father lived in a cabin but took their meals in a boarding-house. He was the only boy in the place and he was spoilt by everyone. However tough the miners and prospectors might be, they respected his innocence.

When bands of Indians drifted into camp, they brought him gifts, moccasins, now a commonplace, and even once a bow and arrows. Now and then they even let him enter their tepees, which revealed a world totally different from that white man's world where mines could suddenly be closed down and starving men driven to mob their fellows. When at night the Indians held their dances, Bob would fall asleep to the throbbing of their tom-toms and dream of their life in the wilds, simple and self-contained.

> They taught me many things. Hunting, for example. Hunting rabbits in the tamarack swamps. If you picked up the trails, you put your dog on one. He begins following the trail and chases the rabbit. All you had to do was to stand on another part of the same trail. The rabbit would come round to where you were because the trail was always in a circle. You had to be patient and wait, and then the rabbit would come loping along and you got him. This was in the depths of winter, when there was deep snow on the ground and the rabbits couldn't burrow.[1]

Such knowledge as this was far more exciting to Bob Flaherty than secrets hidden in school-books. The circumference of a circle might be πr^2 but knowledge of that wouldn't get a hungry man a meal in the North.

And it was in the North that young Bob knew that his future lay. Other people might regard Rainy Lake as an outpost of North American civilization, but to young Bob, as to his father and all the men in the camp with any vision, it was on the edge of a vast land-mass, largely unexplored and unexploited. The Hudson's Bay Com-

[1] This is taken from one of two pre-recorded radio-talks (transcribed from telediphone recordings) made for the B.B.C. in London, 14tb June and 24th July, 1949, in which Flaherty was interviewed by Miss Eileen Molony. Further recordings dealing with *Moana* and subsequent films were also recorded on 29th August, 5th September and 1st October. Mr. Michael Bell also made some recordings of Flaherty which are used later in the book. Hereafter these are referred to as B.B.C. Talks.

pany had of course long been operating; but their interest in the northern territories was confined to fur-trading. Men like Robert H. Flaherty were convinced that to the north lay mineral resources as rich as those of Michigan and Minnesota. These were the ideas which young Bob Flaherty absorbed from his father at Rainy Lake and he took it for granted that when he was older he would be one of the pioneers to open up these mineral resources.

In 1898 Robert H. Flaherty went to Burleigh Mine in the Lake of the Woods country. There he was joined by Susan and the other children. Though Bob had attended school at Iron Mountain, for two important years at Rainy Lake he had no formal education. Robert H. Flaherty obviously thought his son was learning lessons more valuable than he would ever be taught in a class-room. The boy was also an ardent reader and had devoured Parkman, Fenimore Cooper and R. M. Ballantyne, authors who wrote about the world he knew. But Mrs. Flaherty must have realized with a shock how appallingly ignorant her first-born was of the subjects taught in schools. He was dispatched to Upper Canada College, Toronto, as a boarder.

Flaherty described Upper Canada College as 'a public school, something like English public schools with English masters. They played cricket and football. I never learnt cricket. We also played lacrosse, which is a Canadian game, and this I liked very much. It was originally an Indian game'.[1]

This terse account is chiefly revealing in its omission of any mention of work. Sir Edward Peacock, then a master at the College, remembered Bob as a 'tousle-headed boy who had little idea of the ways of civilization'.[2] At table he found it easier just to use a knife and dispense with his fork. But despite his backwoods table-manners, he was

[1] B.B.C. Talks.

[2] Transcribed from *Portrait of Robert Flaherty*, a radio programme of the recorded memories of his friends, devised and written by Oliver Lawson Dick, produced by W. R. Rodgers, and broadcast by the B.B.C. on 2nd September, 1952. Those taking part were Sir Michael Balcon, Michael Bell, Ernestine Evans, Frances Flaherty, Peter Freuchen, Lillian Gish, Oliver St. John Gogarty, John Grierson, John Huston, Denis Johnston, Sir Alexander Korda, Oliver Lawson Dick, Henri Matisse, Pat Mullen, Sir Edward Peacock, Dido and Jean Renoir, Paul Rotha, Sabu, Erich von Stroheim, Sir Stephen Tallents, Virgil Thomson, Orson Welles and the recorded voice of Flaherty himself. Each of the speakers was pre-recorded over a period of months; in addition, not all that was recorded was used in the final programme but we have had access to most of the telediphoned text. Hereafter this is referred to as the B.B.C. *Portrait of Robert Flaherty*.

popular with other boys. They must have envied him the range of his experience; and then, as later, he was wonderful company. But he had already matured too much in practical living to acquire an academic discipline. In later life he wrote with his left hand very clumsily. It is possible that at school he was made to use his right hand and that the confusion this caused made him backward at class-work.

In 1900, Robert H. Flaherty joined the U.S. Steel Corporation and the family moved to Port Arthur on Lake Superior. The one aptitude which young Bob displayed was for mining and prospecting. To give him the technical knowledge he would need, the Flahertys sent him to the Michigan College of Mines. Here at least was a subject allied to his practical interests.

It was no use. Whether he actually took to sleeping out in the woods, as legend has it, is not certain. But it is a fact that after seven months the college authorities, recognizing that he had none of the qualities of an academic mineralogist, told him not to waste his time and theirs.

Robert H. Flaherty, with six other children to educate, decided that there was nothing more he could do for Bob. Hearing of Bob's expulsion, he wrote wishing him the best of luck in whatever he chose to do, but making it plain that from now on he was on his own.

Bob was not completely on his own. Though he hadn't enriched his intellect at the College of Mines, he had made the acquaintance of a girl named Frances J. Hubbard whose sympathies were closely akin to his, though her background was very different.

Dr. Lucius L. Hubbard, her father, was a distinguished mineralogist and geologist, whose hobbies were the collection of rare books, stamps and birds. He had been the State Geologist of Michigan in Boston and on his retirement had gone to live in the Michigan upper peninsula where he began the development of copper mines.

Frances had been educated at Bryn Mawr and academically she and Bob were poles apart. But as a girl she had accompanied her father when he was charting great areas of the forests of Maine for the first time. This had given her a love of life in the wild and of seeing country which hadn't been seen before, similar to that which Bob had acquired in Canada.

When her family settled in Michigan, she tried to recapture that early delight. She would go off alone on her horse, following the faint, overgrown trails of the old logging days. She would pick out on the map some tiny lake or pond hidden in the woods and set off to find it. Sometimes she got lost or darkness fell before she could reach home. Then she spent the night in one of the deserted lumber camps that the forests had swallowed up. What she liked best was to wander all night on the shore of the lake by moonlight.

She went by herself, because she knew no one who could share her feelings. She thought this yearning for the wild was unique until one Sunday young Flaherty came to dinner and she found that he possessed already deep down what she longed to have.

The Hubbards viewed the romance between Frances and young Bob with apprehension. Both were far too young for marriage, but when they learned that there was 'an understanding' between them, they dispatched Frances to be 'finished' in Europe, in the hope that there she would grow out of this infatuation, this dream of marrying and going to 'live in the woods'.

The phrase was Frances Hubbard's, not Flaherty's. *He* was thinking not of the forests of Maine but of what lay north of North Ontario, the unexplored expanses. How he was to get there lay in the lap of the gods. Without technical qualifications, he had only the know-how of a bright lad whose life had never been far from mining camps and prospecting expeditions.

His young manhood was as nomadic as his childhood and seemingly more aimless. He worked in a copper-mine with some Finns for a time. His father, hoping to teach him in the field what he had failed to learn at the College of Mines, took him on several explorations for iron-ore on the pay-roll of the U.S. Steel Corporation. He learnt how to map and prospect. He learnt how to judge geological formations. And what was most important of all, he learnt how to travel and survive in unknown country.

> Even in my teens, I went on prospecting expeditions with my father, or with his men, often for months at a time, travelling by canoe in summer and by snow-shoe in winter. It was sometimes in new country that hadn't been seen before, the little known

hinterland of Northern Ontario. We mapped it and explored it, or at least my father and his men did. I was just an extra.[1]

That phrase 'country that hadn't been seen before' holds one of the secrets of Bob Flaherty's life and work. It is worth examining.

In the first place it isn't true. What Flaherty really meant was that the country had not been seen before by white men. The Indians who roamed the country did not count. They belonged in the same order of nature as the caribou and fish on which they lived. They were denizens of the wonderful other world, which formed such a contrast to the 'poverty-stricken country' in which his family had lived in Michigan. Devoid of the comforts and squalor of civilization, this country was rich in space and splendour. 'More water than land, really. The lakes were interconnected by streams, so that you could canoe for hundreds and hundreds of miles.'

Being the first white man in a place is a wonderful thing, especially for a romantic. But, like walking over freshly fallen snow, one's own presence destroys the pristine perfection. The white explorer may wish to see a world as it was before the white man came; but he can only see it as it reacts to the coming of the first white man. He is looking for the rainbow's end, unless he can imaginatively reconstruct what things would have been like if he had not been there.

This, I think, was a habit of mind which Bob Flaherty acquired while travelling as an extra with his father and his men.

But of course he also acquired the skills of travelling, camping, hunting, fishing, improvising, judging land and weather, surviving in the wild. It was the perfect training for an explorer.

Later he linked up with a picturesque character called H. E. Knobel. Knobel had studied at the University of Heidelberg and then drifted to South Africa, where he took part in the Jameson Raid. Later he had transferred his activities to Canada. A reclusive man, who hated crowds and cities, he lived in a log-cabin away from other people, preferring the company of a piano on which he played Chopin.

All Bob Flaherty's previous expeditions had been confined to Northern Ontario, but with Knobel he crossed the mountains into the Hudson Bay watershed. Their route lay up Lake Nipigon, 'a wonder-

[1] B.B.C. Talks.

ful lake about a hundred miles long, then up one of the rivers running into it to the height of land where the water divides, going south into the St. Lawrence and north into the Hudson Bay'.

When the river became unnavigable, they had to portage over the watershed until they found a navigable northward-flowing stream. This brought them to Little Long Lake, some twenty miles in length.

> Knobel was in his usual position in the bow of the canoe. He'd do his mapping as we went along with a cross-section book and a little compass – a sort of mariner's paper compass.
>
> Suddenly his compass began to turn around very quickly, more and more furiously as we went on. Then it stopped dead. We knew at once what was happening. We were passing over a body of magnetic iron-ore under us in the lake. So with that little compass, we located a large range of iron-ore.[1]

Knobel and Flaherty staked out about five thousand acres of land covering several veins of ore. But it was years before these deposits were opened up and then not by Knobel and Flaherty. Men who make fortunes out of common minerals like iron and copper are not pioneering prospectors. They are the financiers with long purses, who can build railroads as public utilities and then use them for the economical transportation of raw materials. People like Flaherty whose satisfaction is merely in discovery make no money, unless they find something as precious as gold.

Thirty-five years later someone went to Little Long Lake looking for gold and found it. Flaherty was philosophical. 'There's a saying among prospectors, "Go out looking for one thing, that's all you'll ever find". We were exploring only for iron-ore at that time.'

Later on he was to go out looking for something other than iron-ore, for what life might have been like before the white man came, and that was all he found.

What happened after the Knobel partnership is wrapped in legend. Flaherty condensed legend as a mint-julep condenses ice. It was not his nature to deny it. Was he really engaged by the Grand Trunk Pacific Railway, expanding at that time to compete with the Canadian Pacific, to make 'a wide survey'? Did he interpret his brief so liberally

[1] B.B.C. Talks.

that when he was supposed to be working in the Winnipeg area, he delivered a report from British Columbia? Did he reply, when asked what the hell he was doing there, that he wanted to see what the west coast of Vancouver Island was like?

Bob Flaherty never denied the story. He hid the truth in fancies as a buddleia its blooms in butterflies. But Frances Hubbard who followed his progress remembers no assignment with the Grand Trunk Pacific. In 1906 she returned from Europe and spent a couple of months with him on the Tahsish Inlet in the Rupert District on the west coast of Vancouver Island. But he was not making a wide survey for the Grand Trunk Pacific. He was prospecting for marble. During this visit, Bob and Frances became formally engaged.

In November of the same year he was still on Vancouver Island, but now, as actors say, 'resting'. Mr. T. H. Curtis, assistant to the resident engineer of the Canadian Pacific Railway (Island Division), met him in the Balmoral Hotel, Victoria. He found Flaherty, then aged twenty-two, 'a most likeable soul, kind-hearted, generous but improvident'. He seemed to have some sort of allowance from his mother. Although he paid his hotel bills, he spent all the rest on things like books, fancy ties and socks. 'He never seemed to have any specific aim as to occupation or employment. In fact, work in my idea and experience was right out of his ken. He talked at one time of going to Alaska when the spring set in, but to do what I don't remember.'[1]

Probably Mr. Curtis couldn't remember what Bob Flaherty wanted to do in Alaska because he wanted to do nothing except go North, on any excuse or for any purpose.

It is the appalling frustration of late adolescence or young manhood that one has a blind urge which seldom has means of translation into action. If only somebody would do something . . . !

But all that Mr. Curtis could do was to introduce Bob to his friends in Victoria. Among them was Mrs. MacClure, the musical wife of a well-known architect.

Flaherty played the violin and he often went to the MacClures' for musical evenings. There he met a Mr. Russell, the conductor of the Victoria Musical Society, and struck up a friendship, which ended in Curtis and Bob sharing a house with Russell and his brother. 'We more

[1] In two letters to Paul Rotha, 5th and 10th April, 1958.

or less mucked in together,' Curtis remembers, 'and Bob filled the role of house-boy.'

It must have been an even lower point in his career than being sacked from the College of Mines, though the career-minded Curtis did not realize it. With 'house-boy' Flaherty, he went on canoeing trips. Curtis loved fishing for its own sake. Flaherty, used to living on the land and water, was bored by fishing as a sport, but he loved canoeing.

On Christmas Day 1906, they crossed the Victoria Inlet to the Indian Settlement on the other side. Curtis was rather surprised to find that young Flaherty was entranced by the songs and music of the Indians. He took them seriously.

This glimpse of the twenty-two-year-old Flaherty by a man who obviously had little in common with him is interesting. He appeared likeable, kind-hearted, generous, improvident and completely vague. And that was to prove an exterior view of him for the rest of his life.

But the man within was different. He was not articulate. He did not propound an aim and then proceed to fulfil it. He flowed to his end, like a stream, finding its way by a careful exploration of possibilities; and the end was purely and simply to get north and stay north, to cross the watershed of the St. Lawrence which always flowed back to civilization and reach the watershed of the northern flow, where life was still pristine.

I have emphasized the influence which Bob's father had upon his career. The vision of the exploration and opening up of the North was Robert H. Flaherty's. But I think that Bob Flaherty owed the interpretation of that vision to his mother. He never held her religious beliefs. But his quest for the North was spiritual, a sort of humanist Pilgrim's Progress, provoked perhaps by his father but inspired by the sort of religious feeling which his mother satisfied in the Mass.

For the next three or four years he continued his apprentice work. He prospected for a small mining syndicate above Lake Huron. Then he switched to a larger concern and headed north to the Mattagami River over a route that had not been used for 150 years. He discovered iron-ore deposits and staked them for his employers. This staking of claims became almost a routine, which had no relation to future working. He finished his assignment and made south for Toronto.

In Toronto he met his father who had left U.S. Steel and joined the great Canadian firm of Mackenzie and Mann as a consultant engineer.

Sir William Mackenzie was one of the few men in Canada who saw that great territory, despite its climatic difficulties, as a challenge to human endeavour. He brought to Canada the large vision that Cecil Rhodes had brought to South Africa without the need for aggression and its tragic aftermath. Mackenzie had money and he had pull with the Government of Canada.

In 1910 the Government of Canada decided to build a railroad from the wheatfields of the west to the west coast of Hudson Bay for the shipment of wheat through Hudson Strait to Europe. Sir William Mackenzie had the contract to build the railroad, the Canadian Northern. And if wheat could be shipped by that route, why not iron-ore?

In *My Eskimo Friends* Robert Flaherty implied that this idea originated with Sir William Mackenzie. It is possible that the idea was put forward by Bob's father and accepted by Sir William. In proposing his son for the prospecting job, Robert H. Flaherty was not guilty of nepotism. Bob had all the qualifications; even the fact that he had failed to take a degree in mining told in his favour, because he could be hired at a lower salary. He had the practical experience in travel, mapping and prospecting and in the place of ambition to get on in the world he had a burning ambition to go North, to see country which had never been seen before.

And so in August 1910, Sir William Mackenzie interviewed the twenty-six-year-old Bob Flaherty and commissioned him to explore the iron-ore possibilities of the Nastapoka Islands, a chain outlying the east coast of Hudson Bay.

Flaherty accepted with alacrity. This was the chance for which he had been waiting and training all his life.

2 INTO HUDSON BAY

For the first stage of the journey Flaherty's sole companion was a young Englishman named Crundell. The outfit was modest; a seventeen-foot 'Chestnut', beans, bacon, bannock, dried fruit and tea, the usual grub supply of north-country men, a few simple instruments and a carbine Winchester.

They jumped off for the North from a tiny settlement outlying the Northern Ontario frontier, named Ground Hog. The reason for its existence was that it was temporarily the rail-end until the Ground Hog river had been bridged by the Grand Trunk Pacific.

Down the little Ground Hog, into the big Mattagami and on into the smooth mile-wide Moose was only five days' travel, for though the distance was nearly two hundred miles, the rivers were high and flowing strong.

During this, and subsequent journeys, Flaherty wrote up his impressions. His mastery of language shows that the buying of books, to which Mr. Curtis alluded, was no idle extravagance to be lumped in with fancy ties.

> Hudson Bay is a mysterious country. The grizzled old fur traders and the fur brigades of strange Indians curiously garbed, with hair

shoulder-long, whom we sometimes ran into, seemed to be people of another world.

The rugged granites over which the Mattagami breaks, long 'saults', smoking falls, and canyon-slots through the hills, give way about half-way down to a vast muskeg plain which extends for the remainder of the river courses to the sea – a great desolate waste, treeless save along the margins of lakes and streams. Unbrokenly level, in Devonian times, as the fossils in the limestone of its underlying formation show, it was the floor of the now distant sea. Through it to the Mattagami, a deep groove loops and winds.

Wide scars of burnt forests, chafing tangles of tree trunks barked and bleached by the weather, alternate with live forests of fir, silver birches and long-stemmed sea-green groves of poplars. Huge portions of it, undermined by the icefields of break-up time in spring and by the floods of the high-water season, lay avalanched in chaos on the lower slopes. Trunks, branches and foliage of the wreckage swayed like deadheads at midstream.

There was little wild life. The raucous cries of wheeling gulls, the 'quawk, quawk' of wood duck, were infrequent enough to be startling. Even in the forest places the cawing of some 'Whisky Johnny' for bits of bannock and bacon rind, and the forlorn cries of 'Poor Canada' were the only sounds. Of natives we saw only signs – gaunt tepee frames, sleeping patches of weather-rusted boughs, and here and there poles that, as they inclined upstream or down, pointed out the travellers' direction, or message sticks bearing scrolls of birch bark covered with charcoal writing in the missionary's syllabic Cree.

The Moose begins, impressively large, where the Missanabi from the west and the Mattagami meet. By nightfall it broadened to three miles. The forests of either shore gave way to dreary wastes of muskeg and to spectres of solitary wind-shaped trees. Seaward were long leaden lanes and smoky haze and the mirage of islands in the sky.

On the river's last large island, we reached the great fur stronghold of the North, two and a half centuries old, Moose Factory – an enchanting panorama enchantingly unwinding – tepees, overturned canoes, green cultivated fields, meadows, hayricks, grazing cattle, prim cottages and rough-hewn cabins, a little old church with a leaning red tower, and in formal array, red-roofed, weather-worn post buildings.

A few curious half-breeds and their wives stood at the edge of the bank as we climbed from the landing. The men slouched, hands in pockets, gazing intently, and the women, in the abashed manner of the country, peered from the hooded depths of their plaid shawls. In the background a group of Indian women and their children lingered furtively. Dogs innumerable, enervated by the warmth of the sun, lay sprawled on the green – short-haired Indian curs, and here and there a splendid husky from the barrens of the Eskimoes far northward. On the green stood an elaborately staged flagpole flanked by two old bronze field guns; adjacent, the trade shop, over its entrance the Company's emblazoned coat of arms; and deep-set from the green an old three-storied fur warehouse, alongside of it the forge of the armourer and the boat-yards of the shipwrights and carpenters; and facing them all the master's white red-roofed mansion with dormer windows and a deep encircling veranda.

With the post officers – they wore informal tweeds and white collars – we dined in the mess-room of the mansion, where a moccasined Indian served us from a sideboard array of old silver plate. Travel on the river, the high or low water, and such countryside topics as the approaching goose-hunting time 'Hannah Bay way,' Tom Pant's silver foxes, Long Mary's good-for-nothing husband, and, of course, what the free-traders were doing, were the topics of conversation. We were somewhat nonplussed that none showed more than perfunctory interest in news from the frontier or concern for the mail we had brought – towards the latter not half the avidity one of us would display towards a morning paper. It must be remembered, however, that most of these men are recruited in their teens from the Old Country. Growing up in the service from clerk apprenticeships, they become inured to the monotony of post life, its staid conventions and narrow, unchanging round of duty. One interest predominates – the Indian hunter and his fur.[1]

At Moose Factory, Flaherty was told that the chief factor was at Charlton Island, some seventy miles out in the bay. The factor was the man to make arrangements for the farther stages up the Bay from Charlton.

[1] R. J. Flaherty, *My Eskimo Friends*, Doubleday, 1924.

> We were provided with an open 'York' boat and a crew, one Captain John Puggie, a half-breed post servant, and three upland Indians, one of whom (but not distinguishable save that he was sulkier) was Chief of the Moose River Crees. The Indians with their moccasins and hooded trade capotes, belted thrice around with varicoloured sashes, looked anything but seamen.[1]

Despite a storm which swept the rudder away, with only a sweep to hold her, Captain Puggie landed them on Charlton before nightfall. But to Flaherty's dismay, the chief factor dismissed his plans for immediately journeying north as impossible at this late season. They must wait at Charlton for a schooner, which would take them north to Fort George. There they must winter until the sea ice formed, when they could proceed by sledge with Eskimos.

Flaherty began to learn the tempo of Hudson Bay travel. The 200-mile-voyage to Fort George took ten days. Head winds held them weather-bound at various small treeless islands, at which, however, they killed geese and roasted them on spits.

When they reached Fort George, snow was flying and ice gripped rails, deck and rigging. The factor gave what he had in the way of food and shelter and promised dogs, sledge and two drivers as soon as the sea ice formed.

By mid-November, heavy frost was in the air; but it was not until the first week in December that the arrival of hungry 'coasters', bringing little or no furs but heavy tales of distress, showed that the sea was now safe for travel.

The factor gave advice about camping grounds, the missionary presented him with little notes in syllabic Cree to members of his flock and with his two Indian drivers, Flaherty was off across the sea ice.

While they were still in Indian country below the tree-line an amusing encounter took place, which he was to lift word for word from his journal and use in his novel *The Captain's Chair* (published by Hodder & Stoughton, and Scribner, in 1938).

> Darkness caught us while we were still sledging. Nowhere could we see a suitable place to cross the rough tidal ice which was piled high along the shore. We had to keep on. An hour passed. I was hungry and cold. Suddenly we sighted a light flick-

[1] Op. cit.

ering through the darkness ahead. It was the fire-light of an Indian tepee.

The bark-covered tent was filled with Indians, young and old, but they made room enough to put us up for the night. Through the evening they sat in circles round the tepee's leaping fire – the old hunters, their grim, weathered faces as set as so many masks, in the first circle; the younger ones, their faces dancing in the flicker of the fire's light, on their knees behind them; and the women and children, timid and shy, hovering in the background of shadow beyond.

These Indians seldom saw white men other than traders. They watched every move I made – what I ate, how I ate, how I smoked my pipe.

'See!' exclaimed one, as I struck a match for a light. 'He is too lazy to reach to the fire for a coal.'

The women marvelled at my queer costume, clucked over the colour of my eyes and hair. 'See!' said one. 'His skin is like a child's!'

'Wait till he gets beyond the trees,' said another.

'Yes,' said still another, 'then he will surely freeze.'

'Yes,' they all agreed. 'He will surely freeze.'

They were consumed with curiosity as to why I was undertaking such a journey. My drivers told them I was making it for no other reason than to look at the stones of a certain little island which, if good stones, might one day be boiled over big fires and made into iron – such iron, for instance, as their guns were made of. The tepee shook with laughter. Was it possible that I believed that by boiling stones I could get iron such as their guns were made of? They had still another laughing fit.

The humour of this is typical of Flaherty. There is nothing patronizing in it. Not only within their limitations were the Indians quite logical; but they were more sensible. In the North matches shouldn't be wasted when a live coal will serve as well. Later he was to pay tribute over and over again to the Eskimos who saved his life by their better adaptation to the climate than his.

As they drew out of Indian country, forests gave way to sparse clumps of dwarfed trees. They crossed the peninsula of Cape Jones and came on their first encampment of Eskimo.

They were post-trained, three men, their wives and a host of children, incongruously clad in a mixture of trade clothes and native fur costumes. One woman wore fur trousers over a tattered gingham skirt.

To the headman, Wetunik, the Indians passed over the responsibility of taking Flaherty to the Hudson's Bay Company at Great Whale, the nearest outpost to the Nastapoka Islands, and then they took their leave.

Flaherty couldn't speak a word of Eskimo, but he made do with mime and the whole encampment turned to and made him a camp. Wetunik and his wife lent a hand with the cooking and he loaded them up with sea biscuit and tobacco.

From this first contact with the Eskimo Flaherty seems to have felt an instinctive sympathy. The Indians, apart from the family described above, he found corrupted by contact with white men. But even post-trained Eskimo had retained their racial dignity.

To Great Whale from Fort George was reckoned an eight-day journey. He reached it late on Christmas Night after twelve days sledging, just a single square of yellow light shining like a beacon through the darkness across the black glare ice of the Great Whale River.

He was met by Harold, the post interpreter, half-Indian, half-Swede, who was astonished to see a strange white man at such a season.

> I followed him to his cabin, a snug little place, snow-walled to the eaves. A great two-decked stove, its side glowing red, centred the single large deal-panelled room. An old calendar, a few missionary lithographs, and some firearms hung on the wall.
>
> Groups of Eskimoes utterly silent and staring whenever my eyes were turned away, stood back to walls around me, and old Harold's wife, who for all her white-man's shoes and dress of flowered calico, was an Eskimo, crouched before the stove. Old Harold sat beside her, embarrassed and ill at ease, gazing into space and silent save when I questioned him. All of this to the lash of snow against the cabin walls, the dogs' mournful howls, and the drifters' unending drone.[1]

[1] *My Eskimo Friends.*

Old Harold's embarrassment was understandable. Great Whale was a Hudson's Bay Company post. Though 'the Governor and Company of Adventurers of England trading into Hudson's Bay' had enjoyed a monopoly by royal charter only from 1670 to 1859, it had since then by the strength of its economic empire held the free fur-traders at bay. Free fur-traders were not assisted by Hudson's Bay Company servants.

Flaherty was an example of a new sort of white man, interested not in furs but in minerals. One of these had appeared during the summer in the year before. His name was Dr. C. K. Leith and he was a geological expert on Northern Minnesota and Michigan. He, like Robert H. Flaherty and others, had been pursuing the theory that the fabulous iron-ore deposits of Northern Minnesota would reappear farther north. The prospecting which Robert H. Flaherty had done in Northern Ontario had shown iron-ore float similar to the Minnesota ores in the boulder debris in various parts of the height of the land. But the source was never found.

In his brief summer visit Dr. Leith had detected in the Nastapoka Islands deposits similar to those of the Lake Superior region, but not in his tentative opinion sufficiently rich to exploit.

It was this judgement which Bob Flaherty had been dispatched to re-examine. Flaherty had letters of credit and documents authorizing Harold to give him whatever assistance he needed.

Harold lent Flaherty for the last 150 miles of his trip an Eskimo named Nero who spoke a few words of pidgin English, a post-servant Eskimo and a spanking twelve-dog team.

> Nero constituted himself my special bodyguard. On drifting days when to bare my hands to fill and light a pipe was much too cold, he performed that office for me. He was master of the grub-box and sleeping-bag. With his teeth he pulled off my boots of sealskin at turning-in time at night and was master of ceremonies at every camp along the way.[1]

The fourth day out from the Great Whale they came upon an Eskimo encampment, which makes an interesting comparison with the domestic picture of the Indians quoted above.

> From the black voids of igloo tunnel mouths came shaggy

[1] Op. cit.

beings on hands and knees and the bounding forms of dogs. Leather-faced as I was, and dressed as were the men, the Eskimoes took me, for the moment, to be one of their own kind, but when they found their mistake there was a peal of laughter, and peering close, they wrung my hand again, with unintelligible exclamations the while as to the novelty that Nero had brought amongst them.

On hands and knees through a low tunnel I followed Nero who, whip-butt in hand, cowed the dogs as we brushed by them, and within twenty feet squeezed through a door into a large igloo dome. The housewife, her naked babe nestled warming in the depths of her kooletah hood, turned from the trimming of her seal-oil lamp which lit the white cavern with a feeble yellow cast, and welcomed us. Her babe, too, poked out its tiny naked arm for the hand-shaking.

A frozen seal carcass which lay on the snow floor, a nest of yelping puppies in a niche of the igloo wall, willow mats, and robes of bear and deerskin were the igloo's furnishings.

A supply of black plug tobacco, needles, and bright coloured trade candy was a principal part of my outfit to be given as presents to our various hosts along the way. Nero, of course, officiated on occasions when the presents were given out – 'sweetie-give-'em' was his name for it, which at this camp obtained the proportions of a small festival.

The result of 'sweetie-give-'em' – flinging handfuls to the scrambling, squealing throng, up-ended, their seal-booted legs thrashing air – attracted the grown-ups from the igloos adjoining and packed our igloo full. The odour of skin clothes and seal-oil lamp became increasingly intolerable until Nero, noticing my distress, shoed them out into the open again, explaining diplomatically that 'Angarooka' (the white master) 'him sick nose!'[1]

When at last Flaherty reached the Nastapoka islands, he spent five days breaking off rock samples here and there and taking close-up photographs of the iron-bearing cliffs. He had come 600 miles and travelled for months from Ground Hog and he had to go through the routine of fulfilling his task. But even with his limited knowledge of mineralogy, he was certain that Dr. Leith had been right. The deposits on the Nastapokas were of no economic value.

[1] Op. cit.

This was a disheartening experience. What he had hoped was the beginning of a career in Hudson Bay had come to just as dead an end as all his previous ventures.

He was going to pack up and strike south, when Nero pointed out across the frozen sea and said, 'Big land over there. Husky (Eskimo), him say so.'

When Nero said that, Flaherty remembered an incident on Charlton Island, while he was waiting for the schooner. He had been with the Hudson's Bay Company interpreter, Johnny Miller, examining the curios in the sea-chest of an Eskimo named Wetalltok.

Wetalltok had been at Charlton for eighteen years, but he loved to talk of his hunting grounds in the islands.

'Where are these islands?' Flaherty had asked, producing his Admiralty map.

Wetalltok looked at the map, perplexed. But at last he pointed to a little scatter of islands called The Belchers, a series of dots. 'He says the white man,' Johnny Miller said, 'makes his islands small enough.'

Then from his sea-chest among a litter of tools, ivory carvings, harness toggles and harpoon heads, Wetalltok drew out a tattered lithograph on the back of which was crudely drawn in pencil a very different map of the islands which were just a scatter of dots on the Admiralty Chart. With astonishing detail he spoke of his hunting grounds, of a lake so long that it was like the sea, when you looked across it you could see no land the other side. If Wetalltok was right, the Admiralty charts were very, very wrong.

Flaherty had accepted the map as a memento, thinking no more than that this was an interesting contrast between European science and Eskimo fantasy.

But when Nero gave him corroborative evidence, he suddenly took hope. Nero said that the cliffs of these great islands were blue, yet when you scratched them they were red. If that was so, they might be the northern continuation of the Minnesota iron-ore bearing rocks. In that case, it would be a reprieve. He could go back to Sir William Mackenzie and sell him a second season of exploration.

It took fourteen days back to Great Whale in the worst weather of the year. For four days they were marooned on an island. While they slept, the sea ice driven by a nor'easter upped anchor from the coast and swept out to sea. When the west wind drove it back again, it came up-ended in broken pans and rafted fields. Dogs fell between the floes. Nero freeing their toes from cutting ice particles muttered 'Damn hard time.'

Back in Great Whale Flaherty tried Wetalltok's theory of the great Belcher islands out on Harold. Harold was sceptical. Eskimoes from the islands came in every year. None of them boasted of the size of the islands.

Why indeed should they, thought Flaherty, if they hadn't seen the Admiralty Chart? He asked how many Eskimo had come in from the islands.

There was a long colloquy between Harold, Nero and the servants and they agreed that at least a hundred and fifty heads of island families had in recent years come in to trade at Great Whale.

Comparing that figure with the Eskimo on the mainland between Cape Jones and Gulf Hazard, Flaherty convinced not merely himself but Harold that the Belcher Islands must be much bigger than the Admiralty chart showed.

As he retraced his way to the Ground Hog railhead in the early summer of 1911, his spirits rose. Maybe Dr. Leith was right about the Nastapokas, but he, Bob Flaherty, had discovered the possible existence of a group of islands so rich in iron-ore that Sir William Mackenzie would send him back to explore them next season.

3 ACROSS UNGAVA PENINSULA

When Flaherty returned to Lower Canada, he found Wetalltok's report confirmed by an independent source. In 1884, a Dr. Robert Bell had stated that when in Nastapoka country he had received from Eskimo who had come in from islands out at sea, fragments of rock which led him to think that the rock system of these islands was similar to that of Minnesota. A later geologist, A. P. Low, who mapped the east coasts of Hudson Bay and James Bay, had contemplated an exploration of the Belcher Islands but had been forced to abandon it because of heavy westerly winds and the piling up of thick ice.

Sir William Mackenzie authorized Flaherty to attempt to reach the Belcher Islands from Moose Factory. Travelling by the same route, down the Ground Hog, Mattagami and Moose Rivers, Flaherty took with him this time a marine engine, which he fitted to the *Nastapoka*, a diminutive 36-footer which he secured at Moose Factory.

This took time and the 1911 season was well advanced before he reached Great Whale River. The Eskimos looked askance at the tiny craft and its loudly-popping engine. But 'much bargaining, tempting offers, good old Harold's "fur trade" support, and Nero's argument that "all same noise like gun never mind, scare 'em seal, that's all", finally overcame their prejudices'[1].

For three calm sunlit days they cruised north. There were seals innumerable and whirring flocks of ducks and eider. Food was in plenty. By nightfall on the third day, they reached a small island, outlying Gulf Hazard five miles, from which they planned to strike across the open sea to the Belchers.

In the only harbour available, exposed to all winds save the western which then prevailed, they anchored for the night.

But within an hour the wind veered and blew down from the north. A gale rose as the black night settled. They paid out all anchor chain, hoping to hang on until morning. But foot by foot, all anchors dragging, the *Nastapoka* was forced shorewards. By midnight she was aground and breaking seas flushed gear and food from the cabin and open hold.

At dawn, they surveyed the battered *Nastapoka* half heeled on the sands. The Eskimo went in search of food. When they did not return, Flaherty went in search of them. He found them huddled behind a heap of boulders, bent double, clutching their stomachs with their hands and groaning. Lying close were empty containers of dried apples of which they had eaten their fill before drinking water!

After three days patching, caulking and re-rigging running gear and mending the tattered sails, they limped back to Great Whale Post and by the time they reached there the sailing season was over.

Nothing further could be done until the sea froze; but Nero promised Flaherty that in 1912 during the six weeks in February and March when the ice-fields were crossable by dog and sledge he would take him to the Belchers.

What to do with the intervening five months? Mavor, the factor of Great Whale, had barely enough food for his own needs. The nearest alternative was Fort George, 180 miles south. For such a trip the battered *Nastapoka* was useless. No 'York' boat crew was available at this late season, for fear of being trapped in the ice. Canoe was the only transport.

Mavor, who had spent eight years at Great Whale unrelieved and

[1] Op. cit.

was suffering from loneliness, decided to go with Bob, leaving old Harold as his deputy.

Despite Harold's prophecies that they would be frozen up, they made Fort George safely and five and a half months later Flaherty returned to Great Whale to meet Nero who had come down a hundred miles from his hunting grounds to act as driver.

Once again Flaherty was frustrated. Though the ice seemed strong at Great Whale, the annual immigration of the islanders bringing furs to Great Whale had not taken place. They were weeks overdue.

Then the night before Flaherty had decided to go all the same, news came that three sleeps to the north the ice was driving out to sea. At least one team of dogs had been seen on a driving-pan, entangled in their harnesses.

It was sheer bad luck. In the twenty-eight years of Harold's experience, this was only the second time the ice had broken. But Flaherty was not a man to come so far and return with nothing accomplished. If he could not cross the sea to the Belcher Islands, he could attempt the traverse of the Ungava Peninsula via Lake Minto and the Leaf River which had defeated A. P. Low and the Rev. E. J. Peck, when they essayed it: and perhaps return to make a crossing to the Belchers in the summer.

The Ungava Peninsula had fired Flaherty's imagination even in childhood. In R. M. Ballantyne's *Ungava* he had read the story of Dr. Mendry's traverse from Richmond Gulf, following the Clearwater, Larch and Koksoak rivers in 1824 for the Hudson's Bay Company and as a young man he had studied A. P. Low's account of the same crossing, made in 1896 for the purpose of mapping and geological study.

But the Richmond Gulf crossing, till then the northernmost achieved, was through Indian country well within the tree-line. Peck had analysed his failure to make the Lake Minto traverse. 'We were not able to carry a large supply of provisions, but we expected to meet with reindeer and other animals which frequent these parts. In this, however, we were disappointed. For eleven days we struggled on over the frozen waste, but not a vestige of animal life could be seen. We were therefore with heavy hearts obliged to retrace our steps or perish by starvation.'

Of the route which Flaherty proposed to take, the only part which had been reliably mapped was the forty-five miles from the Hudson Bay coast to Lake Minto which had been surveyed by A. P. Low. All the other details of lakes and streams were merely copies of maps made by the Eskimos.

Flaherty proposed to fill in some of the blanks left by Low. How big was Lake Minto, described by the Eskimo as upwards of a hundred miles long? What of the river flowing from it to discharge itself 250 miles away in Ungava Bay? And what of the west coast of Ungava Bay itself? Two hundred miles to the south, along the lower reaches of the Koksoak an inaccessible iron-ore series had long been known to exist. Would he find an extension of it, perhaps more accessible, near Fort Chimo?

> With old Harold and Nero I discussed ways and means. The distance from Great Whale north a hundred and fifty miles to White Whale Point, then inland across the great interior to what Nero called the eastern sea (Ungava Bay) was roughly, as we should wind, seven hundred miles – not a great distance, as Nero pointed out, for sea-coast travel; but inland where 'him, no seal, no tooktoo, no nothing', a more difficult matter. 'Since I am small boy,' Nero went on, 'deer, him all same gone.' Meaning that the vast herds of countless thousands that once wandered through the illimitable barrens were now no more. 'Dogs him starve,' said Nero referring to his journey with Low to Lake Minto until the starving condition of the dogs forced them to retreat.[1]

Flaherty could not persuade Nero's wife to let her husband go all the way to Fort Chimo. So it was arranged that Nero with one team of dogs should go as far as he had explored with Low, about a quarter of the total distance, and then with the weakest dogs and only enough food to enable him to regain the coast, he would return, leaving Flaherty to go on with two other Eskimos, Omarolluk and Wetunik.

Omarolluk had a reputation as a great hunter and sledging man. His wife was won over by Harold's promise that she and her children should live on rations at the post during his absence; and Omarolluk himself was beguiled partly by a wage triple that of the post and even

[1] Op. cit.

more by the guarantee that he could take part in the big deer-killing at Koksoak River in the spring.

Wetunik was supposed to be familiar with the country between Lake Minto and Fort Chimo, though he proved, in the vast confusion of inlets and identical-looking waterways, to be a poor guide.

The journey along the coast was familiar ground. All was easy travelling until they came to the rough ice off Gulf Hazard. Here Nero's sledge pitched twenty feet over a sheer wall of ice. One of its two-inch plank runners broke sheer across the grain and they had to retreat a dozen miles to the encampment of an Eskimo from whom they bartered a new sledge for goods to be obtained from the Great Whale Post on Flaherty's account.

The journey up the coast took a week but during that time they failed to kill a single seal. They were reduced to 50 lb. of blubber with which to supplement the dogs' diet of corn-meal. Before leaving the sea, should they camp and try to kill a seal? But if they failed to kill, they would be so many days short of rations. They decided to push on, leaving a cache of food, marked by a monument of stones, to help Nero on his return, and themselves as well, if they were forced to retreat.

Turning inland up the coastal slopes, they found the going much harder. In four days they covered only thirty miles. Often they followed up a valley to find at the end a sheer wall facing them. To work out of the valley meant harnessing both teams and themselves to a single sledge.

Along the coast they had had driftwood fuel. Now there was only the occasional stunted tree in a wind-sheltered pocket. As they worked higher, even these disappeared. All that was left were creeping willows and trailing spruces which they burrowed for beneath the snow on hands and knees, using snow-shoes as shovels.

On the fifth day they crossed the watershed. The valleys began to curve away to the east and below them they saw miles and miles of snow-smoking plain, sprinkled with multitudes of boulders 'which stood out of the satiny waste like pin points of jet'. Then as they wondered which valley to choose, the snow-smoke settled and in the middle distance they saw a vast sweep of ice whose far horizon was a landless rim. It was Lake Minto or as the Eskimo called it Kasegaleek, the Great Seal Lake.

Richard Griffith in *The World of Robert Flaherty* quoted the following extracts from Flaherty's journal of this expedition. They give a more vivid sense of the day-to-day tensions than Flaherty's account in *My Eskimo Friends*.

March 13th. They clustered about me as I hung the thermometer on the ridge pole of the tent tonight. Of course I had to explain it all to Nero in our amusing 'Pidgin English' fashion. He in turn explained it to his friends. But even then Omarolluk couldn't understand him very well, couldn't see that if that slender thread of mercury went down to the black mark, all water would freeze. He was sure that the cold made water freeze, not my thermometer.
March 16th. Fed the dogs on seal blubber tonight. The dogs were tired and ravenous. Since we had no convenient way of tying them for the night, they were free. The scene just before feeding-time was unforgettable. Omarolluk had to stand guard with his 6-fathom whip while Wetunik cut up the blubber. The dogs acted for all the world like wolves. They kept crawling up on their bellies from every direction, even braving the whip, a cut from which is certainly a painful affair. They are as quick as lightning in snatching, a wolf's trait on the ground. Their fierceness and murderous temper as the odour of the seal meat came to the crouching circle of them is beyond telling. They foamed at the mouth. What would happen to us without them?

March 18th. Our Waldorf fare of Army rations, jam and canned steak will soon be exhausted, then beans for ever. Nero spoke of the flies inland, that often kill the deer. He had seen them inches deep on the deer, the deer's face being raw and swollen by their work. In July this happens when there are hot days and calm. He had seen them after being killed, and says they are bloodless through the flies' work. The Eskimoes keep their dogs in their tents during this time, imagine the smell. At one point this a.m. we reached the summit of a portage and started descending, but barely managed to stop short of a 75-feet precipice. With our sledges that continually strain for speed, it was no small matter to stop in time. We also shortly discovered that while we were looking over for a new course, we were standing on a snow overhang which projected from the cliff about 25 feet. There are many snow formations like that in the rugged area here, and south along the

Richmond Gulf country. The snow is everywhere wind-driven and packed to a picturesque extent, such as is not possible southward. This overhang of which I speak resembles the eave of a house on a huge scale. Many a hunter has lost his life through unconsciously walking to their edge, then suddenly breaking them off. Two men of Little Whale River plunged hundreds of feet to their death in that manner.

We are camped in a tiny valley which contains a handful of stunted trees one of which is 5 feet high. Camped early as the dogs are tired with their trying journey today. Do not seem to be in good condition. When we get to the deer herds they will improve again.

March 19th. This entire area is barren of soil silt and trees. The rounded hills are everywhere interlaced with small lakes that are in shadow most of the day. The snow on the shadow sides of the lakes and slopes and cliffs of the hills never disappears. It truly is a desolate area. The confusing network of lakes in today's travels were too much for Wetunik, and we were consequently delayed while he climbed the hills to locate our course. At 2 p.m. we descended on to the surface of Lake Minto, though having lost the Eskimo route to it, we came on to it in strange country, so that Wetunik wasn't sure we had hit it until we travelled eastward some four or five miles and he did some further scouting on the hills. We saw two partridges, one of which Nero shot. It was given to 'Beauty' tonight for his supper. Would an Indian give his dog a lone partridge?

March 21st. . . . Omarolluk gave further information about whales last night. He said there were many whales on the north coast, that they were black, had divided spray, white about their mouths, and were very large. These are the Ottawa Island whales of which he speaks, and other unknown islands west of Hope's Welcome. At one time the Eskimoes managed to kill one and the bones of it are still there. . . . This is Nero's last day with us. He turns back tomorrow for Great Whale River. We missed the Eskimo trail completely coming to Lake Minto, it seems, and entered it on the south side. By tonight expect to be half-way across it. We depend upon getting to deer herds, and expect to see signs of them today. At lunch-time Nero and Wetunik climbed one of the hills to look for our route, as Wetunik had become confused again. When they came down they proposed camp so that they could devote the morrow looking for the route. Made them go on however as we started late today. Wetunik located himself again. We then made for shore and camped. Camp will remain here for tomorrow. Dogs will have a rest which they need as they are very thin. Hope we get to the deer herds soon so as to get dog food. Wetunik says we are more than half-way across the lake now. Very fine day, brilliant sun which hurts my eyes very much though I wore goggles part of the time. Clear, calm. Aurora and sun dogs.

March 22nd. Sun and snow reflection almost blinding. All but Nero off to north and south of lakes looking for deer. Nero baking bannock and fishing through ice. Hunters returned at sunset, and Wetunik saw fresh signs of about eighty deer. We push on tomorrow for east end of lake, there men will hunt for a day. Nero returns to Great Whale River tomorrow. Splendid calm and clear day. Nero drew map of lake for me in evening and we had a conference together afterwards covering route, deer herds, etc. Dog food is our greatest worry.

March 23rd. Said good-bye to Nero at eight o'clock and then started on our way to Fort Chimo. I felt lonesome at seeing him go. No one to speak to now. My men cannot understand a word of English and I have a vocabulary of about twenty-five Eskimo words. Nero will arrive at Great Whale River in about seven days' time. He's one of the most remarkable men I've ever seen. Clever, a Jap's keenness for novelty and information, the greatest hunter of his people, a daredevil on ice or in a kayak, and the model generally of all his tribe, always smiling and alert, likes to be on journeys with white men, admires them, tho' withal intensely Eskimo. Nero is an illustration of the development of the Eskimoes are capable of. I parted from him this a.m. with regret indeed.

Wetunik confused again and later completely lost. We have travelled some forty miles today and are now camped within two miles of last night's encampment. But are located correctly this time! The lake is a maze of long finger-bays and islands. The saucer-like hills on every side hardly vary, and it is hard to pick up landmarks. And then everything is snow and ice, with no forests to relieve the colour. Distances on that account are most deceptive. Have twelve dogs in fair condition but a very heavy load, about 800 lb. in all.

March 24th. Head wind made a disagreeable day of it. About one o'clock Wetunik became confused again and the men climbed one of the high granite hills for sight. The lake is a monster and will prove to be the largest in Labrador, not excepting Lake Messtassine, I think.

March 25th. There seems to be no change in appearance of country as a whole, everlasting hills of granite and at wider and wider distances little patches of dwarf trees, snuggled in the valleys away from the winds. Heavy load for our dogs, one of which shows signs of giving way soon. I hope we see the deer.

March 26th. Arrived at the end of the lake about ten o'clock. The discharge is a small open rapid. We travelled on a mile farther, then camped as the drift is blinding and wind very strong. Trees are increasing in size and number, and we are camped in quite a grove.

March 27th. Very cold day with a typical March wind and blinding drift. Became partly snow blind, and eye is very sore indeed this evening. About 2 p.m. came across deer tracks on river ice. Omarolluk went after them and Wetunik and I went on with the team. Camped at about three o'clock and no more than had it made when Omarolluk came with the news of two deer killed. He was as happy as a child over it as he has never even seen deer before, being an islander of Hope's Welcome. It means a great deal to us and nothing could have been more opportune. We all shook hands in high glee over it. The men returned at eight o'clock with the deer, cut and quartered, having given the dogs a feast while cutting them. At noon they killed two ptarmigan which they are now eating.

March 28th. Laid up with snow blindness, and a painful affair it is. The men are off after the deer with dogs and sledge. It seems Omarolluk wounded one besides the ones he got. It being a very stormy day, the deer will not travel but keep in the valleys. Omarolluk killed his deer yesterday with 30.30 shells in a .303 gun He gave me to understand the bullets were very loose. The men returned at three o'clock minus deer. At supper tonight the men tried to tell me in signs and in our very limited vocabulary that the dog I purchased from Jim Crow died today, but I thought they said they were going back to Great Whale River. For a moment was alarmed and angry, but I caught their meaning in time. Much laughter.

March 29th. Our travel was most trying and were in seemingly impassable places at times. All of us done up, Wetunik with snow blindness, Omarolluk with a lame knee, and I with cramps and headache after my snow blindness. Wetunik making me a pair of Husky goggles. Cached 80 lb. of dog food. Sledge is very heavy.

March 30th. Very fine travelling and in grateful contrast to yesterday. Dogs working well after deer meat diet.

March 31st. It was funny to see Omarolluk running ahead, and imitating a seal waving flippers in the air, to urge the dogs out of the ice-jam we were stuck in today. Have acquired a few Eskimo words and our crazy-quilt conversations are laughable indeed.

April 1st. Overcast and high southerly winds. Wetunik suffering agonies from snow blindness. Gave him some Cloridine [*sic*] for appearance's sake.

April 2nd. A late start, 9 a.m. Poor Wetunik in a bad way, cannot open his eyes and racked with headache. Have just put him in his blankets, a very sick Husky. Trouble at noon today. The men, I discovered, have been keeping their sealskin boots in my cooked-bean bag. The day is the warmest we have had. The icing on our runners wore off quickly and part of our earthen shoeing is gone. Noted Omarolluk's method of baking bannock this evening: two handfuls of baking powder to about four pounds of flour – and we live!

April 3rd. Ruined our earth shoeing and had to run on the runners today. Tonight the men have made new shoeing. At feeding time one of the dogs mistook Wetunik's hand for deer meat and made a considerable mess of it. It's one damned thing after another with Wetunik. Omarolluk's knee giving him trouble.

April 4th. Last evening at camp noted a Canada Jay, first bird other than the ptarmigan seen on the trip. Travel very tedious and slow owing partly to the spring day, which makes both men and dogs very sluggish. We are all on edge now, expecting and wondering when we shall come to the sea.

April 5th. About 1.30 arrived at the mouth of the river. Was much surprised and delighted as were the men. The river empties into a fiord of Ungava Bay. The mouth was choked with ice and we had a very hard time of it indeed. We were from 1.30 to 6 p.m. travelling about three miles, and then we had to camp on sea ice and walk about a mile for a few pieces of driftwood for a fire, with the result that we did not get into our blankets until about 9.45. Very tired but happy.

April 6th. One of the most trying days we had. We camped on the sea ice last evening and broke camp this a.m. at eight o'clock. Very soon we were into impassable and treacherous ice, where at times we had literally to chop our way. Heart-breaking work. Left the team, climbed the hill-side of the mainland and saw our course was hopeless. Open water in the distance and detached floes packing shoreward. There we were, like a fly in glue. Men and dogs done up. While in the thick of the ice, a snow squall came upon us with great force and blotted out everything. Fortunately was not of long duration. Pitched camp on mainland and tomorrow will attempt to travel overland and come out on southerly side of the bay, clear of the rough ice-fields.

Work tried our tempers but all right now. Omarolluk baking bannock and singing fragments of Eskimo songs, and every little while humming the tune of 'Waltz Me Around Again Willie' which he has heard on some phonograph at Fort George or Great Whale River. Our very limited conversations bear altogether on Fort Chimo and our arrival.

April 7th. Stuck here for the day, a miserable camp with everything wet. Men off in the hills looking for a course for our trvael tomorrow. Slight snow blindness again. Wetunik went off again this p.m. to see the ice-fields from the top of the range. Returned at 5.30 saying ice was all broken. Expect we shall have a hell of a time tomorrow. Omarolluk and I pouring [*sic*] over maps this p.m. The most miserable of all days, everything melting.

April 8th. Started on our cross-country travel to avoid the rough ice-fields. About 100 ptarmigan assembled on a distant knoll to see us go. Very hard and long climb to an altitude of about 600 feet accomplished by noon in 100-feet jobs, with the usual Husky-dog conversation at each one. In the true barrens now and away from trees. One long climb was compensated by a galloping coast down the long slopes this side of the range. Encamped on the main coast of Ungava Bay with another broken ice-field staring us in the face. Fort Chimo seems farther away every day.

April 9th. Wetunik confused and does not know the route from here to Fort Chimo. He is certainly a useless guide and 'attulie' has been his cry ever since we left Nero. It seems from what I can gather from the men that the sea coast is impossible to travel by sledge and the Ungava Bay is open water. An Eskimo route starts in from this Gulf Lake overland for Fort Chimo. As Fort Chimo is more than 75 miles away in a straight line it is most important that we find the trail. The maps are misleading extremely. Travelled inland no more than a mile when in a clump of trees we found a fresh Eskimo cutting. Camped, then looked for tracks underneath the soft snow, found many Eskimo tracks but none of a sledge and as yet cannot tell if these cuttings indicate a sledge or not, which is an important thing to know. The signs indicate the Eskimoes have camped here about seven or eight days ago. Wetunik went off to a distant mountain to scout, but returned with no information. Our grub looking ill. Wetunik is a pin-head, I'm thinking. He has hunted this country and should know it. But Omarolluk makes up for him. Full of resource and brain, a 'good Husky'.

April 14th. Westerly wind all night, heavy, still strong, less drift, partly clear. Travel fast and the excitement of nearing Fort Chimo a stimulus even to the dogs. We plied Charlie with anxious questioning all through the day trying to fix our location and nearness to the post. At about 4.30 we suddenly stood out on the last of the terraces. Fort Chimo, the great broad river, and a valley stretching to a blue haze of dazzling sun, lay before us. The white buildings of the post from our vantage looked like a strange far-off village. The descending sun shot into the innumerable windows. Bolts of light threw the surging figures of Eskimoes, men and women, now aware of the arrival of a strange party, into vivid profile. The day and heat were made for our entry there, the colour of sunset of the sky caught by the snow affected us strongly. The white mass of days of travel was at an end.

These diary extracts give a sense of the mounting tensions in a journey which, as all three men were conscious, might never reach a successful end. They do not emphasize that throughout Flaherty was not merely struggling to reach Fort Chimo safely but was also mapping the country through which he was passing. Nor do they record Flaherty's excitement when first sighting Leaf Gulf he saw 'islands of strangely familiar form, table-topped, grotesquely slanting, as if they were about to topple into the sea . . . formations identical with the iron-bearing formations of the Nastapoka islands – the link I had hoped to find between Low's discoveries of the interior some hundred miles southward and his later discoveries 300 hundred miles northward on Ungava Bay'.[1]

At Fort Chimo, Omarolluk and Wetunik went south for the big deer-killing; and during the fortnight they were gone, Flaherty went back with the post-driver to Leaf Gulf hoping to examine the iron-ore formation more closely. But already the ice and snow was melting rapidly and he had to return to Fort Chimo to wait for the break-up and open water.

Once again he was dogged by ill luck. The old hands at Fort Chimo could not remember a winter that had lasted as long as this of 1912. The mile-wide river ice, rotten enough to prevent trips afield, still showed no signs of breaking.

Flaherty abandoned the project of returning by canoe to Great Whale up Leaf River and through Lake Minto and making another attempt to reach the Belcher Islands that summer. With the late break up, he would reach the Hudson Bay too late.

Omarolluk and Wetunik set off alone to return to their anxious wives at Great Whale, while Flaherty planned with Fort Chimo Eskimo to make a more northerly traverse up the Payne River across the main divide and down the Povungnituk River into Hudson Bay, then northward along the coast to Cape Wolstenholme to await a ship which would take him back to Lower Canada.

> Overnight I decided upon the attempt. The little post of Fort Chimo hummed (if a fur post can ever hum) with active preparations. The factor of each post, Hudson's Bay and Revillon's, vied with one another to help with the outfitting. The Hudson's Bay people gave me one Nuckey, their best man, and Nawri, and young Ahageek, son of the old Ahageek, who was chief of his tribe, and Ambrose, son of the Dog woman. From trade canvas secured from Revillon's a native seamstress fashioned a fly-proof tent, sewing every seam of it with the sinew of a deer. My food supply – beans, bacon, dried fruit, jerked deer meat, sugar, tobacco, and tea – was estimated to be sufficient to last the five of us two months. The canoe was a huge Peterboro, 25 feet long capable of a load of 4500 lb. – one that the Revillon factor had imported some years before for a party of Nascopie packeteers for use in the big rapids of the Koksoak. The Indians, however,

[1] Op. cit.

refused to use it. A 'man killer', they called it, too heavy for the portages; so for years it had lain idle in the loft of the fur post. It was just the kind of craft we needed, however; big enough to weather the seas along the hundreds of miles of sea coast we must travel.[1]

The Peterboro was taken aboard a diminutive sloop, the *Walrus*, already loaded, rails down, with four Eskimo hunters, their wives, their children and dogs with a yelping litter of pups. The *Walrus* had an open hold and 29 feet of keel.

For two days they sailed slowly along before light catspaws with the hunters in their kayaks scooting like waterbugs ahead, alert for seal.

The tides on this fantastic coast rose and fell 40 feet. At low tide long fangs projected miles out to sea, littered with gigantic blocks of sea ice gleaming white and green. And when the tide flooded, the islands disappeared and the blocks rode off in the wind to form new formations on the ebb.

On the third day the wind came scudding from the east, driving the sea ice shorewards. The great white shapes of bergs sailed with a majestic menace in with the ice pack from the open sea. Before nightfall, the *Walrus* was prisoner on a small high island rock. The raft ice piled around in a monstrous ring.

For three days the gales blew in from the east, piling it seemed the drift ice from all the North Atlantic to wall them in.

When the gale died, the sea was solid. But soon the ebb and flow worked channels, winding like ribbons through the pack-ice. Through these capricious lanes, the *Walrus* found her way, signalled on by the exploring kayaks. But winding as they did, they often made in a day only a few miles as the crow would have flown, if it could have existed in that savage climate. And as often they were held prisoners for days on end. But finally on a day in June they reached the wide open arms of Payne Bay and sailed to the head of it, where the river which A. P. Low had named the Payne burst through a multitude of boulder channels to the sea. The *Walrus* had reached her journey's end. All hands debarked and camp was made ashore amid a confusion of sea-drenched garments spread on boulders to dry. For two days the

[1] Op. cit.

women worked on mending boots and clothes and Flaherty's crew on repairing the outfit, checking food and loading up.

Flaherty found the Payne River magnificent, with its great terraced slopes towering hundreds of feet above and the narrow level plains along the river edge carpeted with mosses and with purple, white and yellow flowers in solid banks of colour and among them bees and butterflies.

> There was never a more happy and carefree crew than we five. Banter, smiles and laughter were our stock in trade. Day and night to us were almost the same, and there was no watch to space them. We ate and slept when we willed.[1]

This was the joy of Bob Flaherty in the North, which was such a contrast with, for example, the rather morbid excitement of Jack London, who could only feel that he was in life in the midst of death. For Flaherty it was a very simple thing. Danger may have given a sharper edge. But to draw another line across the uncharted interior of the Ungava Peninsula was something on which he was prepared to stake his life. In terms of human discovery it was worth the gamble.

Working up the Payne River, they fed splendidly on salmon and on the great lake trout, which they caught on cod hooks, baited with pork and red flannel. They came to where the river divided. The left fork, which was larger, led to the great lake which the Eskimos called Teeseriuk, but which is called Lake Payne on modern maps. There was ice still stranded on either shore, which, Nawri argued, meant that if they went south to Lake Payne, they would meet big ice. And so, reluctantly because he wanted to see this, the largest lake in the Ungava peninsula, Flaherty agreed to take the northern fork.

Ice or no ice, the northern fork could hardly have been more difficult. The stream, narrowing to a V-shaped trough, was a white race of water for miles on end. The canoe had to be tracked, or towed, using the treacherous surface of ten-foot banks of ice stranded alongshore. Usually three of the crew tracked the 'man-killer' while Nawri, standing in the stern, worked her nose around the shoals, boulders and blocks of ice. In one rapid the current was so swift that Nawri and

[1] Op. cit.

Flaherty had to join the men on the tow-line, while the Peterboro awash to the gunwhales came on by inches.

For three days they toiled. It seemed as if the rapids would never end. The last rapid was the worst. It seemed as if they were over it, when the sealskin tow-line, catching a sharp-edged boulder snapped. The canoe with all their worldly goods, swung broadside on and began to race downstream. If the canoe was lost, it was more or less certain death. They raced along the ice banks, knowing that their chance of catching the canoe was more or less hopeless.

But Nawri was still in the canoe. He waited until the river doubled around a point. Then he jumped in to his waist and steadying himself with his paddle, he caught the dangling end of the tracking line and held the heavy 'man-killer' until the crew relieved him.

Up and up they went. Larger and larger grew the banks of snow. The river became a series of links between lakes and ponds, so shallow one could almost wade across them. By 17th July, they came to a point where the river had been reduced to a frothing creek. They were near the main divide and they decided to split up next day and each explore the possible rivers running down to Hudson Bay.

But in this height of land man proposes and God disposes. That night a gale scattered their fire and sheets of rain extinguished it. Next morning thick wet snow was flying and for two days they were prisoners in the flapping shelter of the tent with cold water to drink and sea biscuit to eat.

The third day the weather cleared and on the following day they found a possible route and for a couple of days more they portaged the outfit and the man-killer across the head of land. From then on it was like free-wheeling down a hill often without brakes until on 1st August they reached at last the Hudson Bay.

Flaherty had every reason to congratulate himself as an explorer. In one year he had made two traverses of the Ungava Peninsula which had defeated all previous explorers, drawn two new lines across the blank map of the Ungava interior. But though he was now on a coastal belt sparsely inhabited by Eskimo, he had nearly 300 miles of hazardous Hudson Bay waters to navigate before he reached Cape Wolstenholme.

They never did reach Cape Wolstenholme in the man-killer. In a storm they were driven ashore in a tiny cove. But by the Providence which always guided him it was only a comparatively short distance to the Wolstenholme Post.

The twenty-eight-year-old Flaherty had failed to reach the Belcher Islands. But he had earned his salary. He knew as he waited for a ship to take him back to Lower Canada that Sir William Mackenzie would back him on another expedition in 1913.

4 THE BELCHERS AT LAST

Flaherty may have been expelled from the Michigan College of Mines, but when he returned with his reports to Sir William Mackenzie, he found that he had great prestige. By succeeding where A. P. Low had failed he had graduated with first-class honours in the difficult school of exploration.

Sir William was not interested in the Leaf Bay iron-ore series. The location did not fit in with his railroad operations,[1] but he was impressed by the exploring abilities of Robert H. Flaherty's boy. He had drive. He had independence. If he was headed off in one direction, he found another in which to employ his talents without sitting down and waiting for new orders and he had a capacity for survival which was obviously based on his ability to get on with the Eskimo. He liked them. Going North was like Going Home.

'Get a ship,' he said, when Bob Flaherty told him of the failure of the little *Nastapoka* with its built-in engine. The Belcher Islands, if they were as rich in iron-ore as Leaf Bay, could very well provide alternative cargo to Western wheat.

[1] The Leaf Bay deposits are being worked currently by the Cyris Eaton Co. In the words of Prof. Edmund Carpenter, Dept. of Anthropology, Toronto University, they are now 'bringing in untold wealth to the New World'. Letter to Paul Rotha, 24th May, 1959.

There was no suitable ship in Hudson Bay. But at St. John's, Newfoundland, was a topsail schooner, the *Laddie*, 75 feet over all and 85 tons register. Built at Folo, Newfoundland, she had been through the Hudson Strait before.

The *Laddie*, in dock for four weeks, was re-rigged and overhauled from bow to stern, and belted with greenheart to shield her from the ice. And while this was being done, Sir William had another brainwave.

> Sir William said to me casually, 'Why don't you get one of these new-fangled things called a motion picture camera?' So I bought one, but with no thought really than of taking notes on our exploration. We were going into interesting country, we'd see interesting people. I had not thought of making a film for the theatres. I knew nothing whatsoever about films.[1]

To Richard Griffith, Flaherty gave a different version – or perhaps it would be truer to say that he did not challenge the rather journalistic version which Griffith submitted for his approval. 'When Flaherty excitedly declaimed his enthusiasm for Eskimo life to his employer, the ever-receptive Sir William agreed that he should take a movie-camera along with him on his next expedition.'

I prefer Flaherty's own account. But it doesn't matter. What is certain is that when Flaherty got his first camera, a Bell & Howell, he went down to Rochester for a three-week course in motion-picture photography and that was the only training he ever received as a cameraman.

In 1913, this didn't appear as ridiculous as it would have appeared even five years later. Flaherty, always an extroverted man, was quick in picking up techniques and gadgetry. His tests with the Bell & Howell were not very successful. But he decided that if he was going to make pictures he would have to know how he was going on. So in addition to some modest lighting equipment and a fair amount of film stock, he bought a portable developing and printing machine. With the confidence of an amateur, he planned to set up a sub-arctic film laboratory.[2]

Though, as I have said, his travel diaries were vivid, Flaherty wanted

[1] B.B.C. Talks.

[2] From a letter to Paul Rotha from David Flaherty, 29th June, 1959.

a more direct language in which to speak. Film might provide a lingua franca, the Esperanto of the eye.

But at this time, it would be wrong to think that Flaherty was primarily concerned with making moving pictures. He wanted to get to the Belcher Islands and prove that their iron-ore series were profitable. He was a mining prospector ostensibly, who was secretly an explorer.

What with the re-rigging of the *Laddie* and Flaherty's camera course at Rochester, they sailed too late in 1913. A thousand miles northward up the coast of the Ungava Peninsula and into the Hudson Strait the *Laddie* ran into trouble. It was plain that she couldn't reach the Belcher Islands and get back without being frozen in and perhaps crushed during the winter.

With three of the crew, Flaherty landed on Amadjuak Bay in Baffin Island, arranging to winter there while the *Laddie* beat south to avoid the freeze-up and return next summer.

With forty Eskimo, Flaherty and his party made north to the great lake of Amadjuak. Before the camp could be established there was 2,000 miles of sledging backwards and forwards. And when they were established, there was the usual prospecting to do. It was not until February 1914 about the time of his thirtieth birthday that Flaherty began filming.

I think that Flaherty first conceived of film-making as something that would fill in the dreary periods of waiting, in which time dragged so heavily until the weather cleared, a ship arrived or the sea froze over.

> We did not want for co-operation. The women vied with one another to be starred. Igloo-building, conjuring, dances, sledging and seal-hunting were run off as the sunlit days of February and March wore on. Of course there was occasional bickering, but only among the women – jealousy, usually, of what they thought was the over-prominence of some rival in the film. One young mother, whom, with her baby, I was in the midst of filming one clear day, suddenly got up, and despite my threats and pleas, walked away. Neither she nor her husband had been up to snuff of late, so I decided to send them away. 'Don't care,' said she when in the most impressive way we announced her fate, 'seals are the best food anyway.' But old Yew, ever father of his flock, inter-

posed, and what was finally picked out from the crazy-quilt of his pidgin English was that she was not altogether wrong. Two times in as many days I had given Luliakame's (her rival's) baby candy, but I 'no see him hers'.[1]

This was one of Flaherty's first lessons in the direction of actors, who always need handling with sympathy whether acting for fame and fortune or just for candy and comfits. He was to become one of the most accomplished directors of natural actors, binding them to himself with a subtle complex of sympathy and loyalties.

April 1914 came with longer, warmer days. By the end of May Flaherty made sledge expeditions, one west to the mouth of Fox Channel 170 miles and another 150 miles east to Lake Harbour. Hunters came in with tales of deer; and two Eskimo knowing he was planning to film a deer-hunt came in from two sleeps northwards with a live year-old deer on their sledge. They had slightly wounded it and then run it down.

It was an embarrassing gift with so many dogs at large. For three disturbing nights the deer had to be kept in the asylum of their kitchen.

> On the tenth of June I prepared for our long-planned deer-filming expedition, and on the following day, with camera and retorts of film and food for twenty days, Annunglung and I left for the deer grounds of the interior. Through those long June days we travelled far. The thick yellow sun, hanging low in the northern sky for all the hours save the two at midnight, seemed to roll along the blue masses of the far-off hills. Deer were everywhere, pawing up the mosses deep in the valleys, or in long bands winding funereally across the white surfaces of little lakes and ponds. In three days we had climbed to the summit, a wind-swept boulder plain, of the height of land – the divide of the waters flowing south into Hudson Strait, and north through unknown Lake Amadjuak. Behind us lay the welter of the wrinkled hills through which we had come; before us a void of plain.
>
> We were picking out a course when Annunglung pointed to what seemed to be so many boulders in a valley far below. The boulders moved. 'Tooktoo!' Annunglung whispered. We mounted camera and tripod on the sledge. Dragging his six-fathom whip ready to cow the dogs before they gave tongue,

[1] *My Eskimo Friends.*

> Annunglung went on before the team. We swung in behind the shoulder of an intervening hill. When we rounded it we were almost among them. The team lunged. The deer, all but three, galloped to right and left up the slope. Three kept to the valley. On we sped, the camera rocking like the mast of a ship at sea. From the galloping dogs to the deer not two hundred feet beyond, I filmed and filmed and filmed. Yard by yard we began closing in. The dogs, sure of victory, gave tongue. Then something happened. I am not altogether clear as to how it happened. All that I know is that I fell headlong into a deep drift of snow. The sledge was belly-up, and across the traces of the bitterly disappointed team Annunglung was doubled up with laughter.
>
> Within two days we swung back for camp, jubilant over what I was sure was the film of films. But within twelve miles of the journey's end, crossing the rotten ice of a stream, the sledge broke through. Exit film.[1]

This was another form of apprenticeship. Flaherty was learning to film – hard in any circumstances – in the most difficult territory in the world. And it amusingly filled in time before the real business of 1914 started with the arrival of the *Laddie* on 19th August.

At last after a couple of years he was ready to attempt with some prospect of success the attack on the Belcher Islands. The winter camp on Baffin Island was broken up and to the Eskimo who had served him so well, he gave out the remnants of his stores ' – a mirror with a gilt frame, old blankets, clothing, old shoes, precious bits of metal and an old alarm clock with one hand, knives, old pots and kettles and pans, and most wonderful of all, some oranges from the *Laddie* – "peeruwalluk pumwa" (the very best of all that's sweet), they said. Enraptured, they rubbed them against their noses.'[1]

They had clear water through the Hudson Straits; the ice-fields had long since passed into the North Atlantic. They rounded Cape Wolstenholme and on the third day, sighted the Ottawas, the northernmost of the chain of islands which parallel the east coast of the Hudson Bay for 400 miles.

In this desolate terrain, they were surprised, exploring for a harbour, to find a ship riding at anchor and ashore a hut with a Union Jack breaking out on the wind.

[1] Op. cit.

She was the *Active*, a veteran whaler out of Dundee. The crew, having completed winter and summer with little success, were about to clear for Scotland. They were in bad shape, practically out of rations and one of the crew, a doleful creature, begged Flaherty for any 'soft' food he had, 'oatmeal and the like, sir'. He opened his mouth and showed his toothless gums. Flaherty was appalled that even a Scotsman would have the hardihood to venture on a whaling expedition without a tooth in his head.

But he was wrong. 'A few drinks before you leave and then the wee bit of an upset the day after, sir, what with the ship's rollin' an' all; so to tell you the truth, sir, I heaved them over the rail, sir!'[1]

This man was lucky. During the winter two of the ship's harpooners had died of *delirium tremens*. Two wooden crosses stood out in silhouette, as the *Laddie* swung off for the south.

All day an ice 'blink' loomed in the west. By next morning great banks of fog lay round the *Laddie*. It thinned to a haze as the morning progressed, but even so they almost bumped into a low-worn rib of rock.

For three days they crept on, with a look-out in the crow's nest and the leadsman always ready in the bow. There were no suns for latitude, but the log showed a southing of 200 miles from the Ottawas which meant they should be approaching the Belchers.

The skipper wanted to lay up in a harbour on the mainland coast until the visibility cleared. They squared away before a light wind and laid course through the night, when suddenly there was a Crash! Bang! and a wild ground swell broke over the stern, picked up the *Laddie* and hurled her into the teeth of a boiling reef.

In that darkness, they could not launch the dories. The sails cracked like rifles, the *Laddie* pounded on the reef, splinters six feet long rising and drifting away. With a human chain, all hands raised the ballast from the hold and dumped it over the rail, and then, there being nothing more to do, they climbed on deck, provisioned the dories and waited for dawn.

The wind died. The sea was smooth as rolled glass, as far as the eye, in fog, could see. But in an hour or so, the fog dissolving, they saw an island, towards which they made in the dories.

[1] Op. cit.

It was a sorry platform of soil-less bedrock, with a ring of boulders which showed that some time Eskimo, caught perhaps in a similar plight, had camped there.

They cached their food and gear and returned to the *Laddie* to salvage what they could before she sank. They found, to their astonishment, that though the tide was nearing flood, there was not much water in the well. They flung overboard the thirty-six casks of oil which comprised the rest of her heavy cargo, dropped an anchor some 300 feet ahead, put on call sails and opened up the engine. With the crew winding at the winch, the *Laddie* came slowly across the reef.

> When a light breeze an hour on tore up the last shrouds of fog which had lain over us so long, it revealed the hole into which we had poked the *Laddie*'s nose. The white boils of reef were everywhere. . . .
>
> "Tis no place for us, sir,' said the skipper, and he hailed the mate and two of the crew who had gone off to the island for fresh water.
>
> 'We've seen big land, sir,' they called as they clambered up over the rail.
>
> 'You mean the mainland?'
>
> 'Naw, sir,' said the mate, 'what land we seen lays to west'ard.'[1]

Before sundown – the log reading 20 miles – the *Laddie* hove-to on the north-eastern portion of that island coast. It is understandable why these islands, first discovered in the seventeenth century, should have become reduced over the years to a series of problematic dots on the Admiralty Chart, when one considers the difficulty which Flaherty had in rediscovering them.

They landed. As the anchor chains clanked through the hawse pipes, flocks of eiders whirred up and a long string of geese flapped honking off. As they reached shore, a gorgeous silver fox scurried for cover.

But Flaherty had come for iron-ore. And here on this first day, he found it, barely exposed, but rich stuff which lay heavy in his hands.

The mockery of it was that the expedition which had been equipped to spend the winter in the Belchers was now reduced to destitution. Almost all the food and gear had been jettisoned. The ship was leaking badly and though Flaherty had proved his point, there was no possi-

[1] Op. cit.

bility of conducting a survey. After three days on the island, they sailed south, making for Great Whale River.

It was a great disappointment to Flaherty, but the fact that they were going to Great Whale meant that he would be seeing old Harold again, who would give him a fine welcome.

The *Laddie* picked up the mouth of the Great Whale too late on the ebb to get over the river bars to the post. With three of the crew, Flaherty unlimbered the launch but, confused by the darkness, whilst threading through the bars, they were caught in a sweep of surf and thrown up upon a narrow spit of sand, about a mile and a half away from the post.

In the distance they could see two squares of light shining from the windows of one of the cabins of the post. So to summon help, the mate lashed a lantern to a long pike pole while Flaherty fired round after round from his Winchester.

For an hour, they waited for help, but no one came. They tried again. Still no one came.

Then the moon rose and they could see their way to get clear. As they landed, they glimpsed bodies flitting past window lights and disappearing into the darkness.

They climbed into the lighted cabin, but there was no one there. They could not understand what had happened. It was a most extraordinary situation.

Then after nearly half an hour, the door began to open and a head was poked round. It was old Harold and when he saw who was in the cabin, the fear left his face, and he became wreathed in smiles. He ran forward and clasped Flaherty's hand. 'My God, sir,' he said, 'I t'ote you was the Germans.'[1]

That was the first news which Flaherty had of the outbreak of the First World War, which though it appeared very far away, was destined to change Flaherty's work in the Hudson Bay as profoundly as the U.S. depression of 1893 had changed his father's in Iron Mountain, Michigan.

[1] Op. cit.

5 FROM ORE TO AGGIE

From Great Whale Flaherty sailed south through James Bay and on along the nine-mile-wide delta of the Moose to Moose Factory. There the *Laddie* was made ready for the slipway where the crew and half-breed ship-wrights of the post were to overhaul her during the winter.

When everything was taken out and the cobble ballast thrown overboard, she filled to the engine-room and would have sunk, but for the shallows in which she rode.

Flaherty took his films, his specimens, maps and notes by canoe back to Lower Canada to report to Sir William Mackenzie.

Mrs. Evelyn Lyon-Fellowes of Toronto recalls that when Flaherty came to that city, she used to chaperon her friend Miss Olive Caven, whom Flaherty appeared to be courting. 'I chaperoned them once at the old Queen's Hotel (now demolished). On this occasion he gave me a wonderful photo of a husky dog, taken I understand in an *igloo*, He gave Miss Caven many beautiful presents including a white fox fur, and numerous photos of Eskimoes which she accepted as she admired him very much. On his last[1] return from Hudson Bay, he

[1] It was not in fact his last return. Mrs. Lyon-Fellowes refers, in this letter to Paul Rotha, to his propenultimate return in November 1914. It is interesting to speculate whether the white fox fur belonged to the fox Flaherty described in *My Eskimo Friends* as 'the gorgeous silver fox' which 'scurried into the crevices of a great pile of rocks'.

spent the first evening with her and left that night for the United States.'

When he saw Frances Hubbard, she (if not her family) must have made it plain that the engagement had been going on too long. There was war in Europe, the future was unsettled, it was high time that they should get married.

This did not fit in with his plans at all. His exploration and mapping of the Belcher Islands was to be the climax of the four years he had spent in the sub-arctic. He was not prepared to abandon it in order to take a Ford Agency post, as the Hubbard family suggested.[1]

Frances Hubbard did not press for the abandonment of his career. But when Bob pleaded that he was broke, a remarkable statement considering that he had returned from over a year in the North where opportunities for spending his salary were small, Frances bought her own wedding-ring and accompanied him to City Hall in New York City to get the licence.

They were married on 12th November, 1914, at the New York City home of one of the Hubbard cousins and they left immediately for Toronto.

There the enamoured Miss Olive Caven was surprised first to be introduced to Bob's bride and then to be asked to find them a house to live in. She had never even been told that Bob was engaged. But she did find them a house and after she had recovered from the shock, 'she married happily and well'.

In autumn 1914 Sir William Mackenzie's main energies were concentrated on the war effort. It is unlikely that he would have bought Flaherty a ship in which to explore the Belchers, as he had done the year before. But the *Laddie* was at Moose Factory, being refitted; and Flaherty had at least established that the Belcher Islands were much larger in fact than they appeared on the Admiralty Chart. Flaherty's proposal to spend the winter of 1915–16 on the islands, making a full exploration, was reasonable; and there was a far better chance of approaching them successfully sailing from James Bay than coming from Baffin Land through the Hudson Strait.

[1] Ernestine Evans, an old friend of Frances and Robert Flaherty relates this suggestion of a Ford Agency in *Film News* (New York), Vol. XI, No. 8, Sept. 1951. It was made, I imagine, contemptuously, to emphasize how unsuitable the young prospector was as a husband for Frances.

Flaherty spent the winter editing the film he had shot in Baffin Land. It was too crude to be interesting. But he had learnt something from it and when he made a second attempt, after finishing his serious work on the Belchers, he hoped to do better.

Frances and Bob had had no conventional honeymoon. It was impossible to take a woman to the Belcher Islands. But Bob thought of a compromise, which could at least give Frances some glimpse of the country to which he had lost his heart. Instead of going north alone in the summer of 1915, he went with a party consisting of his father, his young brother David, Frances and Margaret Thurston, a friend of hers from Bryn Mawr days.

Together they made the, for Bob familiar, journey to Moose Factory. There the *Laddie* was waiting, refitted and ready and together they sailed to Charlton Island, where Bob left his family party to camp for several weeks before they returned on the Hudson's Bay Company steamer *Nascopie*. In their place, he took aboard Wetalltok, 'his wife and three children, his two partners, their wives and seven children, twenty dogs, kayaks, sledges, tents and hunting gear. Their impedimenta topped the *Laddie's* deck load, which was already rail high, while among the boxes and bales in the choking hold, Wetalltok and his tribe made their temporary home. The dogs, chained in the dories which swung from the davits over the rails, whined and yelped and chorused to the skies'.[1]

In their approach to the islands, they were favoured with good luck. They sighted the southernmost outcrop towards nightfall on an almost windless evening. They dropped anchor and rode out the storm which arose after dark. Next morning they crept north and as they found a suitable harbourage for camping ashore, they were approached almost immediately by an Eskimo, who directed them to the main settlement of island families.

Soon the whole energies of the settlement were turned to helping the Flaherty party to establish a base camp at the main harbourage.

Cynically one might say that the Eskimo regarded this expedition as a marvellous stroke of good fortune. As they helped to off-load the *Laddie* and bring the mysterious packing-cases ashore on their catamaraned kayaks, even bent nails and scraps of planed plank were

[1] *My Eskimo Friends.*

treasure-trove. But the spirit in which they gave their help was not self-seeking. In that savage climate, it was an imperative that any human soul should help any other. Life was too tough for human beastliness.

The weeks before the sea ice formed were devoted to preparing the base for winter, getting gear and equipment in shape, making sledges, bartering for more dogs for sledging and laying in fuel, even to the extent of sailing the *Laddie* across to the Great Whale coast to return laden with driftwood – the preparations for the siege of winter.

This was work in which Flaherty delighted. It fulfilled his energetic nature, the communal fight against savage elements which continually threatened life. It demanded the vigour, training, courage and resource which inspire soldiers, but its object was to prevent casualties.

As the news of their arrival resounded through the islands, more and more Eskimo came in to see the Kablunak (white man) and his huts and to learn what he was about.

With each hunter, Flaherty and Wetalltok pored over maps, listening to what he had to say (translating 'sleeps' into 'miles') and seeing the size of those island dots on the Admiralty Chart growing into a complex like the jawbones of an enormous beast.

Before these Eskimo departed, after giving their cartographical information, Wetalltok would tell them about the rocks which the white man sought; blue rocks which when scratched with flint showed scratches like blood and how these rocks when boiled by the Kablunak could be made into the knives, guns and spearheads they held so dear. He showed them samples of iron-ore and several of these hunters of seal and geese and walrus went off to the places where they knew they could find the 'sevick' (iron) rocks, samples of which they would bring back when the sea froze.

One greatness of Robert Flaherty as explorer, man and artist lay in his humility. He knew that in their country, Eskimo knew best. He trusted them as map-makers, hunters and friends. His own knowledge as a white man was severely limited; but within its limits, and tempered by humility, it could help the Eskimo as much as they helped him.

During that winter of 1915–16, there was a strange mixture of civilizations. The Skipper of the *Laddie*, Salty Bill, improvised a Christmas Tree from spruce boughs he had brought from Moose to make spruce beer. On the gramophone there were the songs of Harry Lauder and 'Tipperary', and most popular of all 'The Preacher and the Bear'. The growling of the supposed bear, caused shouts of '*Nanook! Nanook!* The Bear! The Bear!' which made adults roar with laughter and babies clutch their mothers in half fright. There was the miracle of 'Cakeot Nucky', or Pop Corn: and the playing of baseball on harbour ice with the *Laddie*'s starboard side as a backstop. 'If what with our cumbersome fur costumes, the game lacked speed, it did not lack interest for the gallery – old men, women, young and old, and squalling youngsters – especially if one of their kind was fortunate enough to hit the ball, for, as they saw it, the pitcher's role was to hit the batter! Only darkness stopped us.'[1]

On 2nd January, Eskimo came in from the far west with news that the sea ice was fit to travel everywhere to westward. At noon Flaherty with Wetalltok and two of the crew set off with a thirteen-dog team. The Eskimo visitors went with them to a point less than a sleep away where there was an outcrop of sevick rocks, enough they thought to load the Kablunak's ship many many times.

Flaherty was delighted, because it proved to be a rich vein 25 to 30 feet wide, running north and south along the coast. He traced it southward for 30 miles and found at the conclusion of his survey that it was the largest and richest deposit in the islands.

The work of exploring, prospecting and mapping came first in Flaherty's schedule and throughout January and February he concentrated it.

But even so, scenes imprinted themselves upon his memory. One afternoon they struck the sea. Drift filled the air. It was so cold that some of the dogs vomited. Suddenly they all gave tongue. Before Flaherty knew what was happening, Wetalltok was at their head, cracking his long lash like a rifle-bullet. There ahead, crouched over his snow-blind, sat an Eskimo, arms folded on knees and harpoon in lap, watching for seal to rise through a breathing hole no bigger than the butt-end of his harpoon. As quietly as they could, they sheered

[1] Op. cit.

away from him, not to disturb his hunting. Wetalltok said the man had been waiting there since dawn.[1]

Nightfall that day, they saw the orange square of an igloo window. Rainbow, its owner, said he had not killed a seal for eight days. Sea pigeons were all they had to live on. Just before Flaherty arrived, he had killed one – the first in two days – and his wife, who was plucking it, held it up for Flaherty to see. But though they knew Flaherty had little or nothing to give away, they forgot their troubles in making the stranger welcome. Rainbow helped Wetalltok with the dogs, while the wife tidied up the igloo, sending her daughters scurrying out for a pail of clean sea-water snow, while she herself unrolled his sleeping bag, pulled off his kooletah and hung it over her feebly burning lamp so that it would be dry for the morning. As the strangers were eating their beans and bacon, she kept her children away so that they shouldn't prove embarrassing; and when Flaherty crawled in to sleep, they spoke in whispers.

Next morning Flaherty told Rainbow that when he returned to base camp, Rainbow and his family must visit him and he would try to be hospitable. 'Yes,' added the practical Wetalltok, 'and keep one eye open for sevick rocks as you come.'[2]

'I will,' promised Rainbow, 'that is, if I ever kill another seal.' And at this joke against starvation, there was a chorus of laughter.

It was this sort of incident which made Flaherty love living among the Eskimos. They had a simple courage and nobility which echoed in himself when he was among them. Farther south one ran into complications; like taking a girl out to dinner, going away and coming back married and asking her to find you somewhere to live.

Much has been written about the birth of Flaherty the film-maker; most of it pious poppycock. The deepest experience in Flaherty's life had nothing to do with films, art or for that matter with exploration, prospecting and the opening up of the North. It was the discovery of people who in the midst of life were always so close to death that they lived in the moment nobly.

This virtue, which he prized above all others, is an epic virtue. The

[1] Thus Flaherty in *My Eskimo Friends:* when Flaherty told the story on the B.B.C. a quarter of a century later, they came upon the man next day still at the same seal hole.

[2] Op. cit.

Greek heroes had it, as did the Vikings, because they were living in the simplest contexts; and the Eskimo, liable to be separated by a crack of the ice, so that an igloo would split in half and one half of the family would be separated from the other for perhaps ten years before they met again, preserved the same heroic simplicity.

He mapped the Belchers and he gathered his samples of iron-ore. But he was no fool. He had already discovered deposits of iron-ore in Leaf Gulf which he knew were as rich as those in the Belchers and Sir William Mackenzie had said they were uneconomic to exploit.

If the finds in the Belchers had been twice, or twenty times as rich, Flaherty had already demonstrated their unexploitability by the fact that it had taken him four years to land on the islands.

So what new excuse would he have to return to the North after he made his report? For the duration of the war, at least, Sir William Mackenzie would not be interested in opening up new fields, when he could satisfy war-demand from current mines.

Filming provided his alternative. Impressive though Flaherty's exploration had been, it did not compare with that of Vilhjalmur Stefansson, the Icelandic Canadian who had gotten himself through the University of Iowa to Harvard and then established a reputation for exploring 'the Friendly Arctic' which he described as a land of abundance. If anyone was going to invest money in Arctic Exploration, he would choose Stefansson who propounded a northward course of empire rather than Flaherty who loved the North just because life was so hard and could resist the northward course of empire.

So from the end of February 1916, the thirty-two-year-old Flaherty concentrated on what had earlier been a pastime. In January 1916, the mapping and prospecting was finished. With maps of the islands, plans of the deposits covering over 100 square miles and samples of the ore, two members of the crew of the *Laddie* crossed the sea ice to the mainland and made their way south to report to Sir William Mackenzie. Flaherty requested an expert mission to examine his findings; and while he was awaiting their arrival, he concentrated on the filming which had previously been a pastime.

It is impossible to say exactly when Flaherty became conscious that his lifework was to be devoted to making films. One can see from his diary entries that Flaherty was a natural artist in words, when not inhibited by writing for publication. He was also a good violinist, preferring to play without an audience.[1]

But these were skills which Flaherty brought with him to the North. He had learnt them as a boy. His film-making, on the other hand, was taught by no one; and his methods as will be seen later, especially from John Goldman's account of editing *Man of Aran* and Helen van Dongen's accounts of working on *The Land* and *Louisiana Story*, were unlike those of any other film-maker. It was Paul Rotha, pondering this and then reading Professor Edmund Carpenter's *Eskimo*, who had the brilliant intuition into Flaherty's creative method. Flaherty was the first appreciator of Eskimo carvings and drawings.[2] Flaherty had an admiration not merely for the products of this Eskimo art but also for the philosophy that lay behind it.

Rotha suggested to Wright, who agreed, that there was an uncanny similarity between the Eskimo methods described by Professor Carpenter and those employed by Flaherty.

Carpenter, when consulted, endorsed this intuition heartily. Mrs. Flaherty later incorporated it in her lecture notes; and a film was made along these lines. Professor Carpenter's notes to this film express vividly the Eskimo attitude.

> Nowhere is life more difficult than in the Arctic, yet when life there is reduced to its barest essentials, art and poetry turn out to be among those essentials. Art to the Eskimo is far more than just an object: it is an act of seeing and expressing life's values; it's a

[1] Peter Freuchen the explorer met Flaherty in the sub-arctic in 1923. Flaherty was asked by people at the trading post to play his violin. He said that he would play in the room next door and they could listen. While he was playing, one of the man out of sheer love of life got up and started to dance by himself. The man went on dancing after the music stopped and did not notice Flaherty come in from the other room. Flaherty's eyes were blazing. 'That wasn't dance music,' he said. 'I didn't play for dancing.' And then, because the man did not immediately stop, he brought the violin down on the stove and smashed it to smithereens. (B.B.C. *Portrait of Flaherty*.)

[2] His collection of 360 carvings, considered one of the best in existence, was acquired by Sir William Mackenzie and donated to the Royal Ontario Museum in 1933. A photograph of a typical Eskimo carving is reproduced in the *Nanook* Section, together with an Eskimo drawing of Flaherty filming.

In 1915, Flaherty published *The Drawings of Enooesweetok of the Sikoslingmit Tribe of the Eskimo*, with the subtitle, 'These drawings were made at Amadjuak May, Fox Land, the winter headquarters of Sir William Mackenzie's Expedition to Baffin Land and Hudson Bay, 1913–14'. These drawings have now been donated also to the Royal Ontario Museum, by Mrs. Frances Flaherty.

ritual of discovery by which patterns of nature, and of human nature are revealed by man.

As the carver holds the unworked ivory lightly in his hand turning it this way and that, he whispers, 'Who are you? Who hides there?' And then: 'Ah, Seal!' He rarely sets out, at least consciously to carve, say, a seal, but picks up the ivory, examines it to find its hidden form and, if that's not immediately apparent, carves aimlessly until he sees it, humming or chanting as he works. Then he brings it out; Seal, hidden, emerges. It was always there: he didn't create it; he released it; he helped it step forth.

What emerges from the ivory, or more accurately from the artistic act, isn't simply a carving of a seal, but an act which explicates, with beauty and simplicity, the meaning of life to the Eskimo.

In the Eskimo language, little distinction is made between 'nouns and verbs' but rather all words are forms of the verb 'to be' which itself is lacking in Eskimo. That is, all words proclaim in themselves their own existence. Eskimo isn't a nominal language; it doesn't simply name things which already exist, but rather brings both things and actions (nouns and verbs) into being as it goes along. This idea is reflected in the practice of naming a child at birth: when the mother is in labour, an old woman stands around and says as many different eligible names as she can think of. The child comes out of the womb when its own name is called. Thus the naming and the giving birth to the new things are inextricably bound together.

The environment encourages the Eskimo to think in this fashion. To Western minds, the 'monotony' of snow, ice, and darkness can often be depressing, even frightening. Nothing in particular stands out; there is no scenery in the sense in which we use the term. But the Eskimo do not see it this way. They're not interested in scenery, but in action, existence. This is true to some extent of many people, but it's almost of a necessity true for the Eskimo, for nothing in their world easily defines itself and is separable from the general background. What exists, the Eskimo themselves must struggle to bring into existence. Theirs is a world which has to be conquered with each act and statement, each carving and song, but which, with each act accomplished, is as quickly lost. The secret of conquering a world greater than himself is not known to the Eskimo. But his role is not passive. Man is the force that reveals form. He is the force which ultimately conceals nothingness.

Language is the principal tool with which the Eskimo make the natural world a human world. They use many 'words' for snow which permit fine distinctions, not simply because they are much concerned with snow, but because snow takes its form from the actions in which it participates: sledding, falling, igloo-building, blowing. These distinctions are possible only when experienced in a meaningful context. Different kinds of snow are brought into existence by the Eskimo as they experience their environment and speak; the words do not label something already there. Words, for the Eskimo, are like the knife of the carver: they free the idea, the thing, from the general formlessness of the outside. As a man speaks, not only is his language *in statu nascendi*, but also the very thing about which he is talking. The carver, like the poet, releases form from the bonds of formlessness: he brings it forth into consciousness. He must reveal form in order to protest against a universe that is formless, and the form he reveals should be beautiful.

Since that form participates in a real situation, the carving is generally utilitarian. One very characteristic Eskimo expression means 'What is that for?' It's most frequently used by an Eskimo when he finds some object and stands looking down at it. It doesn't mean 'What can I use that for?' but rather something closer to 'What is it intended to be used for?' That portion of the antler, whose shape so perfectly fits the hand and gives a natural strength as well, becomes, with a slight modification, a chisel handle. Form and function, revealed together, are inseparable. Add a few lines of dots or tiny rings or just incisions, rhythmically arranged to bring out the form, and it's finished.

Here, then, in a world of chaos and chance, a meaningless whirl of cold and white; man alone can give meaning to this – its form does not come ready-made.

When spring comes and igloos melt, the old habitation sites are littered with waste, including beautifully-designed tools and tiny ivory carvings, not deliberately thrown away, but, with even greater indifference, just lost. Eskimo are interested in the artistic act, not in the product of that activity. A carving, like a song, is not a thing; it is an action. When you feel a song within you, you

> sing it; when you sense a form emerging from ivory, you release it.[1]

This Eskimo attitude is implicit in all Flaherty's work, though he never stated it more fully than 'First I was an explorer; then I was an artist.' The attitude of reverent exploration 'what is it intended to be used for?' rather than 'what can I use that for?' made the process of film-making painfully slow and as we shall see almost baffling to those who worked with him on the later films.

It also made the actual process of shooting an exploratory end in itself.[2] The most exciting of the film sequences was the 'iviuk aggie', the walrus-hunt. Mukpollo, the hunter, failed to kill. But back in base, Flaherty developed the film and he was happy. Everything was there, including the escape of the walrus.

While waiting for the experts to arrive, supplies of fuel gave out and they were forced to burn the *Laddie* spar by spar. As it burned, Flaherty saw his chances of returning to Hudson Bay going up the chimney. Sir William Mackenzie could not be expected to supply another ship for exploration or filming while the war was on.

For the run-back to Moose Factory, Flaherty had to depend upon the flimsy *Nastapoka*, which had been refitted but was in poor shape.

The experts did not arrive until late August, 1916. On the York boat that brought them was a vaguely familiar figure, which proved to be Robert H. Flaherty hidden beneath two months' growth of beard, and Dr. Moore, a geologist and surveyor, who besides surveying the claims was to make astronomical observations on behalf of the Canadian Government, which was still sceptical about the size of the Belcher Islands.

Flaherty was not surprised at the verdict delivered by his father. The ore was rich, but the difficulties of extracting and shipping it from the Belchers made it an uneconomic business.[3]

Flaherty returned in the *Nastapoka*, which had only room for food, instruments and essential gear. Much that had been brought by the

[1] Prof. Edmund Carpenter: *Notes on Eskimo Art Film*: based on Flaherty's Eskimo Paintings and Carvings. Robert J. Flaherty Foundation.

[2] John Taylor says that on *Man of Aran*, Flaherty sometimes spent hours shooting with no film in the camera.

[3] As with the deposits in Leaf Bay, the Belchers are being currently mined with great success by the Cyrus Eaton Co.

Age about 20

The trading post at Port Harrison

NANOOK OF THE NORTH — 1920–21

'The Laddie' — circa 1915

Flaherty with Nyla, Nanook's wife

Nyla

Flaherty's cabin
(*see page 83*)

Ptarmigan carved from baby walrus tooth (Southampton Island, 1950)

Eskimo drawing of Flaherty filming NANOOK

Laddie had to be left behind. For this Flaherty was glad, because it gave him an opportunity to reward the Eskimo to whom he was indebted with riches beyond their imagining. The hut and all its furnishings were divided out.

Three of the most treasured things were a Winchester rifle and cartridges which went to the generous Rainbow, a canoe that went to the loyal Tookalook and the pianola, the 'big box with the many insides', that went to Wetalltok who regarded it as the most wonderful thing in the world.

A year later, in Lower Canada, Flaherty received letters from Great Whale River, dated three months before, with news from the Belcher Islands. Rainbow, who had made the joke about coming to base camp if he ever killed another seal, had gone mad through starvation. He was at large for days on end, spreading terror among the islanders with the Winchester rifle before they killed him in self-defence.

Within a month of the sailing of the *Nastapoka*, Tookalook catamaraned his kayak with Flaherty's canoe to make the crossing to Great Whale. The canoe was found upturned on the mainland coast, but nothing more was seen of the kayak or Tookalook.

The news of Wetalltok was better. The beloved pianola was too big to go in his igloo; and as winter came, he could no longer live in the hut. There was no fuel.

Wetalltok remembered that Flaherty had told him that Mavor, the factor of Great Whale, prized the pianola. It was the most precious thing on earth and Mavor would pay a good price for it.

And so when the ice froze, he loaded the pianola on his sledge and took it 85 miles over rafted sea ice to the Great Whale Post.

When he arrived to collect his fortune, he found that Mavor had been transferred 180 miles south to Fort George. And so, with supplies provided from the factor of Great Whale on the strength of the sale of the pianola, he set off for Fort George, where many nights later he arrived. 'Here, Angarooka,' he said to Mavor, 'is the box with the many insides.'

'The thing worked, you'll be surprised to hear,' Mavor reported to Flaherty, 'though some of its notes were what Wetalltok called "sick sounds".[1]

[1] *My Eskimo Friends.*

But before Flaherty heard of these troubles, he had his own. He had completed his survey of the Belcher Islands. The Canadian Government had so far recognized the geographical existence of the group as to name the largest island after Flaherty himself. The richness of the iron-ore deposits was acknowledged but they were not immediately useful and to any young man raving about the Eskimo and Hudson Bay, there was the slightly pitying question, 'But don't you realize there's a war on?'

There was only one thing between Flaherty and settling down; the film he had shot, in all some 70,000 feet, or approximately 17½ hours' of screening time.

Working in Toronto, he made an assembly of the print of this, which was despatched to Harvard for a special screening. Then, while he was packing either the cut negative or the whole of the negative, for dispatch to New York, much to his shame and sorrow he dropped a cigarette in it and the whole thing went up in flames. Flaherty tried to put the fire out, but succeeded only in landing himself in hospital with burns.

Among Flahertomanes there has been more nonsense talked about this episode in his career than about any other. John Grierson, the possessor of a memory even more creative than Flaherty himself, can remember Flaherty having carried scars all his life on his hands from this fire. But nobody else, including the authors, detected these life-long scars; and photographs show no signs of them. Some people speak as if the loss of the negative of what is erroneously called 'the first Nanook' was a tragedy, even though Flaherty, who was not a conspicuously modest man, considered the film a failure.

In fact, of all the providential happenings of Flaherty's career the destruction of his Baffin Land and Belcher Island negative was the happiest.

Even if he had known how to shoot film, which he didn't, the conditions under which he had made the Baffinland–Belcher travelogue were such that a director with years of experience would have failed. Making a film is a whole-time activity, not a hobby to be pursued in the intervals of not-mapping and not-prospecting.

He needed this set-back for two reasons; and those who wish may see in what happened the action of Divine Providence. If the negative had survived, Flaherty would have tried to sell his picture to the theatres and he would either have failed and been convinced that he had no talent or succeeded in selling it and seen for himself that the film was a flop.

As it was, he was left with the 'Harvard' print, something which he could look at himself and show to others, but which could not in those days be used for making a duplicate negative.

6 SHOOTING *NANOOK*

The war was on. Sir William Mackenzie was not interested in further exploration in Ungava, Baffin Land or Hudson Bay. The *Laddie* was no more and Sir William was not prepared to buy a ship for a man to shoot another 70,000 feet of film and then set fire to it with a cigarette.

All that was left was the 'Harvard' print and the experience which Flaherty hoped to communicate through it. He showed it to the American Geographical Society, to the Explorers' Club in New York and to friends at his home in New Canaan, Connecticut.

> People were so polite, but I could see that what interest they took in the film was the friendly one of wanting to see where *I* had been and what *I* had done. That wasn't what I wanted at all. I wanted to show the *Innuit.*[1] And I wanted to show them, not from the civilized point of view, but as they saw themselves,

[1] *Innuit* was the name the Eskimo used to describe themselves. Flaherty's translation 'we, the people' implies a contrast with 'them, the masters, the white men, traders and missionaries' or in terms of United States history, 'the people, against the imperial power'. It meant originally 'we, human beings, in contrast to nature and brute creation', the Eskimo at that time being unable to conceive of any other members of the human race.

as 'we, the people'. I realized then that I must go to work in an entirely different way.[1]

The film represented to Flaherty his one uncompleted job. He had found and mapped the Belchers. If others did not exploit the mineral riches, that was their concern. But in the course of prospecting, Flaherty had found a mine of human material as rich as that which Jack London had discovered in the Klondike Gold Rush of 1898. He could not work it out in words. His diaries were vivid; but only as diaries. He didn't possess the novelist's skill, perhaps because he was too gifted with speech. (How many story-writers are failed raconteurs?) And yet for all the stories which he told, which held his listeners entranced, he knew that what he really wanted to say about the *Innuit* failed to get across. It was all glorification of Flaherty. In the film he had hoped to eliminate himself, but he saw he had not succeeded.

> It was utterly inept, simply a scene of this and that, no relation, no thread of a story or continuity whatever, and it must have bored the audience to distraction. Certainly it bored me.
>
> My wife and I thought it over for a long time. At last we realized why the film was bad, and we began to get a glimmer that perhaps if I went back to the North . . . I could make a film that this time would go. Why not take a . . . a typical Eskimo and his family and make a biography of their lives throughout the year? Here is a man who has less resources than any other man in the world. He lives in a desolation that no other race could possibly survive. His life is a constant fight against starvation. Nothing grows; he must depend utterly on what he can kill; and all of this against the most terrifying of tyrants . . . the bitter climate of the North, the bitterest climate in the world.[2]

During the remaining years of the First World War and the terrible aftermath, the Russian, Hungarian and German revolutions, the bloodshed of the trenches and the even more lethal Spanish 'flu epidemic that followed, the orgy of hatred and the calculated cruelty of the Allied Blockade following the Armistice, Robert J. Flaherty went on plugging away at the need for his film.

[1] *The World of Robert Flaherty.*

[2] 'Robert Flaherty Talking.' *The Cinema*, 1950. R. Manvell, Pelican.

It must have seemed to many of his listeners that he had become remote from the world scene and the really urgent problems. But in fact Flaherty knew from personal experience that the message of the film he wanted to make was even more relevant then than it had been in his childhood, when he had found the friendship of men against the hardship of the North the antidote to the class-hatred of industrial Canada and the United States. In the world of war-time bloodshed and post-war hatred, the Eskimo struggle for life provided a much-needed restatement of values.

But nobody wanted to listen to such arguments; and the Flahertys spent lean years, staying for some time with the Hubbards in Houghton, Michigan, and then moving east to Connecticut, living for the most part in Silvermine and New Canaan.

In 1918, he wrote two articles for the *Geographical Review* dealing rather tersely with his explorations in the North. They extended his reputation among a small circle; but they did not go far to supporting his wife and their three daughters, Barbara, Frances and Monica, who had been born meanwhile.

In 1920, when Flaherty was aged thirty-six and was a failure by any material standards accepted by his father or his father-in-law, Flaherty met Captain Thierry Mallett of Revillon Frères at a cocktail party. It is fairly easy to imagine what happened. For Flaherty, Revillon Frères meant Fort Chimo and the 'man-killer' Peterboro canoe, the wonderful rivalry between the Hudson's Bay Company and Revillon Frères to equip him for the east-west traverse of the Ungava Peninsula. Flaherty opened up his charm and eloquence. There were further meetings. Captain Mallett introduced him to Mr. John Revillon.[1] They saw the 'Harvard' print, the pitiful forerunner of what was to be a masterpiece, a vision of the northern territories which the Hudson's Bay Company had for hundreds of years considered their peculiar province.

The public was not sufficiently aware that Revillon Frères had for years been in competition with the Hudson's Bay Company, who started with the initial advantage of being advertised in every atlas by the words Hudson Bay. Supposing that Revillon Frères advanced

[1] Captain Mallett also introduced him to the Coffee House Club, which became for the remainder of his life his favourite New York City haunt.

the money for Mr. Flaherty's film, could the film be shown with the title *Revillon Frères Present*?

'Of course,' said Flaherty, knowing even less about the ethics of film-distribution than he did about the mechanics of making a commercial film. And so at long last the film was financed.

Flaherty had already studied his requirements. He chose two Akeley motion-picture cameras, which were the best to operate in extreme cold, because they were lubricated with graphite, instead of oil or grease. He was fascinated by these cameras, because they were the first with a gyro-movement in the tripod-head, whereby one could tilt and pan the camera without the slightest distracting jar, jerk or vibration.

Today complex camera-movements are commonplace. But in those days they were little used. D. W. Griffith had pioneered the pan or panorama shot (sideways movement of the camera on its own axis) and had used other innovations such as the 'tilt' (an up-or-down movement, or vertical, as opposed to horizontal, pan). In both these shots, it was necessary in the old cameras to wind a geared handle. To try and use both geared handles at once reduced speed and produced a picture so jerky that the scene was often unusable.

The invention of the gyro-tripod, operated by a single arm. was therefore an important technical revolution; and it was one the significance of which Flaherty naturally seized on, because of the demands of his material; how better could he show for example a vast expanse of sea ice, with a solitary seal-hunter at a breathing-hole and the towering of an iceberg?

It was this sort of problem he had been meditating in the years of inaction and although *Nanook* did not in fact contain more than a few pans or tilts, they became an important – indeed vital – feature of his later work in relating his characters to the natural elements.

Revillon Frères chose for Flaherty's base a post of theirs in the sub-Arctic at Port Harrison on Cape Dufferin on the north-east coast of Hudson Bay. To reach there would take two months by schooner and canoe. But Flaherty was determined to take with him full equipment, not merely for shooting and lighting, but for developing, printing and projecting. The 200-mile trip to Moose Factory was familiar; but he had never made it so heavily laden. One portage took two days to pack across.

On 15th August, 1920, they dropped anchor in the mouth of the Innuksuk River. The five gaunt buildings of the Port Harrison post stood out on a rocky slope less than half a mile away.

Of the Eskimo who were known to the post, a dozen all told were selected for the film. Of these Nanook, a character famous in the country, I chose as my chief man. Besides him, and much to his approval, I took on three younger men as helpers. This also meant their wives and families, dogs to the number of twenty-five, sledges, kayaks, and hunting impedimenta.

As luck would have it, the first film to be made was that of a walrus hunt. From Nanook I heard of the 'Walrus Island'. On its south end, a surf-bound beach, there were in summer, he said, many walrus, judging from signs that had been seen by a winter sealing crowd of Eskimo who at one time had been caught there by a break-up of the ice. 'The people do not go out to the island in summer,' he continued, 'for not only is it out of sight of land, but is ringed with heavy surf – dangerous landing for kayaks. But for a long time I have had my eyes on your whaleboat,' said he, 'and I am sure, if the seas are smooth, it is big enough for crossing over, and just the thing for landing.'

Through the busy weeks that followed, time and time again Nanook reminded me of the many, many moons it was since he had hunted walrus. One morning I woke up to see the profile of rising ground just beyond my window covered with topeks. Nanook popped his head in through the door. They were Eskimo from the north, he said, far away. 'And among them,' eagerly he continued, 'is the very man who saw the walrus signs on Walrus Island.'

Nanook was off, to return in a moment more leading the great man through the door. We talked iviuk through the hour. 'Suppose we go,' said I in conclusion, 'do you know that you and your men may have to give up making a kill, if it interferes with my film? Will you remember that it is the picture of you hunting the iviuk that I want, and not their meat?'

'Yes, yes, the aggie will come first,' earnestly he assured me. 'Not a man will stir, not a harpoon will be thrown until you give the sign. It is my word.' We shook hands and agreed to start next day.

For three days we lay along the coast, before the big seas outside died down. The wind began blowing off the land. We broke out our leg-o'-mutton. Before the day was half done a film of grey far out in the west told us we were in sight of Walrus Island. By nightfall we closed in to the thundering shadow that was its shore.

For hours we lounged around the luxury of a driftwood fire, soaking in its warmth and speculating on our chances for the morrow. When daylight came we made off to where the stranger had told us he had found the walrus signs. It was a crescent of beach pounded by the surf. While we looked around, one after another the heads of a school of walrus, their wicked tusks gleaming in the sun, shot up above the sea.

By the night all my stock of film was exposed. The whaleboat was full of walrus meat and ivory. Nanook never had such walrus-hunting and never had I such filming, as that on Walrus Island.

Three days later the post bell clangs out the welcome news that the kablunak is about to show his iviuk aggie. Men, old men, women, old women, boys, girls and small children file in to the factor's house. Soon there is not an inch of space to spare. The trader turns down the lamps. The projector light shoots over the shocks of heads upon the blanket which is the screen.

Then the picture. A figure appears. There is silence. They do not understand. 'See, it is Nanook!' the trader cries. The Nanook in the flesh laughs his embarrassment. 'Ah! ah! ah!' they all exclaim. Then silence. The figure moves. The silence deepens. They cannot understand. They turn their heads. They stare at the projector. They stare at its beam of magic light. They stare at Nanook, the most surprised of all, and again their heads turn towards the screen. They follow the figure which now snakes towards the background. There is something in the background. The something moves. It lifts its head. 'Iviuk! iviuk!' shakes the room. The figure stands up, harpoon poised in hand.

'Be sure of your harpoon! be sure of your harpoon!' the audience cries.

The figure strikes down; the walrus roll off into the sea. More figures rush in; they grab the harpoon line. For dear life they hold on.

'Hold him! Hold him!' shout the men. 'Hold him! hold him!' squeal the women. 'Hold him!' pipe the children.

> The walrus's mate dives in, and by locking tusks attempts rescue.
>
> 'Hold him!' gasps the crowd.
>
> Nanook and his crew, although their arms seem to be breaking, hold on. But slowly and surely the threshing walrus drags the figures nearer sea.
>
> 'Hold him! hold him!' they despair. They are breathing hard. 'Dig in! dig in!' they rasp, as Nanook's feet slip another inch through the sand.
>
> Deep silence. Suddenly the line sags, the crew, like a flash, draw in the slack, and inch by inch the walrus is pulled in to shore. Bedlam rocks the house.
>
> The fame of the film spread far up and far down the coast. Every strange Eskimo that came into the post Nanook brought before me and begged that he be shown the iviuk aggie.[1]

This showing of the rushes to the actors was a deliberate part of a philosophy of film-making which Flaherty had evolved during his years of waiting. *Nanook* was to be a film of the Innuit by the Innuit, 'of the people by the people' insofar as that was possible.

The printing machine he had brought with him was an old English Williamson which he screwed to the wall of the hut. He found that the light from his little electric-plant so fluctuated that it was useless. Instead, he used daylight, letting in through the window an inlet of light, just the size of the motion picture frame and controlling its density by the addition or subtraction of pieces of muslin from the printing aperture.

Worse problems than developing and printing film were washing and drying it, because of the freezing cold. To the hut in which he wintered he built an annexe as a drying-room. His source of heat was a coal-burning stove; and how inflammable film was in those days Flaherty knew to his cost. Perhaps that was why no catastrophe happened. When supplies of coal gave out, the Innuit scoured the coast for driftwood.

Washing film was even more difficult. All winter a hole had to be kept chiselled through six foot of ice without its freezing up. The unfrozen water was loaded in barrels and rushed by dog-sledge to the

[1] *My Eskimo Friends.*

hut. There all hands were used to clear the ice forming in the water, before it could be poured over the film. Deer-hair falling from clothing was as much a worry as the forming ice.

Involving the Innuit in this film work was part of the education he found necessary for making the picture. It began by showing them still-photographs of themselves. 'When I showed them the photograph as often as not they would look at it upside down. I'd have to take the photograph out of their hands and lead them to the mirror in my hut, then have them look at themselves and the photograph beside their reflections before, suddenly with a smile that spread from ear to ear, they would understand.'[1]

With him, Flaherty had taken one of the old gramophones, with a square box and a long horn, together with an assortment of records from Caruso, Farrar, Riccardo, McCormack, Al Jolson and Harry Lauder. To the Innuit, the funniest record was Caruso singing the tragic finale of the prologue of *Il Pagliacci*. Nanook tried to eat one of the records and Flaherty incorporated this in the picture.[2]

Flaherty knew that musical gadgets, like his pianola in the Belchers, had a fascination for the Innuit. The gramophone to them was like a jam-jar to wasps. They would come for miles to his hut and there they would be regaled with hot tea and sea-biscuit and music either from the gramophone or from his violin.

The photograph of Flaherty's hut (which we reproduce) is interesting. The framed portrait on the wall seems to be that of Arnold Bennett. On the shelf below is a model, looking rather like the clown Grock. Top left is a photograph of Frances Flaherty and below reproductions of two old masters, of which one is the Franz Hals young man with a mandolin. The portrait of the man to the left of the clock seems to be signed John Turner. Wherever he went on his expeditions,

[1] 'Robert Flaherty Talking', *Cinema*, 1950, pp. 13–14. Robert Lewis Taylor in the *New Yorker* Profile of Flaherty said that the reason why Eskimo held the photographs upside down was according to Flaherty because they had previously only seen their reflections in a pool of water. This was a typical Flaherty joke, taken literally by a journalist so sophisticated that he had never looked at himself in a pool of water, only at other people on the far bank. If a journalist was such an ass as to take such stuff literally Flaherty wasn't one to spoil the joke. The Profile appeared in 3 parts, June 11, 18, 25, 1949.

[2] The author of the *New Yorker* Profile, who had obviously never seen *Nanook of the North*, said that Flaherty stopped filming just before Nanook bit the record. Flaherty didn't trouble to correct him.

Flaherty took with him in addition to essentials, *lares* and *penates* which were bulky in view of the *portages* involved in their transport.

One of Flaherty's, or rather Nanook's, difficulties was the building of an igloo large enough for filming the interior scenes.

> The average Eskimo igloo, about 12 feet in diameter, was much too small. On the dimensions I laid out for him, a diameter of 25 feet, Nanook and his companions started in to build the biggest igloo of their lives. For two days they worked, the women and children helping them. Then came the hard part – to cut insets for the five large slab-ice windows without weakening the dome. They had hardly begun when the dome fell in pieces to the ground. 'Never mind,' said Nanook, 'I can do it next time.'
>
> For two days more they worked, but again with the same result; as soon as they began setting in the ice-windows their structure fell to the ground. It was a huge joke by this time, and holding their sides they laughed their misfortune away. Again Nanook began on the 'big Aggie igloo', but this time the women and children hauled barrels of water on sledges from the water-hole and iced the walls as they went up. Finally the igloo was finished and they stood eyeing it as satisfied as so many small children over a house of blocks. The light from the ice-windows proved inadequate, however, and when the interiors were finally filmed the dome's half just over the camera had to be cut away, so Nanook and his family went to sleep and awakened with all the cold of out-of-doors pouring in.[1]

Just as Flaherty had learnt on his Ungava traverses that he could not survive physically without entrusting himself to Nero and Omarolluk, so now he entrusted the work of the film to Eskimo deputies.

> To 'Harry Lauder' (one of the Eskimoes christened after the gramophone record) I deputed the care of my cameras. Bringing them from the cold outside into contact with the warm air of the base often frosted them inside and out, which necessitated taking them apart and carefully drying them piece by piece. With the motion-picture cameras there was no difficulty, but with my Graflex (a still-camera) I found to my sorrow such a complication of parts that I could not get it together again. For several days its 'innards' lay strewn on my work-table. 'Harry Lauder' finally

[1] 'Robert Flaherty Talking.' *Cinema*, 1950.

> volunteered for the task of putting it together, and through a long evening before a flickering candle and with a crowd of Eskimoes around ejaculating their 'Ayee's' and 'Ah's', he managed to succeed where I had failed.[1]

In what is today the usual documentary practise, there is a preliminary stage of research – which Flaherty could be considered as having done in his previous expeditions. This is followed by a stage of scripting – which in a very loose way Robert and Frances Flaherty were doing when they were reflecting on what had gone wrong on the first film.

But the idea – a year in the life of an Eskimo family – was vague. What sort of family, for example? Flaherty found that Nanook and the rest weren't really dressed in Innuit clothes and he had to go to great trouble and expense to procure for them the clothes which they should be wearing if they were to appear on the screen as genuinely Innuit as they in fact were.

In historical terms *Nanook of the North* was a costume picture, as in far cruder terms the Wild West shows of Buffalo Bill Cody were.

That very first sequence of the walrus-kill was something which Nanook had done and was prepared to do again to make the 'aggie' but he wouldn't have done it otherwise.

This is the second stage of the process which I pointed out previously. The white man who goes into country which has never been seen previously by white men alters it by the mere fact of seeing it. The white man who wants to show what Eskimo life is like normally has to manipulate it on film; a degree of organization comes in from outside. If the Innuit is side-tracked from his hunting, he must be guaranteed basic rations. The film unit is undermining the very pattern of life it is trying to film.

But even so there were two ways of working. Flaherty could have

[1] *My Eskimo Friends.* Prof. Edmund Carpenter in *Eskimo* says, 'The Aivilik Eskimo are first-class mechanics. They delight in stripping down and re-assembling engines, watches, all machinery. I have watched them repair instruments which American mechanics, flown into the Arctic for this purpose, have abandoned in despair.' This is not as surprising as it might seem. The American mechanic is a specialist used to working in his own environment, which is different from the climate in which the Eskimo is a skilled mechanic of all trades.

squatted at Port Harrison and said, 'Just go on living; I'm not going to help you, except in emergency, until this picture is over. But I'm going to film you in all your sufferings. Just forget I'm here!'

If he had tried to do that, despite his charm, his violin and gramophone, he would have been left high and dry by the Innuit. They needed powerful inducements to break their winter pattern. And the whole discipline of filming was the opposite of their pattern. If you want a walrus, you stalk him and harpoon him. But if you want a film-sequence of killing a walrus, you have to stalk the walrus and wait until the director gives the signal for the kill.

Nanook discussed with Flaherty what would be a good 'aggie', killing a she-bear in her den at Cape Sir Thomas Smith 200 miles to the north. He described how in early December the she-bear denned in snow-drifts, with just a tiny vent or airhole melted by the animal's bodily heat. It would be a wonderful hunt, with Nanook's companions either side of Flaherty, rifles in hand, while Nanook cut into the den, block by block with his snow-knife.

> The dogs in the meantime would all be unleashed and like wolves circle the opening. Mrs. Bear's door opened, Nanook, with nothing but his harpoon, would be poised and waiting. The dogs baiting the quarry – some of them with her lightning paws the bear would send hurtling through the air; himself dancing here and there – he pantomimed the scene on my cabin floor, using my fiddle bow for the harpoon – waiting to dart in for a close-up throw; this, he felt sure, would be a big, big picture (aggie peerualluk). I agreed with him.
>
> 'With good going ten days will see us there. Ten days for hunting on the Cape, then ten days for coming home again. But throw in another ten days for bad weather, and let's see (counting on his fingers) – that makes four times my fingers – more than enough to see us through.'
>
> 'All right,' said I, 'we'll go.' And Nanook, his eyes shining, went off to spread the news.[1]

It was an appalling journey. They travelled 600 miles in the course of eight weeks. Two dogs were lost through starvation. They never saw a bear and they were lucky to escape alive. When they returned, they

[1] *My Eskimo Friends.*

were met by Stewart the post-trader. 'What, no bear?' he asked. 'An' just to think that a week come Friday two huskies got a she-bear an' two cubs in a cave. 'T would have made a fine aggie.'

Film critics were to seize on this sort of 'falsity' to the life of the people that Flaherty filmed, even when he succeeded in shooting pictures. In this case, he would have succeeded filmically far better, if he had just stayed in Port Harrison.

But I suggest that Flaherty enjoyed going to Cape Sir Thomas Smith and not finding she-bears far more than he would have done sitting in Port Harrison waiting for one to appear less than a day away. He enjoyed the hazards of exploring, whether it was to map an unknown route, discover a new series of iron-ore or shoot a picture. In each case, it was the hazards and not the achievement that most delighted him. But at the end he had to deliver something, a map, a geological survey or a film, to prove that he had earned his passage.

Perhaps if he had been given an annuity by Revillon Frères he might have gone on shooting in Hudson Bay until he died, because the camera eye had become to him more perceptive than his own. This life of going off with Nanook on bigger and bigger aggies was just what he wanted. In the end, they were hunting whales with a fleet of kayaks. But by August 1921, the film stock now being exhausted and the yearly ship arriving at Port Harrison, Flaherty had to go back to civilization to render the account of what he had been doing all this time. He had to make a film.

A curious fatality pursued many of those whom Flaherty chose out of their natural settings. The Belcher series I have outlined. Within a couple of years Nanook, the great hunter, died of starvation deer-hunting in the interior of Ungava. Frances Flaherty says that ten years later in the Berliner Tiergarten she bought an 'Eskimo Pie' called 'Nanuk' with Nanook's face smiling at her from the paper-wrapper.[1] It was a tribute to Flaherty's film, if small consolation to Nanook's family.

[1] Frances Flaherty. Lecture Notes. 1957.

PART TWO

7 THE MASTERPIECE THAT PAID

During the winter of 1922–3 Flaherty edited *Nanook of the North* with Charlie Gelb, whom, in Frances Flaherty's words, he had 'picked up around the place'. Carl Stearns Clancy helped write the sub-titles. And at last a show-print was ready for screening to possible distributors, the middle men of the film industry.

Flaherty had had no experience of selling a picture and at this time no friend to advise him how to set about it. In his naïve way, he thought it was only necessary to make a good film for a distributor to say 'I'll buy that'.

If it had been a sensational travelogue like those which Martin Johnson made, it would not have been difficult to sell as a second feature; or if it had been the record of a highly publicized expedition, like Ponting's *With Scott to the South Pole*, it would have secured special bookings. But this was neither a run of the mill travelogue, nor the report of an adventure which had stirred the imagination of the world. It was a work of art, unlike anything previously shown on the screen. If it were shown, people probably wouldn't like it because it was so different. But if they did like it, it would be even worse, because it would be impossible to follow it up with other pictures of a similar type. The exhibitors needed 104 double feature programmes a year to satisfy their regular twice-a-week fans and they could not afford to show films which might disturb that pattern.

Flaherty went to a major distributor, Paramount. 'The projection-room was filled with their staff and it was blue with smoke before the film was over. When the film ended they all pulled themselves together and got up in rather a dull way, I thought, and silently left the room. The manager came up to me and very kindly put his arm round my shoulders and told me that he was terribly sorry, but it was a film that couldn't be shown to the public.'[1]

Flaherty then tried First-National. After screening the film, they refused even to tell Flaherty what they thought of the picture. He had to go round to the projection-room and collect the film, almost apologizing for the waste of their screening time.

Selling a film may not be a fine art, but it takes a great deal of craft. If before showing the film to Paramount, Flaherty had managed to spread the rumour that First-National were all steamed up about *Nanook*, Paramount might have bought it out of spite. But Flaherty, though a natural-born showman, had to learn his craft the hard way.

Revillon Frères were French and the Pathé Company of New York was still controlled by the parent company in Paris. Would a French company venture where Americans did not dare?

At least the distribution staff did not turn the picture down out of hand. The material was interesting. But at five reels, playing an hour and a quarter, it was an impossible length. What about a series of short films?

Flaherty exploded to the Coffee House Club friend, a journalist working with Pathé, who'd made the introduction. 'Wait,' said the friend, 'we'll show it to the big brass.'

The second audience, which included Madame Brunet, wife of the Pathé President, 'caught fire'. Now it was only a question of selling the full version to the general public, or rather to the exhibitors.

No ordinary exhibitor would handle so off-beat a picture. But Roxy, who had introduced the three-console electric organ and re-vamped the Victoria Cinema as the Rialto, 'a temple of Motion

[1] 'Robert Flaherty Talking', *Cinema*, 1950.

Pictures; a Shrine of Music and the Allied Arts', might take *Nanook*, if properly approved.

Flaherty's friend planned the operation, knowing that capturing Roxy was as hard as filming Nanook harpooning a walrus.

The sister of the publicity chief of Pathé was a friend of Roxy. She and her friends were shown *Nanook* and told when to applaud when they saw it in Roxy's projection-room at the Capitol. They mustn't say a word to Roxy himself; just murmur their appreciation, as if he didn't exist. Roxy, a magnate with his ear to the ground, ignored anything said to him direct.

The plan succeeded. When the lights went up in the Capitol projection-room, Roxy babbled words like 'epic' and 'masterpiece'. He booked it.

Aware that they could fool some of Roxy some of the time but not all of Roxy all of the time, Pathé decided to 'tin-can' or 'block-book' *Nanook* with Harold Lloyd's first big feature, *Grandma's Boy*, for which every theatre manager in New York was scrambling. When Roxy's manager of the Capitol saw *Nanook*, he exploded with rage. Roxy tried to back out, but climbed down when told, no *Nanook*, no *Grandma's Boy*.[1]

So *Nanook* opened on Broadway during a hot spell as a second feature. Robert E. Sherwood says it took $43,000 business in a week, but he does not mention whether this was the gross for the two pictures or *Nanook*'s share.[2]

In 1923 serious film criticism, as we know it, did not exist. Notices of movies were necessary to sell publicity space and the professional film critic merely gave the public an idea what type of picture could be expected and how successful it was in that type. The professional critics did not know what to make of *Nanook* and they hedged. Favourable notices came from columnists and free-lance journalists able at last to hail a motion-picture which was not an insult to the intelligence, a film which was in its way as original as had been D. W. Griffith's *Birth of a Nation*.

The most considered verdict came from the critic and playwright

[1] Op. cit.

[2] The above account is Flaherty's own. David Flaherty in a letter to Paul Rotha stated that *Nanook* did not run as second feature to *Grandma's Boy* but ran a week at the Capitol as a sole feature, grossing $36,000, an increase of $7,000 over the previous week's film.

Robert E. Sherwood, who wrote in *The Best Moving Pictures of 1922–3.*

> There are very few surprises, few revolutionary stars and directors of established reputation. *Nanook of the North* was the one notable exception. It came from a hitherto-unheard-of source, and it was entirely original in form . . . there have been many fine travel pictures, many gorgeous 'scenics', but there is only one that deserves to be called great. That one is *Nanook of the North.* It stands alone, literally in a class by itself. Indeed, no list of the best pictures of the year or of all the years in the brief history of the movies, could be considered complete without it. Here was drama rendered far more vital than any trumped-up drama could ever be by the fact that it was all *real.* Nanook was no playboy enacting a part which could be forgotten as soon as the grease-paint had been rubbed off; he was himself an Eskimo struggling to survive. The North was no mechanical affair of wind-machines and paper-snow; it was the North, cruel and terribly strong.'

This sort of praise meant little to the multitude. There might be a minority public waiting anxiously for films which broke new ground. But there were not enough such films to bring these people into cinemas twice a week; and even if there had been, the numbers of the minority would not have made up for the numbers of the majority, who would have stayed away. *Nanook* might be a masterpiece, but it was dangerously, uncommercially different.[1]

Nanook of the North did not do good business in the United States. But then in London and in Paris, where the exhibition machinery was more flexible, *Nanook of the North* ran for six months and the prestige of its metropolitan success created a demand for it in the provinces.

There was a kind of specialized form of exhibition in the United States, the system of 'road-showing' such as was used for *The Birth of a Nation* or *Intolerance.*[2] But for these pictures there was the financial

[1] Of all the films shown in 1922, the only one re-issued twenty-five years later was *Nanook of the North.* In 1947 it was shown at the London Pavilion in a sound version and in New York, it played at the Sutton Theatre shortly before the première of *Louisiana Story* in 1948. In 1950–51 this version was released for 16mm. distribution. It has been televised in the United States, Britain, Western Germany, Italy and Scandinavia.

[2] Compare *Gone with the Wind* or more recently *Spartacus* and *Ben-Hur.*

justification that production costs had been very high; and the studios were able to put pressure upon their distribution affiliates. *Nanook*, on the other hand, had cost comparatively little to make; and what little it had cost had been advanced not by a commercial film company but by Revillon Frères. So there was no inducement for the American industry to give it special treatment.

A summary of *Nanook* is given in Appendix One. From what has already been said about the shooting of the picture and about Flaherty's adoption of the Eskimo approach to art, the nature of its originality must be clear. 'In many travelogues you see, the film-maker looks down and never up to his subject,' wrote Flaherty. 'He is always the big man from New York or from London. But I have been dependent on these people.'

But there was one aspect of Flaherty's originality which was misunderstood in *Nanook* and also in his subsequent pictures. It was due partly to the intimacy with which Flaherty used the film medium. He made a greater demand upon the viewer than any previous film-maker, because he did not state in advance what the viewer was going to see. This was famously demonstrated in the sequence of Nanook spearing the seal. During his enormous fight, there is no indication of what is struggling at the end of the line with such tremendous force until the seal is finally hauled on to the ice. Jean Renoir described this method of engaging our curiosity as if the director was making the picture for each individual member of the audience.

Because Flaherty makes each of us the witness of something taking place before our eyes (rather than something which happened at the time of filming), it has an impact of actuality in some ways greater than that, for example, of Ponting's *With Scott to the South Pole*. The statement is not 'This happened to us' but 'this is how life is with Nanook and his family'.

As I have said, the mere fact of filming Nanook automatically changed the actuality of the lives of Nanook and his characters. It was not a newsreel record, nor even a re-enactment of daily life. It was a distillation of reality into a form of poetry; and though the raw material appeared to be the Eskimo, the poetic echoes resonated around the world.

We fail to understand *Nanook*, if we think only of what was on the screen; an almost equally important part of the film was what was in the minds of the audience. Few of the audience were as near to death by starvation, by exposure to the elements, by the caprice of nature. And few of the audience were as free from fear of their fellow men, as naturally generous and loyal and brave. The pure simplicity of *Nanook* is a gentle reminder that our anxieties are luxuries that can be dispensed with.

But of course such a reminder, though it may be inspiring, does not solve the problems of a slum mother in the windy city of Chicago in the depth of winter when fellow creatures, equally driven, have lost their generosity. A miner out of work in the Ruhr or the Rhondda Valley was in no position to go out and kill a seal. And a child running barefoot to the compulsory school could not hide beneath the skins on the snow-bed of an igloo.

A certain resentment built up against *Nanook*, which found its spokeswoman in Iris Barry in 1926. Iris Barry had done secretarial work for Professor Vilhjalmur Stefansson before she became the film critic of the London *Daily Mail*. In *Let's Go to the Pictures*, she described *Nanook* as an 'enchanting romance' which 'convinced us it was fact, though it wasn't at all'. '*Nanook* was actually taken in the latitude of Edinburgh and acted by extremely sophisticated Eskimos.' Though the type of attitude described by Prof. Carpenter above may truly be sophisticated in comparison with the crudity of Admass culture, Iris Barry did not mean it in this sense; and though the latitude of Port Harrison may be the same as that of Edinburgh, its climate is arctic. She added that Vilhjalmur Stefansson said it was 'a most inexact picture of the Eskimo's life'.[1]

Stefansson had done nothing of the sort. In his book *The Standardization of Error* he showed great understanding of the sort of difficulties under which Flaherty had laboured and was most generous as propagandist of the 'Friendly North' to the poet of the 'Bitter Arctic'. He understood that in order to get the type of truth he needed, Flaherty had been forced into artificial aids. Nanook could not build an igloo

[1] On the revival of *Nanook* in 1947, Campbell Dixon, film critic of the *Daily Telegraph* wrote an article *Is Nanook a Fake?* which resurrected the criticism in its distorted form. He quoted from a letter which said, 'To put it mildly, *Nanook* is a phoney . . . I can still remember with what delight I came across Stefansson's exposure of the impostor . . .' For 'delight', one should perhaps read 'relief'.

large enough and with enough light for his family plus the camera, so as Flaherty had admitted in *My Eskimo Friends*, part of the igloo had to be cut away and one could see the steaming of the family's breath, as one wouldn't if they had really been inside an igloo. The seal fishing was unauthentic in that part of Ungava; the seal when landed was patently dead.

Flaherty himself made no pretence of actuality. 'Sometimes you have to lie,' he said. 'One often has to distort a thing to catch its true spirit.'

But all this was in the future. In 1923, having launched *Nanook of the North*, Bob Flaherty settled down with the help of Frances to produce the book of making the film, *My Eskimo Friends*.

What he would do after that, he hadn't the faintest idea. He was out of the world of exploring and prospecting. But his future in the world of films was uncertain.

8 IN SEARCH OF SEA MONSTERS

Mr. Jesse M. Lasky, the production head of Famous-Players-Lasky, the studio end of Paramount Pictures Corporation, was crazy about exploration. As a boy he'd gone on fishing trips with Dad in Maine. Zane Grey, the Western writer, took him camping and he spent vacations on pack-trips with hired guides in Alaska, the High Sierras, the Canadian North-West and down the Colorado River.

Paramount had turned down *Nanook of the North* and yet it had proved good box office overseas. It had cost peanuts to produce compared with even the run-of-the-mill pictures from the studio.

So in his argument with the distributors, Lasky decided to hire Flaherty. In Lasky's autobiography there is no mention of hiring Flaherty, but Flaherty, for whom the words prove the watershed of his career, was emphatic what they were.

I WANT YOU TO GO OFF SOMEWHERE AND MAKE ME ANOTHER NANOOK GO WHERE YOU WILL DO WHAT YOU LIKE I'LL FOOT THE BILLS THE WORLD'S YOUR OYSTER.

This is Flahertyism: the beginning of falsity in the Flaherty story, the snapping of the naturally grown roots of what had been the consistent life of the son of a mining prospector, who became a mining prospector and then because he loved the North so much went back there to make a film.

From this moment on, Flaherty was a film director, an explorer in search of film subjects and the money to make them.

One can understand the feelings of Frances Flaherty. She had married Bob because she loved the primitive life. But for nine years, she had been stuck at home while Bob had done all the exploring. Why couldn't Bob select a part of the world oyster in which she and the girls could be with him?

'Why not?' said Bob and they both went to New York to see Frederick O'Brien, the author of *White Shadows in the South Seas*, at The Coffee House Club.

O'Brien brought along George Biddle, a rich American who had been painting in Tahiti, and Grace Moore, who was beginning to sing in the Metropolitan Opera House.

According to the *New Yorker* Profile, 19th June, 1949, O'Brien said that after years in the frozen North, 'Flaherty should go south to Polynesia.' Grace Moore and Biddle agreed. Samoa was the only place with a truly Polynesian culture. 'Go to Safune on the island of Savaii,' O'Brien said. 'You still may be in time to catch some of that beautiful old culture before it passes entirely away.'

'What about the children?' Frances asked. They were aged six, four and two. 'Of course,' said Flaherty, 'we'll all go. They shall be schooled in the ways of nature. The world is our oyster.'

Frances Flaherty was a very active woman – and indeed still is. Frustrated for years at Bob's vanishing away to make moving pictures, she had taught herself still photography. She had been following his methods, and if she went to Samoa, she wasn't going to be just a mother. A nursemaid must be hired to look after the children.

The party was snowballing. But it hadn't finished. Young David Flaherty was working in a coal and wood office in Port Arthur when he received during the 'coldest winter on record' a telegram. ALL ARRANGED WITH FAMOUS-PLAYERS-LASKY MAKE FILM IN SOUTH SEAS STOP SAILING SAN FRANCISCO FOR SAMOA APRIL 24 STOP COME EARLIEST STOP SALARY TWO HUNDRED DOLLARS MONTHLY BOB.

'It changed the course of my life,' says David Flaherty. 'Within two weeks, I had joined Bob and his family in New Canaan and a few weeks later we were on the bosom of the broad Pacific, far from snow and ice, coal-dust and clinkers.'

Frances and David Flaherty were to become the hands and organizing brains of what had been a single operation in the North.

They sailed on s.s. *Sonoma* from San Francisco in April 1923; Bob, Frances, David, the three girls and a red-headed nursery maid. Before he left New York, Flaherty had been given a glowing description of Savaii by Frederick O'Brien. It was the last remaining island uncorrupted by Western civilization. The inhabitants were an almost Grecian race, as beautiful as their landscape. In the village of Safune, there lived one white man, familiar with the Polynesians and their language, a German trader named Felix David, to whom O'Brien gave Flaherty a letter of introduction.

Flaherty did not take Lasky's 'another *Nanook*' very seriously. *Nanook* came from years of living, working, travelling and thinking in Eskimo country. He knew that he would never make another film from so deep a level of his being even with the most sympathetic of backers. Paramount would not want it, even if he did. They wanted something exotic, exciting, spectacular, the tropical equivalent of hunting seal and walrus and bear. In an island as paradisal as Savaii, the land was too beneficent. On the *Sonoma*, the Flahertys discussed the possibilities of sea-monsters, sharks or a giant octopus. If there were such creatures, it would presumably be possible to dream up a story in which the Samoans might have to fight one for their lives, even though any sensible inhabitant of an island paradise would stay ashore.

In fact Savaii was by no means the island paradise which Frederick O'Brien had described. According to Newton A. Rowe, author of *Samoa under the Sailing Gods*,[1] a District Inspector of the Island of Savaii 1922–6: 'The administration of justice in Savaii during 1923 and 1924 amounted to a scandal I should think without modern parallel in a British possession'[2].

There would have been a possible film about the very strange

[1] Putnam, London, 1930.

[2] The islands were under League of Nations Mandate to New Zealand. The maladministration which led to the machine-gunning of High Chief Tamese and ten others in Apia, on 28th December, 1929, was already established.

complex of government, missionary and trading endeavour in Savaii and its effects upon the people; a film of great anthropological-sociological-political-and-whatnotical interest. But Flaherty was no more interested than Jesse Lasky in that stuff. He wanted to find Felix David, Frederick O'Brien's contact man with his finger on the pulse of Polynesia.

> 'I don't think that either of us will ever forget the morning we stood off the reefs at Safune waiting to get in,' Flaherty said. 'We waited a long time before at last daybreak came, I've never seen such big seas. They were higher than the boat was long.
>
> 'When we got into the lagoon, we were like a cloud floating through the sky . . . When the schooner finally berthed at the long slender wharf, we could see the man we had come so far to meet. From the upper veranda he gazed at us through binoculars, The natives streamed down the wharf and gave us the friendly welcome that so endears one to the Polynesians[1].

The unsophisticated party of film-makers with their children and nanny landed and was conducted up the beach to the gates of the compound and thence up a stairway to the veranda where they were greeted by their host, Felix David. White-haired, moustachioed like the ex-Kaiser, Herr David preferred to his legitimate description of Trader the title King of Savaii.

He gave the Flaherty party a vast breakfast consisting of mummy apples, breadfruit, pineapples, coco-nuts, roast wild-pig and the rarest of rare mangoes. The breakfast lasted hours. But when it was over Herr David took them into his living-room, the great doors of which gave on the blue sea and the white surf of the coral reef.

Flaherty was curious, though never psychologically intrusive. He was puzzled to see on the walls old lithographs and photographs of the great figures of the German stage and opera. In contrast to them was a painting of a Prussian officer, holding a sword in front of him, almost like an exorcist. And in one corner stood an old piano, of the 1880's, laden with fly-specked music.

Over the prolonged breakfast Herr David had told Flaherty that he had informed the island chiefs that a motion-picture would be made about them. They had never seen a motion-picture; any more

[1] B.B.C. Talks.

than he had, having left the Fatherland in 1896. David indicated that if one was shown to his subjects, he would be prepared to watch it. But films, he intimated, weren't what the Savaii people really liked. It was an astonishing thing. They loved opera. And that was what was so marvellous. When he was a young man, he had been trained to sing baritone. 'But his father,' and he looked up at the only painting among the photographs, 'his father didn't approve.'

So he had come out to Samoa, which in those days was German, and settled down as a trader and had sold and bought during the day and at nights he sang opera to his 'subjects'. His *tour-de-force* was Siegfried's death scene from *Götterdämmerung*, which according to Flaherty had been heard by some of the older inhabitants of Safune some five thousand times.

Flaherty had brought with him some entertainment films. Paramount had given him copies of *It Pays to Advertise*, *The Miracle Man* and *Sentimental Tommy*. But the most popular film among the islanders was Henrik Galeen's *The Golem* made in Germany in 1920. The massive stone figure of the monster, played by Paul Wegener, so struck the Safune people that for years later children could be found named after the Golem.

It might have been thought that this German film would appeal most to Felix David for patriotic reasons. But on it he came to concentrate the fury provoked by Flaherty, who overshadowed him with his dominant personality, undermined him with the excitement of his film project and deprived him of his operatic audience by providing more popular entertainment.

This however was not immediately apparent. Felix David promised full co-operation, with the guarantee that if *he* said so, there would be no trouble.

Before they arrived at Safune, sixteen tons of equipment had been landed, the lighting-generator, projector and other apparatus for the laboratory. For insurance purposes they had been labelled with high-priced values and Flaherty was known as the 'Melikani Millionea'.

For days a chain of natives carried boxes and bales up to an old, disused and overgrown trading post, which was to be used as their headquarters when it had been made habitable by a second team. This house, where Frederick O'Brien had lived, was sited among giant palms within view of Herr David's house. In due course a green sward was cleared under the trees so that a cinema-screen could be erected at one end and the lighting-plant and projector at the other. A little hut was built at the mouth of a cave which was to be converted into a laboratory. It was sheltered beneath a huge out-spreading bread-fruit tree.

Herr David arranged a meeting in the village guest house to introduce Flaherty to the chiefs of the island. Twenty-five chiefs were present, all drawn from the village of Safune.

With Felix David as interpreter, Flaherty tried to explain to them why he had come to Samoa, and to Safune on Savaii in particular, to make a film of the Samoan people and their way of life. The chiefs promised every sort of help and there was a great feast.

But the Flahertys knew that the Samoans had no idea of what they intended to do; even less than Flaherty himself, who could think no further than finding a Samoan equivalent of Nanook, a sturdy, dignified chief and head of a family, and then build the picture round him, substituting for snow and ice the dangers of the sea. 'We would present,' in Mrs. Flaherty's words, 'the drama of Samoan life as it unrolled itself naturally before us, as far as possible untouched by the hand of the trader, the missionary and the government.' It was an irony that in order to do so they had to use as interpreter a trader who considered himself King of Safune.

They began by trying to tell the islanders in a booklet about the Eskimo and the purpose behind filming *Nanook*. Through Herr David, Flaherty spoke of how he lived with the Eskimo people, won their friendship and confidence, made his picture because 'love overflowed in his heart for the people of that country, on account of their kindliness, etc.'[1] The men in New York saw that Mr. Flaherty had done a very useful thing. 'Such pictures as this will create love and friendship among all the people of the world.' So the men in New York had sent Mr. Flaherty to make another such picture among the descendants of the pure Polynesian race of ancient times as they were in the days before missionaries and traders had arrived to change their customs.

Though Jesse L. Lasky would have been surprised to learn that his motive for sending Flaherty to Samoa was so that 'misunderstandings

[1] Mrs. Flaherty, quoted in *The World of Robert Flaherty*.

and quarrels between the nations will cease' and though this statement made as little impression on the islanders as the screening of *Nanook* some weeks later, it is confirmation that Flaherty saw his first picture as a contribution to world peace, at least after the event.

While the organization of unit headquarters and equipment went ahead, Flaherty took pains to establish good relations with Herr David. He went over to the trader's house in the evenings and drank his mummy-apple beer. Herr David had a daughter, whom he was careful to keep away from the visitors, but whom he hoped to send back to 'civilization'. The money the film unit would pay him for his services might give him the chance he had been waiting for. '*Ach Gott!* the new art! Are we not brothers in the craft?' As the beer flowed, he grew maudlin about the operatic triumphs that had been denied him. But between depressive bouts, he was very helpful at the outset, sending his servants scouring the island for whatever Flaherty wanted.

The trouble was Flaherty didn't know what he wanted. For weeks he searched the deep-sea caverns underlying the reefs for the giant octopuses or tiger-sharks which might have menaced a chieftain of the pure Polynesian race of ancient times. He was assured by white residents of long standing that no such creatures existed. But he refused to believe them and he inquired about monsters from any native visitor to Safune, until finally after months a party of chiefs from up the coast reported that a giant octopus had been spotted in the passage of the reef at Sataua. Its body was as big as one of the Safune village houses.

This did not surprise the Flahertys. Hadn't an octopus been washed up on the coast of Madagascar with a carcase bigger than that of any known whale? There was also talk of tiger-shark in the deep-water reef at Asau Bay on the way to Sataua. They decided to go and see for themselves, sending word in advance of their arrival.

But when they reached Asau, what awaited them was a formal ceremony with speeches and drinks which had to be gone through before the business of tiger-sharks could be broached; and though the chiefs agreed that it would be the easiest thing next morning to lure sharks with bait placed on the rocks and spearsmen ready to kill them, meanwhile what about the dance that had been arranged in their honour?

MOANA — 1923–25

The village of Safune

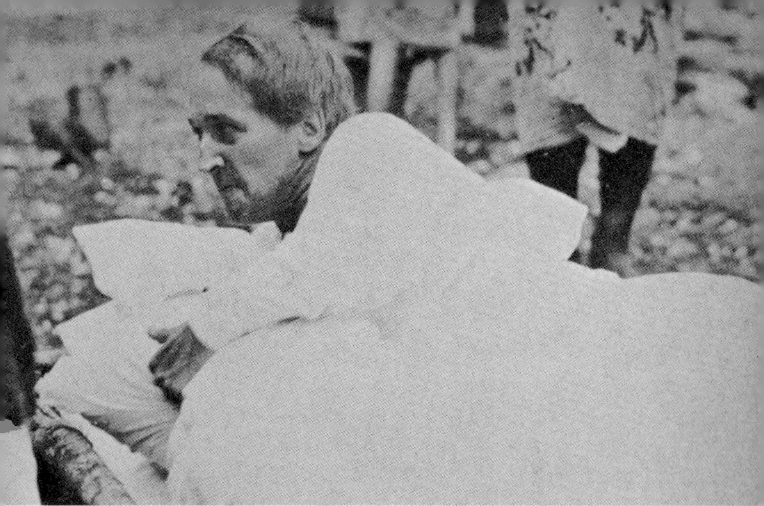

Flaherty on the way back from Tufu
(see page 110)

Making the bark cloth for lava-lavas

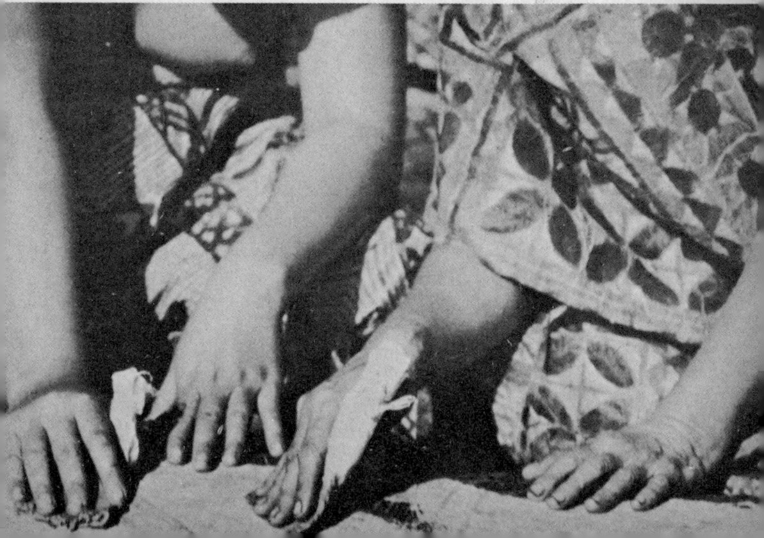

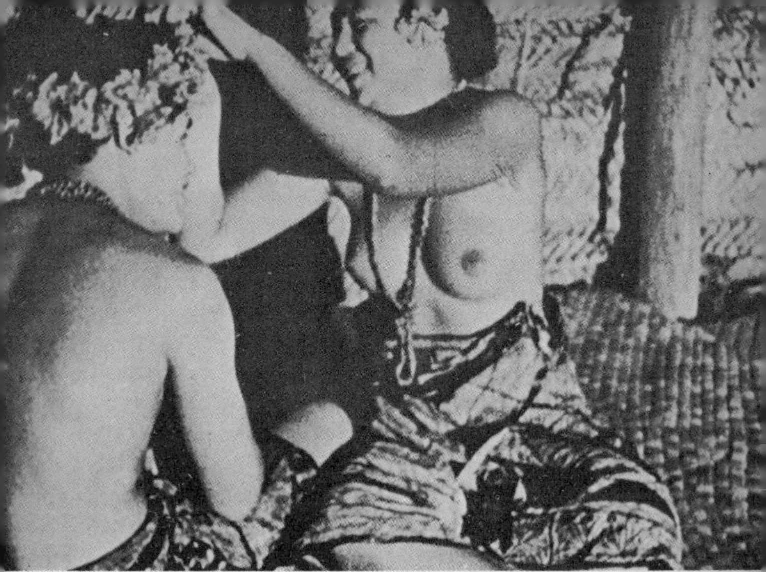

Making ready for the ceremony
(enlargement from film)

Rehearsal for the siva

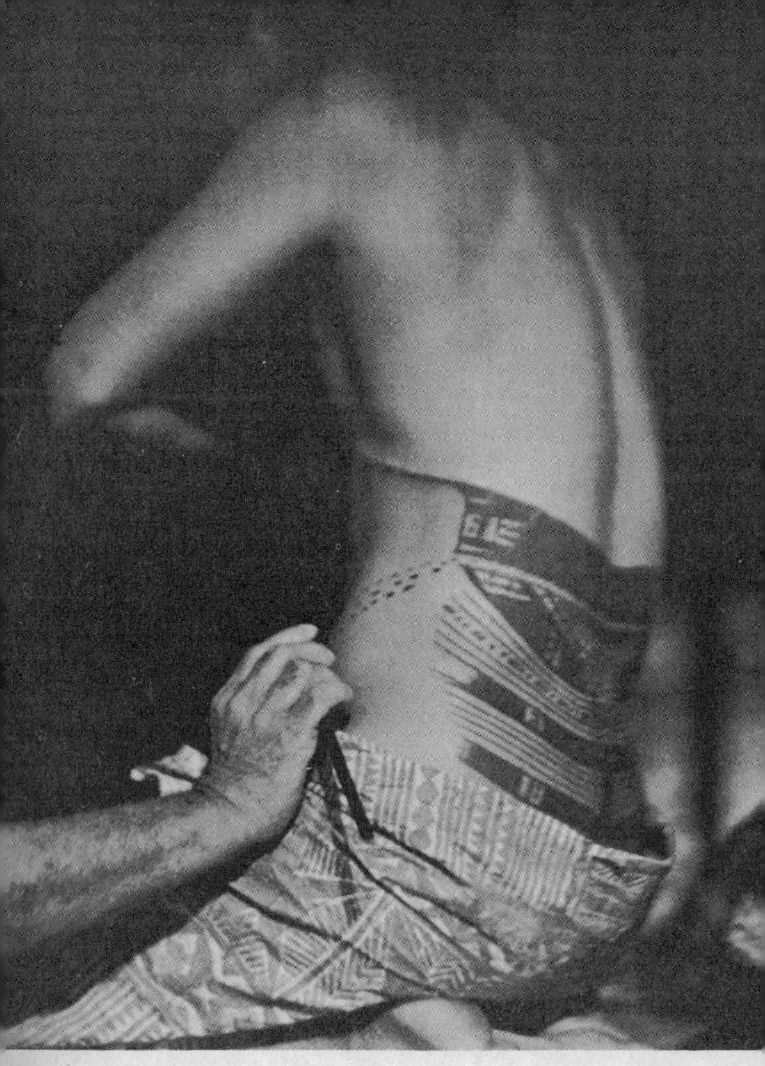

The tattoo

The dance was elaborate so that the dances staged by the villagers they were to visit later should appear insignificant in comparison. But next morning, though the bait was on the rocks and the spearsmen ready, there were no sharks. Nor was there an octopus in Sataua; only more feasting, dancing and affability.

As a prospector, Flaherty had observed that you find what you go out to see. Looking for iron, he had not observed gold. Looking for sharks, he failed to see what must be the subject of his film.

The fact that the Flahertys had chosen Safune as their location had stirred up jealousy in all the other villages. Why should the Melikani Millionea spend his millions in Safune rather than Asau or Sataua?

While he wasn't looking for sea-monsters, Flaherty was searching for photogenic types and shooting atmosphere scenes, useful for testing his organization. Even before he had decided what the story should be, he was looking for a beautiful young girl to be the heroine. He inspected the maidens of Safune but none of them was what he wanted. This so distressed the chiefs of Safune, who had been lording it over the chiefs of all the other villages that theirs had been the village chosen for the film, that they even offered Flaherty the taupou of Safune as his heroine.

The taupou, it must be explained, is the principal maiden of a Samoan village. She is the highest in rank and theoretically the most beautiful. She is treated like a minor princess. She officiates at all ceremonies, especially the making of kava when visiting chiefs arrive. Her tribal destiny is to marry a visiting chief, the higher the better.

Flaherty had already rejected the taupou of Safune in his own mind. She was neither young, nor attractive. Now with all the diplomacy he could command, he turned down this proud offer.

Soon after, he found the girl he wanted, the taupou of the neighbouring village of Sasina, a real beauty named Taioa.

When Flaherty announced his choice, the chiefs of Safune received the news with arctic coolness. No two villages in Savaii hated one another more than Safune and Sasina.

'When, after a feast of pigs, taro, breadfruit, wild pigeons, mangoes and yams, to the accompaniment of siva sivas and Ta'alolos hours and hours long, I bargained for and bought her from the proud and haughty, albeit canny, chiefs of Sasina, and she and her handmaid came up the palm-lined trail to Safune, the old women here told her between their teeth that they would see that she was killed by dawn.'[1]

Flaherty appealed to Felix David to solve the difficulty. Taioa was given space for her sleeping-mat on the Flahertys' veranda. She survived the night and submitted to film tests, smiling and strumming her guitar.

'How did you fix it?' asked Flaherty.

'I just asked them if they wanted you to go and make the picture at Sasina,' David answered.

Having solved that difficulty, Flaherty turned his mind to other problems. But within a month Taioa had vanished from the veranda; and from the village one of the boys had vanished too. 'The Safune chiefs just laughed and laughed.'

Undeterred, Flaherty found another girl, Saulelia, not quite as fascinating as Taioa but with beautiful long hair. The tests were good and altogether Flaherty shot thousands of feet on her.

Then one morning she arrived with her hair cropped like a man's. Flaherty exploded with rage. Weeping, the girl explained that she had been deserted by her lover and, fa'a Samoa, she had to crop her hair.

With his third girl, Fa'angase, Flaherty succeeded. She was almost a child when the unit first arrived in Safune and had followed Flaherty around shyly wherever he had been filming. Sometimes she brought him a flower. Now with the months, she had blossomed.

She came from the other end of the village. Her father was an important chief. He agreed that his daughter might take part in the film provided 'Lopati' as they called Flaherty treated her like his own daughter. The chief explained that his end of Safune was high in rank but where Lopati lived was low and always had been. The village boys round Lopati's house were low-class and Flaherty must see they behaved when Fa'angase was around.

Flaherty promised. Filming restarted. But the 'low-class' boys were difficult to restrain. Flaherty had trained two of them to work in the cave laboratory. They worked in semi-darkness and sang and laughed to keep away the evil spirits. When rushes of Fa'angase came through, they teased her unmercifully, shouting 'Oh, Fa'angase, her legs are

[1] Picture Making in the South Seas, *Film Year Book*, 1924.

bowed . . . and her eyes . . . one looks one way and the other looks the other way.'

Fa'angase took the teasing in good part. But her father got news of it and one day there was a meeting in the high-class end of the village. It sounded angry, and Flaherty went to ask Herr David what was happening.

There was trouble between the two ends of the village, David said, and the chiefs from the high-class end were coming to take Fa'angase away from the film. To lose his third leading lady seemed the end to Flaherty. He stopped shooting and waited to see what would happen.

A small river divided the high-class end from the low-class end and that night a deputation of chiefs came across the bridge towards Flaherty's house. It was obvious to him that they had come to take his third leading lady away; and he must have been debating whether to go to another village or another island, when his interpreter, a woman named Fialelei,[1] ran up to say that the chiefs of the low-class end were hiding among the trees with knives in their hands.

By this time the high-class chiefs had reached Flaherty's house. Their spokesman asked a favour of Lopati. Knowing it could not be refused, Flaherty asked what it was.

'Would Lopati mind going with us to the bridge across the river?'

No word was said about Fa'angese.

Flaherty hesitated a moment; then he and Frances went with the chiefs to the bridge down the path in the half-light past the men, waiting with their drawn knives, hidden in the trees. Nothing happened.

Nothing, that is, except that next morning Fialelei said Willy, the house-boy, wanted a holiday.

'Why?' asked Flaherty.

'He's married.'

'Married?' said Frances. 'To whom? When?'

And then it came out that while the chiefs had been visiting Flaherty the night before, the boys who had worked for Flaherty had slipped across to the other side of the river and abducted as a bride for Willy

[1] In March 1942, Flaherty published the story of Fialelei in the *Reader's Digest*, Vol. 40, No. 239.

the not-so-young-or-very-beautiful, but high-class taupou whom Flaherty had rejected as his first leading lady.

The summer of 1923 passed with Flaherty still searching for his characters and his theme instead of waiting for his theme and characters to come to him. He was conscious that he hadn't got all the time in the world and he was deliberately trying to make a Polynesian *Nanook*; and yet every experience he had had since landing on Savaii had proved that he was trying to impose on the Polynesians a Rousseauesque Noble Savagery which was quite foreign to them.

They had none of the heroic Eskimo virtues. Life was exceptionally easy. The sea wasn't an implacable enemy. It was a heated bathing pool crammed with sea-food. The land was so rich that 'farming' wasn't work, but fun. Climatically Samoa was a denial of all the epic virtues which Flaherty had come to accept as the axiomatic contrast to the industrial situation which he loathed.

He was thirty-nine, a self-educated man who had learnt his lessons the hard and limited way of personal experience. Samoa was difficult to absorb.[1] If he had been a younger man, less conditioned by earlier experience, he would have saved months of labour. But if he had saved these months, it is possible that he would have missed the technical discovery which made *Moana* photographically the most beautiful picture ever shot till that time and which revolutionized the use of film-stock throughout the world.

The technical discovery was due to chance. Flaherty had taken his two Akeley cameras for black-and-white work. For those he used the normal orthochromatic stock, such as he had used in *Nanook*. In *Nanook* the orthochromatic stock had been splendid, because the backgrounds had been white, against which shades of darkness stood out well. But in Samoa, the enormous richness of colour, the golden-bronze of the people, the green subtleties of foliage, the brilliant red of the flowers the villagers wore in their hair were all reduced to the same imprecise darkness.

Flaherty had also brought with him a Prizma colour camera, together with the new type 'panchromatic' stock which was colour-

[1] Just as it had been difficult for Jack London with a similar Arctic experience in youth to readjust to Hawaii and places south.

sensitive. When the Prizma broke down, Flaherty loaded an Akeley with a roll of panchromatic, perhaps out of curiosity, perhaps feeling that for tests which wouldn't be used in the final film he might economize on his orthochromatic.

When the rushes were screened, though in black-and-white, 'the figures jumped right out of the screen' according to Frances Flaherty. 'They had a roundness and modelling and looked alive and, because of the colour correction, retained their full beauty of texture. The setting immediately acquired a new significance.'[1]

Flaherty decided that the whole of his film should be re-shot on panchromatic stock. This enormously complicated the production. In the cave laboratory, orthochromatic film could be developed in red light; panchromatic stock had to be developed and fixed in utter darkness.

Then again the manufacturers, Eastman Kodak, had warned Flaherty that panchromatic was tricky. It was good for cloud effects but it had never been used for a full-length production.

Flaherty had already shot 40,000 feet of orthochromatic. He knew its quality was poor, even when the content was right.[2] So he cabled Eastman Kodak for more panchromatic, though he didn't inform Mr. Lasky.

Flaherty's use of panchromatic film was not merely one of the reasons why even today *Moana* is photographically brilliant but also one of the main factors for its subsequent adoption in black-and-white cinematography throughout the world.

There was a contributory factor to the brilliance of the photography of *Moana*.[3] This was that Flaherty shot the picture in either early morning or late afternoon, when the sun was low and its rays threw long shadows to create an effect of depth and perspective.

But before Flaherty achieved this technical triumph, there were physical setbacks. The first was a personal one. Used to endure extreme cold, he was distressed by the exposure to extreme heat. While the Flahertys were still hunting for strange sea-monsters, he was

[1] Quoted in *The World of Robert Flaherty*.

[2] This was rather like the footage he had shot in Baffin Land and the Belchers which had so conveniently gone up in flames.

[3] Told to Rotha and Wright by Flaherty himself in 1931.

suddenly taken ill in a little village called Tufu. It was a distance from Safune. He couldn't eat anything, could only take doses of some pain-killer. He grew too weak to move.

A messenger was dispatched to Fagamalo, whence a radio message was flashed to Apia to send a boat immediately to Falealupo, the port (a mere opening in the reef) nearest to Tufu. It would take five days for the boat to reach Falealupo; but Mrs. Flaherty gave instructions for a litter to be made to carry her husband to Newton Rowe's house there. Rowe headed the progress mounted on his horse, followed by a native Samoan missionary, Mrs. Flaherty and Bob in his litter. (See Illustration.)

At one point, Rowe found that he had ridden ahead without anyone following. When he turned back, he saw that the procession had stopped. The missionary insisted that Flaherty, ill as he was, should leave the litter and walk a short distance.

Frances Flaherty thought it was nonsense. But Rowe told her to agree seeing that all the Samoans advised it. He did not learn till later that Flaherty had to walk because he could not be carried across the spirit-path which led to a rock from which the dead spirits dived into the sea to Polutu, the land of their dead.

It is ironic that Flaherty, who had come to Savaii in order to film the rich life of the ancient Polynesians before traders, missionaries and government officials had arrived to corrupt their culture, would have died if he hadn't been looked after by Newton Rowe, a District Officer, and Father Haller, a Roman Catholic missionary whom the islanders wanted to burn, until the *Lady Roberts*, a tug designed for inland waters, arrived with a Dr. Ritchie, who took Flaherty for treatment to Apia, the capital on the main island.

After a month Bob was back in Safune, but it wasn't until a year later that he found what had caused his illness. He only discovered it then because his panchromatic rushes began to go wrong. The developed negative had dark flashes on it at regular intervals and the positive film projected in the coco-nut grove theatre was unusable.

Perhaps Eastman Kodak's warning was valid. They stopped shooting and through June and July, 1924, carried out tests to find out what was wrong. Flaherty sent a young Tasmanian, Lancelot Clark, to

Hollywood and then to Eastman Kodak to find out what the trouble might be.

But while Clark was away, David Flaherty discovered what had spoilt the film and poisoned Bob. A Government chemist in Apia on the other island had suggested that the water in the laboratory cave had been too salty and gave him some silver nitrate with which to make a salinity test.

David Flaherty found that all the time they had been developing film, the silver nitrate instead of being washed away by the tide had been accumulating in the bottom of the pool in ever-increasing quantities. This was the reason why the film had developed the dark flashes. It was the cause also of Bob's mysterious illness, because he had been in the habit of drinking water from the pool.

Over a year had passed. The unit had not shot a foot of usable film. Flaherty had discovered a method of shooting on panchromatic stock. But in May 1924 it still remained for him to discover a proper theme. And he found it, not as a more sociological director might have done in the conflict between the ancient pattern of Polynesian life and the rival interests of traders, missionaries and government officials, but in Fa'a Samoa, the combination of social convention and ritual, which had resisted all Flaherty's attempts to impose his own preconceived ideas.

9 *MOANA*

The twelve months' shooting had not been an utter waste of time. Flaherty had accumulated the experience and characters from which he was to make his final picture.

First there was Tu'ungaita, who was to play the part of the mother of Moana's family. She first came to the Flaherty house selling baskets she had made from strips of sun-dried pandanus leaf. Frances thought it would be good if her daughters learned how to make them and Tu'ungaita stayed on as their teacher.

The old lady proved equally skilled in making tapa, a bark-cloth from which lava-lavas had been made in earlier times. It was a dying craft, as most lava-lavas were made of cotton, woven and printed in Manchester or Japan. But when the old lady made this tapa, the younger women and girls of Safune gathered round in admiration; and Flaherty, with his love of traditional skills, filmed it with care to detail.

The screening of the tapa-making and other scenes opened Flaherty's eyes to the possibility of making his film out of the picturesque incidents of everyday life, fishing, hunting, making bark-cloth and so on.

But from Flaherty's point of view, Samoan life was still too easy. The climate did not provide the challenge which was the necessary discipline for the formation of character. And for some time, Flaherty was at a loss for a fitting climax. He found it in the tattooing ceremony, an idea suggested by Newton Rowe. In *Samoa under the Sailing Gods*, Rowe writes: 'A Samoan who is not tattooed . . . it extends almost solid from the hips to the knees . . . it has been remarked, appears naked beside one who is; and in no way can the custom be considered disfiguring. Indeed, it enhances the appearance of a Samoan. The missionaries . . . with the exception of the Catholics . . . hated it, and still hate it, as a relic of 'heathenism'. It matters nothing apparently to them that, while the custom stands, it militates against immature mating; and that it is the one test in these islands, where life is so easy, that the youth has to go through.'

Flaherty leapt at the suggestion – perhaps all the more eagerly because, like tapa-making, tattooing was obsolescent. Newton Rowe had had a tiff with the old tattooer of Asau; but cupidity got the better of the old man and Rowe persuaded him to move to Safune to perform the tattooing of Moana.

Moana[1] (played by Ta'avale) in the sequences which had already been shot had been portrayed as pursuing a romance with the heroine (played by Fa'angase). But until he was tattooed, Moana, no matter what his age, was still a boy (at least according to the premises of the film). The tattooing ceremony, therefore, made the turning point of his life, the initiation to manhood.

Flaherty, who had watched the process on two previous villagers, filmed it in great detail. It was very painful. Needle-points of bone, like a fine-tooth comb, impregnated with dye, were driven into the skin under the steady tapping of a hammer. The skin was held taut and the surplus dye and blood were wiped away along the lines marked out for the pattern. The pattern, like fine blue silk tights, extended from above the waist to below the knee, solidly. The pain was such that only a small area could be tattooed at a time.

According to Frances Flaherty,[2] 'Tattooing is the beautification of the body by a race who, without metals, without clay, express their feeling for beauty in the perfection of their own glorious bodies.

[1] Moana is the Samoan word for Sea, the only relic of Flaherty's original concept that the sea should be the main theme of the film.

[2] Quoted in *The World of Robert Flaherty*.

Deeper than that, however, is its spring in a common human need, the need for some test of endurance, some supreme mark of individual worth and proof of the quality of the man.' How valid this was, or had been, of the Samoan cultural pattern is hard to say. But certainly it is true of Flaherty's symbolism.

Ta'avale would never have been tattooed if it hadn't been for the film. He dreaded the ordeal. It meant six weeks of torture with Flaherty filming at each stage and another fortnight of recovery. But after some hesitation he endured it according to Frances Flaherty[1] because it 'was not only his own pride that was at stake but the honour of all Samoa' and also more plausibly because 'he was certainly the hero of the film now'.

It would not be cynical to add that Ta'avale was well paid by Flaherty to undergo the traditions of his race.

In all, Flaherty shot some 240,000 feet of film, making *Moana*. By modern standards this would not be much for a major-feature picture, but it was a fantastic footage for a single director-cameraman on a single location.[2] Mr. Lasky did not complain. Never had such footage been so cheaply developed and printed by two native boys in a cave remote from any labs.

But during the final weeks of production, the film was nearly wrecked because of these two lab boys, Samuelo and Imo.

A youth travelling from Sataua with a government party which spent a night in Safune on a tour of the island made advances to a girl who was the wife of the native missionary's son. Imo and Samuelo took it up as a violation of fa'a Samoa. In the quarrel that ensued Imo stabbed the youth in the neck with a 'bullet-tipped cane'. The thrust reached his spine and twenty-four hours later he was dead.

Samoan native law demanded an eye for an eye, a life for a life. Women and children were evacuated from Safune, while the men patrolled the village all night expecting a counter-attack. The Flahertys bolted themselves into their bungalow. The immense footage of film was stored in camphor-wood chests on the veranda and the three adult Flahertys took turns to stand guard over it with a shotgun.

[1] Op. cit.

[2] It should be remembered though that of this 40,000 feet of orthochromatic was scrapped and an unknown quantity of panchromatic ruined by 'fogging'.

Robert Lewis Taylor in his Profile of Flaherty (*New Yorker*, 18th June, 1949) stated that Felix David had begun the trouble by making the two lab boys drunk. In notes to the authors, David Flaherty flatly contradicted this.

On the other hand, the continued presence of the Flaherty unit had undermined the German trader. His kingship of the village had been challenged. Nobody wanted to hear him sing when they could watch *The Golem*. Whatever money he might make out of the film, Felix David began to hate the film-makers. If he could hinder the film by jailing the two lab boys, he would do so.

Police came from Apia, and arrested the two boys. The Flahertys wrote to the authorities, stressing their good character and behaviour and their importance as film technicians. Felix David wrote direct to the Resident Commissioner accusing the Flahertys of 'obstructing the course of justice'.

In the final showdown, Imo was sentenced to five years imprisonment for manslaughter and Samuelo to two for aiding and abetting. But counter-charges levelled against the Resident Commissioner and Felix David had graver consequences. Both of them were homosexuals, who had seduced Samoans. When the Resident Commissioner at Matautu was told by the investigating commission that the charges against him would be dropped if he left the country, the Resident gave the Commissioners an excellent dinner and told them he would give them his answer by the morning. Next day they found him sitting in his office dead. An army rifle was lying on the floor, the trigger tied to his toe.

Felix David, arrested on the same charge in Safune, was taken to Apia, tried and banished. He did not long survive.

Before the unit left Samoa in December 1924, Flaherty had eliminated much of his inessential footage. But when they reached Hollywood, there were months spent, more in the projection-room than in the cutting-room, producing a rough-cut and fending off executives.

Flaherty had learnt at least part of the lesson about making his sort of film for commercial film companies. Before he showed anything to the high-ups, he sneaked a long version to Laurence Stallings, a well-known playwright who wrote a regular column for the *New York World*. Under the heading 'The Golden Bough', Stallings wrote, among other things: 'I do not think a picture can be greater than this Samoan epic.'

In the course of two years, Famous-Players-Lasky had almost forgotten that they had a guy Flaherty making a picture in the South Seas. But suddenly Paramount, the eastern office of Famous-Players-Lasky, summoned him to New York to finish editing there.

In view of Stallings's article, Famous-Players assigned Julian Johnson one of its top-paid writers to write the sub-titles and the final screen credits read 'Edited and Titled by Julian Johnson'. David Flaherty however is emphatic that Bob and Frances Flaherty wrote the titles and edited the film. The addition of Julian Johnson's name was a form of collateral insurance.

Finally a twelve-reel cut of the picture was shown to Jesse Lasky, Adolph Zukor, Walter Wanger and other executives. The response was enthusiastic. It was too long. Flaherty should reduce it to six reels. But then they might put it out on a road-show release playing at selected theatres at special increased prices.

Flaherty went away to boil the film down to half its length and by the time he had done so, enthusiasm had evaporated. Far from hailing it as a worthy successor to *Nanook*, by then acknowledged a world classic, the salesmen said it had nothing they could sell. 'Where's the blizzard?' one asked. There were no octopuses, no tiger-sharks, not even a hurricane. There was a slender love interest, but Moana and the girl didn't *do* anything. The idea of road-showing the film was dropped.

For months Flaherty argued that *Moana* was a picture people would like, if given the chance to see it. At last he screened the picture to William Allen White and Otis Skinner, critics respected by the industry, and got them to write to Paramount.

'All right,' he was told. 'We'll put the film out in six towns with no more and no less advertising than our usual run of pictures. These six will be the hardest boiled on our list. If it gets by, O.K., we'll put it out on general release.'[1]

[1] The six tough spots were Poughkeepsie in New York State, Lincoln, Nebraska in the middle-west, Pueblo, Colorado in the far west, Austin in the huge state of Texas, Jacksonville in the deep south of Florida and Asheville, N. Carolina, in the mid-south. 'There was a saying in the theatrical world,' observed Flaherty, '"If you think your act is good, try it on Poughkeepsie!"' Robert Flaherty Talking, *Cinema*, 1950.

Flaherty knew *Moana* was good, but it was different from the usual run of films, and if given the same type of publicity, it was bound to fail. He went to Wilton Barrett, head of the National Board of Review of Motion Pictures in New York, and Col. Joy of the Hays Organization. Both liked the picture. Mailing-lists of magazines and lecture societies were obtained, containing the names of discriminating people, not habitual movie-goers, who formed 'the latent audience'. The National Board had leaflets printed about *Moana*, describing the sort of picture it was and the aims of Flaherty, the director of *Nanook*, in making this new film. This leaflet was mailed to thousands of people in the neighbourhood of the six test towns.

When shown in Poughkeepsie, *Moana* did not flop; nor did it do record business. But there and in the five other towns the week's run was rather better than average.

The Paramount executives were so elated that they even revived the idea of road-showing the film. But on second thoughts they decided on an ordinary release. They turned down any specialized promotion of the type used in the six test towns. Instead, when *Moana* opened at the Rialto on Broadway, 7th February, 1926, with snow lying deep on the fake palm trees of the façade, they dreamed up the advertisement – THE LOVE-LIFE OF A SOUTH SEA SIREN.

In *Moana*[1] Flaherty for the first time used close-ups, sometimes very large indeed, in a succession of shots, not in isolation but in continuity – usually, in order to show a process. Three outstanding and beautiful examples are the making of the bark-cloth, the preparation of the meal and the tattooing. In the last especially, the contraction of Moana's facial muscles at the pain of the bone-needles, the anguish on his mother's face as she fans the tortured waist and limbs, shown large on the screen provided for audiences of the time an agonizing experience of actuality. The way these sequences were shot could not be bettered today and Flaherty himself never surpassed this choice of camera set-ups and camera-movement in his later work.

Moana also showed increased use of camera-movement, panning and tilting to follow or anticipate action. No other director-cameraman used such camera-movement at that time. The Russians favoured in

[1] For synopsis see Appendix 2.

the main a static camera. The Germans mounted the camera on wheels to give it mobility. The Americans copied the Germans but increased the complexity. Only Flaherty used the camera on its gyro-head to capture and interpret movement. Pe'a's climbing of the coconut palm is the classic example of Flaherty's camera-movement, but there are many others in *Moana*, including that final slow pan-shot which relates the parents in their hut to their sleeping son.

Long-focus lenses were also used more daringly than before, perhaps a corollary of Flaherty's development of the close-up. When he found that he could not approach an object he was filming by moving his camera nearer (as when shooting the giant waves breaking over the reef and canoes coming in on the surf), he brought it close with the long-focus lens. No professional cinematographer, Flaherty learned by trial and error; and in all the films he made as director-cameraman, he used only two filters.

The visual quality of *Moana* is very lovely. Seeing the film today on copies taken from dupe-negatives, we still feel no need for colour, even though some of the original quality has been lost.

The film has a wonderful organic unity. Every incident is an integral part of the family's everyday life. It is a lyric of calm and peace. Even the dances and the tattooing have no violent or aggressive qualities.

For all its human feeling and warmth of approach, *Nanook* had a detachment, as if the characters were being watched from outside. The triumph of *Moana* was its intimacy. The audience felt they were really there with Moana, Fa'angase and the others on Savaii. Apart from the use of close-ups, etc., mentioned above, this intimacy was achieved because Flaherty was his own cameraman. His unit was so small the natural actors were not inhibited. Today with the complications of sound-recording equipment and the personnel requirements of British and American trade unions, such intimacy would be impossible to achieve, even for a director as sympathetic as Flaherty.

Moana was well received by many critics in New York. The most perceptive and laudatory notice appeared in the *New York Sun* over the pen-name of *The Moviegoer*. It was written by John Grierson, who used for the first time an adjective which was subsequently to take different shades of meaning. '*Moana*, being a visual account of events in the daily life of a Polynesian youth, has documentary value.' The word documentary in this sentence was a translation of the French *documentaire*, used to describe serious travel and expedition films as opposed to boring travelogues. Grierson had only one point of criticism. 'Lacking in the film was the pictorial transcription of the sex-life of these people. It is rarely referred to. Its absence mars its completeness.' But apart from that '*Moana* is lovely beyond compare'.

Praise came also from Robert E. Sherwood, Robert Louis Stevenson's son-in-law Austin Strong, and Matthew Josephson, who remarked 'Flaherty has done more than give us only a beautiful spectacle. With his broad vision he has suddenly made us think seriously, in between the Florida boom and our hunting for bread and butter in Wall Street, about the art of life. Here, he says to us, are people who are *successful in the art of life*. Are we that, with our motor-cars, factories, sky-scrapers, radio-receivers?'

The chiefs from Safune saw it in Apia. According to Mr. C. H. Hall who was present at the screening, they said that it was 'good exceedingly' 'fa'a Samoa' and something sacred! beyond the comprehension of the alien *papalangi*.'

The alien *papalangi* in France thought very highly of the picture. In Britain, its protagonists were members of the documentary movement that was to follow. While Bryher in *Close-up* 1928 recommended it as a film for children, Rotha wrote in *The Film Till Now* (Cape, 1930) that of Flaherty's two films, '*Moana* was perhaps the finer'.

But unlike *Nanook*, *Moana* was not listed among the ten best films of its year. It came among the Honourable Mentions. And because it was not given generally the specialized promotion which Flaherty had stimulated in the six test towns, it grossed only 'about $150,000 in a period when Sidney Kent was distributing Gloria Swanson pictures for a million apiece'.[1]

Paramount's head distribution executive told Flaherty that if he had had a series of good, modest-budget pictures, he could have built up the sort of specialized distribution Flaherty wanted. But economically it wasn't worthwhile to do it for a single picture. Appreciating that his problem concerned not merely Paramount, but the cinema industry as a whole, not merely himself, but other directors of 'off-beat' films, Flaherty approached the Rockefeller Foundation with the

[1] *Motion Picture Herald*, 11 August, 1951.

suggestion that a special organization should be built up to draw the attention of the 'latent audience' to unusual films from any part of the world. A meeting of their board was arranged to discuss the project and a representative of the Hays Organization was invited to attend. This representative agreed that the proposal was interesting, but its implementation ought to come within the province of the Hays Organization rather than of a special foundation.

And that was the end of that.

In 1950, Flaherty said[1]: 'Some years ago, fearing that the negative of *Moana* might somehow get lost, I wrote to Paramount and asked them if it would not be possible to turn it over to one of the film museums so that it might be preserved. The letter was never answered. And only recently, while getting the prints of *Louisiana Story* made at the company's laboratories on Long Island, I learned that the negative of *Moana* no longer existed; to make room, no doubt, for other newer films, it has been destroyed.'

This was an act of vandalism towards a work of art whose effective commercial life was over. But the failure to exploit *Moana*'s distribution had a far worse effect on its maker. His reputation slumped in Hollywood, chances of his having another film financed appeared remote and he was already forty-two.

[1] 'Robert Flaherty Talking', *Cinema*, 1950.

10 SHADOWS, WHITE AND DARK

It is the terrifying experience of the film director that he is at the mercy of a financier. Flaherty's earlier career of prospector had been hazardous enough. But his new career was far more dangerous. Between the completion of *Moana* and its première in New York, Flaherty divided his time between New York and his home in New Canaan, Connecticut. As his reputation sagged in Hollywood, it rose among the lovers of film art in New York, who unfortunately were less rich.

In 1926, Flaherty made two short sponsored films. The first, financed by the actress Maude Adams, a great admirer of Flaherty, for the Metropolitan Museum, was *The Pottery Maker*. A humble experiment using the new Mazda incandescent lamps instead of mercury vapour lights, it was shot in the Museum basement in collaboration with the Arts and Crafts Department. It proved to be important only as a preliminary study for the pottery-making sequence in *Industrial Britain*, and also perhaps in the humiliating discipline of the sponsored film, which Flaherty never accepted.

The inspiration coming from Flaherty's side, Maude Adams tried to raise the finance for a colour film based on Kipling's *Kim*. The project fell through, but it shows that Flaherty was already thinking of India as a future location.

His second project in 1926 was *Twenty-four Dollar Island*, a film of Manhattan in two reels 'financed by a wealthy socialite'[1] for a purpose which is not clear. This journalistic commission was outside his competence. He shot a lot of material from the tops of skyscrapers, producing a curious, flat, foreshortened effect. 'The film had a viewpoint of New York that people in the streets never have,' he is reported to have said, ignoring the fact that many of the people in the streets of New York worked in those high buildings. 'It gave the effect of deep, narrow canyons thronged with the minute creatures who had created this amazing city.'

Flaherty regarded this shooting not as a film, but as a sort of notebook and he felt no annoyance when it was used as a backdrop for the stage ballet, *The Sidewalks of New York*, cut to one reel for presentation at the Roxy Theatre.

And then, much to his surprise, in the summer of 1927 Howard Dietz of M.G.M. asked him if he would like to work on a film of Frederick O'Brien's *White Shadows in the South Seas*. Flaherty, though puzzled how that book of travel impressions could make a film, answered 'Yes'. So Dietz passed the acceptance on to Irving Thalberg, 'the brilliant young genius' who had become General Manager of Universal Pictures at the age of nineteen and Production Manager of M.G.M. at twenty-five.[1]

Thalberg called Flaherty by long-distance telephone and asked if he would co-direct the picture with W. S. Van Dyke II, an M.G.M. staff director, known for successful Westerns. Frances Flaherty was suspicious; but Flaherty accepted. He had a child-like enthusiasm for new proposals; and he realized that to become a professional film director would involve his taking the jobs offered. If all worked out well, Frances could join him with the children on the Tahiti location.

[1] *Film Index Series*, No. 6 (Supplement to *Sight and Sound*, pub. British Film Institute, May 1946) by Herman G. Weinberg. David Flaherty says the film was financed by Pictorial Clubs, of which the moving forces were Mrs. Ada de Acosta Root, Col. Breckinridge and their business manager, Mr. Pearmain.

[2] Thalberg produced among others, *The Big Parade, Ben-Hur, The Good Earth* and *Grand Hotel*. He is assumed to be the original of Scott Fitzgerald's *The Last Tycoon*.

Arrived in Hollywood, Flaherty found Thalberg had bought O'Brien's book not for its denunciation of the degrading impact of white civilization on the Marquesans but for its intriguing box-office title. Laurence Stallings, author of the successful play and later film *What Price Glory?* was called in to work with Flaherty on a story-line. They started by trying to persuade Thalberg that he could make a far better film of the South Seas out of Melville's *Typee*, but Thalberg was sold on *White Shadows* and Stallings quit the job.

His place was taken by an M.G.M. staff-writer, Ray Doyle, who shared with Jack Cunningham the final film credit for the 'original story'.

The producer assigned to *White Shadows* was Hunt Stromberg, who invited Flaherty to give a showing of *Moana*. When it was over, the yes-men who filled the theatre waited for Stromberg's reaction. 'Boys, I've got a great idea!' he is supposed to have exclaimed. 'Let's fill the screen with tits.'

Headed by Van Dyke, with Raquel Torres and Monte Blue as the stars, a full-scale technical unit, with assistants and assistant assistants, set sail for Papeete. In this Armada of technicians Flaherty felt uneasy from the start. Any naturalness would surely be ruined by such a crowd; and when, early on in the shooting with the Polynesians singing Polynesian songs in the coconut groves, he came on the cameramen down on the sand beside a radio, listening to Abe Lyman and his band from the Hollywood Coconut Grove, he said disgustedly, 'Why not go back and make the picture in the Coconut Grove?'

Soon Flaherty realized that he had no contribution to make, and despite the financial loss it involved he resigned from the picture and returned to Hollywood.

But in early summer 1928, the Fox Corporation engaged him to make a film about the Pueblo Indians in New Mexico. This seemed a genuine Flaherty project and he went down with Frances and David and started to make a picture of Acoma Indians, based upon their tribal life and ceremonies with a small Indian boy as his hero.

Towards the end of 1928 David Flaherty was recalled to Hollywood before being sent as technical adviser on a film that Fox intended to make in Tahiti, based on a story-outline Bob and David put up about Trader Felix David. Berthold Viertel was working on the script.

Through him David met the great German director, F. W. Murnau, who was most complimentary about Bob. 'Your brother makes the best films,' he said. What Murnau went on to say about Hollywood was not so complimentary.

When he had arrived in Hollywood in July 1926, Friedrich Wilhelm Murnau, a tall thin Westphalian, was aged thirty-six, five years younger than Flaherty. His film *The Last Laugh*, scripted by Carl Mayer and starring Emil Jannings, was already accepted as a screen classic. *The Last Laugh* and the two films that followed, *Tartuffe* and *Faust*, had made a deep impression in the United States; and in securing him as a director William Fox congratulated himself. On Murnau's first Hollywood picture, *Sunrise* (made also from a Carl Mayer script), Fox lavished all the resources of his studio. But the pretentiousness of Fox did not mix happily with Murnau's sincerity. *The Four Devils*, to which a dialogue sequence was added at the last moment, was even less successful.

Then Murnau, who had hitherto always worked in a studio, suggested making an epic film of life in the Dakota grainfields, revolving round farming customs and traditions. Much of it was shot at a farm at Pendleton, Oregon. But when the film was nearly finished, William Fox panicked. Sound was on the way in; and this epic with wheat as the never-changing symbol seemed all too grave and old fashioned. Talking sequences were added, comic gags inserted; but the more it was changed, the worse it grew. It was finally released in an abbreviated version as *City Girl*, but it never played New York or other big cities.

When David returned from Tahiti a few months later, Murnau summoned him urgently to his 'castle' in Beverley Hills. Murnau said he was through with Fox. He had just bought a yacht, a Gloucester fisherman, called *The Pasqualito*. Murnau produced photographs of her – a beauty. The name was to be changed to the *Bali*. That was the island he'd make for. He'd stay at Tahiti on the way.

'You'll never believe an island could be so beautiful,' David said. 'I'll give you letters.'

He was also going to Samoa. 'I'll give you letters there too,' David said.

Murnau looked at him. 'Like to come along?'

David said he'd give his right arm to, but he'd got to go back to New Mexico and the Pueblo film.

Fox was just about to call the Pueblo film off, Murnau said. The camp at Tucson had been burned out. Flaherty and Fox weren't seeing eye to eye. Fox wanted to write in a love story and Bob refused.

Murnau unfolded his plan. Flaherty was through in Hollywood. He, Murnau, was fed up with it. Why not join forces, go to Tahiti, Samoa, Bali and make the films they wanted to make and to hell with Hollywood? Murnau was sure he could get the finance.

Then and there they put in a call to Tucson and fixed to drive down the 500 miles to see Bob Flaherty next day.

At Tucson, Bob told Murnau the story of a pearl diver which he had heard during his unfortunate *White Shadows* experience in Tahiti.

Murnau was enthusiastic. 'This,' he said, 'will be the first Murnau-Flaherty Production.'

Murnau had business flair. He put out the news story that Murnau and Flaherty were shaking the dust of Hollywood off their feet in order to make films in far-off places. The combination of Murnau's experience and Flaherty's treatment of the drama of primitive peoples soon brought a contract with Colorart, a young company as hungry for prestige as William Fox had been a few years before. Murnau-Flaherty Productions Inc. was launched to make pictures independent of the major studio companies.

There was no question this time of Frances Flaherty working with her husband. The daughters were growing up; and thinking that European education was not only cheaper, but also better, than Bryn Mawr, Frances took them east to Germany as Murnau and David sailed west from San Pedro in April 1929.[1]

Bob Flaherty left a month later by mail steamer; but he arrived in Papeete well ahead of the *Bali*, which had stopped at the Marquesas and the Paumotos. And when he met Murnau on the quay, he had grave news. Colorart had not made the payments called for by their contract. He, Bob, had been living on credit.

There followed weeks of cabling back and forth, before they resigned

[1] Frances Flaherty claims that she anticipated the Wall Street crash in 1929 and the Second World War in 1938, says Newton Rowe. Though it altered her residence in each case, we do not know how it affected her investments.

themselves to the fact that Colorart was unsound. They were stranded. Finance could not be negotiated from Papeete. Flaherty was broke, as usual. So Murnau decided that he would have to finance the picture himself, making every possible economy. He paid off the American crew and sent them back to California, replacing them by Tahitians. The Hollywood cameraman, unit-manager and laboratory man dispatched by Colorart without funds to pay their wages were put on the next boat home, while Flaherty set up a lab in a back-street shed and trained a seventeen-year-old half-caste boy in film-processing. Bill Bambridge, another half caste, a member of an influential commercial family, acted as major-domo, interpreter and (with David Flaherty) assistant-director. Bambridge had acted in the same capacity on the M.G.M. productions of *White Shadows* and *The Pagan* and became an indispensable member of the Murnau-Flaherty unit.

But there were difficulties within the unit from the start. Murnau and Flaherty might be partners, but they scarcely knew one another and were temperamentally opposite. 'Had Murnau been by nature prodigal and Bob frugal,' David Flaherty says, 'the arrangement might have worked out well. But since Murnau was by nature frugal and Bob notoriously the opposite, it brought little comfort to either. Neither one had asked for this situation; there it was.' And Murnau held the purse-strings.

Flaherty wanted to make the sort of picture M.G.M. wouldn't let him make of *White Shadows*. He didn't want another *Moana*. Instead of recording the fading forms of fa'a Samoa, he wanted to record why they were fading – the impact of civilization on a primitive culture.

O'Brien had written of the Marquesans, 'They were essentially a happy people, full of dramatic feeling, emotional and with a keen sense of the ridiculous. The rule of the trader crushed all these native feelings. To this restraint was added the burden of the effort to live. With the entire Marquesan economic and social system disrupted, food was not so easily procurable, and they were driven to work by commands, taxes, fines and the novel and killing incentives of rum and opium. The whites taught the men to sell their lives, and the women to sell their charms. Happiness and health were destroyed because the white man came here only to gratify his cupidity.'[1] This was the story,

[1] Frederick O'Brien, *White Shadows in the South Seas*, Grosset & Dunlap, 1928.

as true of Tahiti as of the Marquesas, that Flaherty was now ready to tell.

But Murnau, fresh to the South Seas, was still, so to speak, in the aesthetic *Moana* stage; and being a studio man, he wanted a strong story-line rather than the tenuous threads which contented Flaherty. He found his plot in a legend derived from the age-old Polynesian custom of the *tabu*. A virgin is consecrated to the gods and as a result is forbidden to men. If any man violates the *tabu*, even from the motive of the deepest love, tragedy will overwhelm him. So the young pearl-fisher who falls in love with the sacred virgin is consumed by the sea. The gods have been avenged.

When Flaherty protested that this story bore no relation to the one he had outlined in Tucson, apart from the fact that the hero was a pearl-fisher, Murnau eagerly agreed. 'That means Colorart can't sue us for the money they advanced. *We aren't making the picture they contracted for.*'

There was nothing Flaherty could say. Murnau was financing the film. He was a most gifted film-maker and Flaherty admired his work. But their approaches to film were utterly divergent. The greatest contribution which Flaherty could make was to withdraw tactfully into the background as far as he could, consistently with the fact that he was the cameraman.

Then Flaherty's Akeley, the only camera on the job, began to give trouble and in December, when they were on location at Bora-Bora, it broke down altogether. 'If only Floyd Crosby were here with his Debrie!' said Murnau. (He had met Floyd Crosby fleetingly on his trip to Tucson when Crosby was acting as second cameraman on the Acoma Indians picture.)

Next day, a schooner arrived from Papeete with a cable, addressed to Murnau-Flaherty: JUST FINISHED FILMING IN CARIBBEAN STOP MAY I JOIN YOU FLOYD CROSBY.[1]

His arrival on the next mail steamer enabled Flaherty to recede into the background even further. That retirement was made still easier by

[1] Among many documentaries, Crosby photographed *The River*, *The Fight for Life*, parts of *The Land* and *Man Power and the Land*. One of the finest realist cameramen in the U.S.A. he includes in his feature credits *The Brave Bulls*, *High Noon* and *The Wonderful Country*.

Viscount Hastings,[1] who met Flaherty and Murnau and sized up the situation. 'Both my wife[2] and I fell under Flaherty's spell, were charmed and loved to listen by the hour to his stories. He related them so vividly that I can still clearly see Flaherty driving his team of huskies with the inevitable violin tied to the top of the load. . . . I was puzzled how two people with such divergent points of view as Murnau and Flaherty had decided to make a picture in partnership. . . . Murnau thought that he had the certainty of a release for the film but only if it turned out to be the sort of picture which *he* considered would be acceptable and sure of a box-office success. Flaherty was only interested in making what he believed would be a work of art with integrity. He refused to compromise or have anything to do with a "dramatic" story; for him the drama was in the life of the islanders.'

This picture of Flaherty as the man of inflexible integrity is over-simple. He had combed the seas around Samoa for tiger-sharks and octopuses and scoured the Arctic for mother-bears. Supposing that Flaherty had been in Murnau's shoes, supposing that is to say that he had ever saved enough money to invest it all in a film (as indeed he might, if he had been a canny business man) would he have invested it all in a denunciation of the impact of white civilization on primitive life? Even if Murnau had been urging him to do so, I doubt it. But the real conflict was between two personalities, both dominant, and yet trained in totally different traditions. As Flaherty spellbound the Hastings with his irrelevant Eskimo exploits, Murnau must have fumed at the comparative insignificance of his triumphs in the studios of Neubabelsburg.

The position deteriorated. The Wall Street crash echoed across the Pacific. Money grew even shorter than tempers. In September 1930, Flaherty, tired of his pin-money, offered Murnau his share in Murnau-Flaherty Inc., for $5000.

Jack Hastings, in appearance a typical English aristocrat, in fact a socialist, pupil of Diego Rivera and a sensitive and shrewd man, was still in Tahiti. 'As I had call on some capital from a small film company of which I was a director, I decided to join Murnau and get the consent of the other directors to invest in this project.'

[1] Now the Earl of Huntingdon.

[2] Cristina, daughter of the Marchese Casati, Rome.

By a strange irony Flaherty disapproved of *Tabu* because it elevated an ancient superstition to the level of truth, while Murnau, not believing in the superstition, thought it good box-office. On Bora-Bora Murnau chose as his location a small atoll in the main lagoon called Motu Tapu. It was convenient and undisturbed, but the islanders were superstitiously reluctant to go near it. Though the ancient *tabu* on the dedicated maiden had lapsed, this *tabu* was very strong. 'From then on everything went wrong,' writes Hastings. 'Film stock was lost. Schooners failed to arrive. Reri (our leading lady), became pregnant, we nearly all contracted mumps and Bob Reese, the young assistant, got so badly burned in an accident that he had to spend weeks in hospital.'

But in spite of these mishaps, *Tabu* was finished to Murnau's satisfaction by the end of the year and the unit, including Flaherty, sailed back to California.

There is no need to analyse *Tabu*. It was Murnau's picture, not Flaherty's. Floyd Crosby won an Oscar for his photography and Murnau, having ventured $150,000 of his own money, earned an equal sum in profits; but for his estate, not for himself. He was killed in a car crash in March 1931.

By Rotha and Wright, *Tabu* is regarded as a meretricious film, with 'special effects' of fake moons and rubber sharks shot in Hollywood to heighten the dramatic effect. As an outsider, I can say that as a young man, *Tabu* gave me a vision of the world as vivid as that which *Nanook* had produced in me earlier and more vivid than *Moana*. Perhaps this was because I was starting to write novels, and not documentaries. Perhaps it was just that I, like most filmgoers, enjoyed the fictional employment of the imagination.

11 BERLIN AND INDUSTRIAL BRITAIN

Having sat out the shooting of *Tabu*, Flaherty joined Frances and the family in Germany for Christmas 1930. There was no future for him in Hollywood. Murnau's nostalgia for the country in which he had done his best work may have led Flaherty to hope it would hold out opportunities for him also. *Nanook* and *Moana* had been well received in Germany and were popular both with the general public and among the intellectuals.

He was, however, deeply shocked by Berlin. The whores lining the *rennbahn* of Friedrichstrasse, the open sale of pornography, straight and perverse, the proliferation of bars and night-clubs for pansies, lesbians and cross-dressers horrified him. When he came to London, later in the year, he would speak about Berlin sex life again and again in terms of uncomprehending repulsion.

But in Berlin he explored the possibilities of finding finance for his sort of film. He had been enormously impressed by Eisenstein's *Potemkin* and in Berlin he saw for the first time Dovjenko's *Earth*, which he described later as 'the greatest of all films'. The Soviet Union seemed to be a place where he would be encouraged to make the sort of serious films which American movie tycoons hated.

He met the Dutch left-wing film-director, Joris Ivens, Pudovkin, the director of Gorki's *Mother*, and Fedor Ozep, a Soviet director who had made a German-Soviet co-production *The Living Corpse* in which Pudovkin had played the leading role.

Flaherty, either because he had been approached by Eisenstein or someone else in the Soviet production of films or because he made the first overtures through the Soviet Film Distribution agency in Berlin, started discussions on the possibility of making a co-production in the U.S.S.R. with U.F.A. supplying the film stock and the Russians the facilities, the Russians to have internal rights with the proviso that they could cut anything they disliked but put nothing in, while Flaherty had other world rights with a similar proviso.

Fred Zinnemann, who met Flaherty early in 1931, says that Flaherty wanted to make a film about the dying civilizations of Central Asia, while the Soviet officials, admitting the location, insisted it should be about the sovietization of primitive life.[1]

The Soviet flirtation proved even less rewarding than the Hollywood. So a group called the Porza tried to set up a film for Flaherty in Germany, but with equal ill-success.

Ernestine Evans met Flaherty one day on the Kurfürstendam and they went to see René Clair's *Le Million*. In the same bill was a *kulturfilm* by Dr. Nicholas Kauffman about forestry in Rumania.[2] Flaherty was so fascinated by the sequence in which the huge tree trunks cascaded down steep wooden chutes that he sat through Clair's film twice in order to see *Turbulent Timber* three times.[3]

In March 1931, Murnau was killed in a car smash and all repayments on the sale of Flaherty's share in Murnau-Flaherty Production Inc., were stopped.[4]

[1] Grierson insists that Flaherty wanted to make a film of 'The Russian Woman'. Zinnemann in those days was associated with a progressive film *Menschen Am Sonntag*. Later that year he went to Hollywood. His later films include *High Noon, The Men, A Nun's Story* and *From Here to Eternity*.

[2] When shown in England, this film was called *Turbulent Timber*.

[3] *Film News* (New York), Vol. XI, No. 8, September 1951.

[4] Not only had the estate to be settled, but Colorart brought, as Murnau had expected, a suit to recover their outgoings on Flaherty's story idea. Thanks to Murnau's change of story line, the suit was lost and in 1932 Flaherty's money was paid to him. It is worth realizing that if Flaherty had prevailed over Murnau, Colorart would have won the case.

During the summer of 1931, it became more and more plain that there was no future for Flaherty in the U.S.S.R. or in Germany and one evening, after six, when the telephone calls were cheaper, Frances Flaherty put through a personal call to John Grierson, the dynamic Scotsman who had been Flaherty's champion in the *New York Sun* and his companion in New York bars, and who was now production chief of the Empire Marketing Board Film-Unit in London.

Jimmy Davidson, the staff-cameraman, was the one member of the unit still in the office when the call came through from Berlin. He ran down to the Coronet, the pub just off Soho Square, where the unit congregated after work, and said, 'There's a Mrs. Flaherty calling you from Berlin up in the joint.'

The Empire Marketing Board had been set up in 1926 to promote the sale of Empire produce in the United Kingdom. Sir Stephen Tallents, its imaginative secretary, made it the first government body to exploit public relations, using all publicity media. In John Grierson, Tallents found a man with a propagandist flair and a love of films, a twentieth-century radical, shrewd, forceful, no poet but a social prophet, an oxy-acetylene firebrand with the showmanship of Barnum and Bailey and the sincerity of Moody and Sankey. Grierson was a man with the realism to accept a totally inadequate budget to make an inadequate film which would produce a larger but still inadequate budget to make a more ambitious film.

Grierson listened to Frances Flaherty and told her he could do nothing until he had spoken to Tallents. But he held out hopes. He had the Scotsman's ability of adding two and two together to make a career, a fortune or a movement.

Next morning, Grierson saw Tallents. He warned him that Flaherty was profligately extravagant, but any material that he produced would be first class. The experience of working with Flaherty would give his school of young film-makers the fillip they needed.

Also, he may have added, getting Flaherty would show the Government how important the Empire Marketing Board had grown and losing him again would show the Government how inadequate their financial allotment was for films.

A few days later the Flahertys arrived at the York Hotel, Berners

Street, a very crooked stone's throw away from the Oxford Street offices of the Empire Marketing Board Film Unit.

Flaherty was a conservative individualist of the nineteenth century, with more of Herman Melville in him than of Jack London. Grierson was a twentieth-century man, who had studied the new methods of Public Relations and was dedicated to their employment, using public money to further as far as possible his own sociological aims. 'There was the run-away from the synthetic world of contemporary cinema,' Grierson wrote in his preface to Paul Rotha's third edition of *Documentary Film* (Faber & Faber, 1952), 'but so also, as I remember, did documentary represent a reaction from the art world of the early and middle twenties . . . Bloomsbury, Left Bank, T. S. Eliot, Clive Bell and all . . . by people with every reason to know it well. Likewise, if it was a return to "reality", it was a return not unconnected with Clydeside movements, the Independent Labour Party, the Great Depression, not to mention our Lord Keynes, the London School of Economics, P.E.P. and such. Documentary was born and nurtured on the bandwagon of uprising social democracy everywhere; in Western Europe and the United States, as well as in Britain. That is to say, it had an uprising majority social movement, which is to say a logical sponsorship of public money behind it.'

This was an insinuating lingo to which Flaherty was alien. He belonged in a simpler world, in which words were used precisely to express meanings, not imprecisely to conceal intentions.

Rotha and Wright recall Flaherty's arrival in London. 'We well remember Flaherty and his wife being conducted round the two floors of the unit's premises. We remember too going to their hotel-room to look at the superb photographs of Savaii which Frances Flaherty had brought with her. We remember especially Flaherty's delight at discovering the English-made, spring-driven, Newman-Sinclair camera with its easy portability, the ease with which magazines could be exchanged and its range of lenses, and the extensions which could be inserted for ultra-close work.'

According to Newton Rowe, Flaherty gave a press conference at the York Hotel to announce his entry into British documentary and hint at his availability for larger assignments. Frances and the children were out of town and before the conference started, Newton Rowe, who had left New Zealand Government service and was working as a free-lance journalist, came along to dinner bringing with him E. Hayter Preston, the associate editor of the *Sunday Referee*. It was a typical Flaherty evening. The wine flowed at dinner and at the conference the whisky gushed.

After the journalists staggered down for taxis to take them to catch the last trains home, Flaherty detained Rowe and Preston. 'You stay,' he said.

With the night porter bringing fresh supplies as needed, they talked and drank and laughed and smoked and coughed till it was light next morning. Rowe says that men were already working on the road, when he and Preston left; and Preston regaled them on the riches of his political understanding.

Who paid that bill, one wonders? Certainly not Flaherty, who was broke. Not Mrs. Flaherty, who was out of town. So it must have been one of the first charges on *Industrial Britain*.

The Secretary of the Empire Marketing Board had managed to rustle up £2,500 – a fortune for the Empire Marketing Board – to make a film about industrial craftsmanship. Anthony Asquith had been asked to make it, but he had refused, perhaps because otherwise committed or the money wasn't enough. So the subject went to Flaherty.

There had been a tradition in exterior photography, due partly to the insensitivity of early film, that one could only shoot in bright sunshine. This was something which the slender budgets of the E.M.B. could not afford. 'There remained to be destroyed the belief that the industrial life of Britain and her grey city atmosphere could never be portrayed on the screen,' said Tallents later, 'the real point of bringing in Flaherty at this moment was to destroy that fallacy.'[1]

[1] In the B.B.C. *Portrait of Flaherty* programme, Sir Stephen indulged his aetiological fancy. E.M.B. cameramen had been struggling to shoot in all weathers long before Flaherty drifted on the scene.

In this programme, one of the most moving contributions came from Erich von Stroheim, who had contributed almost as much to film history as Flaherty and had lost his backers far more money. Stroheim, with a sob in his voice, described the meeting of the two masters for the first time in the flesh, though they had known and admired one another for years. It couldn't have happened any way but this, if they had ever met. Which they didn't.

Grierson knew Flaherty's methods; £2,500 might be exhausted in preliminary shooting before a foot of usable film was taken. He knew that he could only employ Flaherty for a short period and he devised a way of using him to the best purpose, limiting his expenditure.

Basil Wright was going out to shoot his first film, finally known as *The Country Comes to Town*, some of the locations of which were in Devonshire. Grierson said that it would help Flaherty in shooting a film about *Industrial Britain* to go to Devon and watch Basil Wright shoot his film about cows. He was as much concerned with what Flaherty could teach his young men as he was with what Flaherty might ultimately shoot.

'So I found myself,' recalls Wright, 'driving Flaherty whom I regarded with immense awe – in a dilapidated Buick two-seater roadster from London to Exeter and points west. He was extremely nervous and round about Runnymede he said this was because he had been deeply affected by Murnau's death in California.

'But when he reached Camberley, he said he was in need of refreshment. I pulled into a pub and here the unpredictability of the great man hit me for the first time. I wanted to reach our Devon location as soon as possible; but over pints of bitter (which I think he didn't like but drank for experience) he saw a shove ha'penny board. He wanted to know everything about the game. More interesting is that before he even learnt the rules, in a tactile series of gestures he had appreciated the qualities of the board, the silky smoothness of the wooden surface and the craftsmanship of the brass strips which, carefully hinged, separated one "bed" from another. As soon as he betrayed his interest, we became involved in a series of games.[1]

'With a lot of, as I thought, nervous tact, I finally got him back into the car. He soon fell into a doze and I took the Basingstoke-Stockbridge run at full speed, passing my favourite pub whose architecture and position in a glorious landscape would have caught Flaherty's eyes, if they had not been shut.

'After an indifferent lunch at Salisbury, I could not get away before he had seen the Cathedral. We drove to the Close. He was rapt

1 At The Highlander, the Dean Street pub which succeeded The Coronet, as the documentary 'local', Flaherty became a shove ha'penny adept. It was the sort of skill he loved.

in admiration, gazing at it from a variety of angles. Then he went inside and took one look round. "It's an exterior job," he said.

'We pressed on towards Devon, but on the outskirts of Salisbury, where the road crosses the railway and heads for open country, there were a lot of chaps looking over a wall. "Stop!" cried Flaherty. "What's going on?"

'It was a cricket match.

'Flaherty was fascinated. Finding he could not see well standing on the floor of the car, he climbed precariously on to the seat cushions. "You must explain what they're doing," he said.

'I disliked cricket then even more than I do now. My explanations were punctuated by hints about the tightness of shooting schedules and the problems of E.M.B. Unit expenditure. But it was about twenty minutes before I could get Flaherty to sit down.

'At last we established ourselves at a tiny pub, The Lamb, between Exeter and Cotley, where the farm was that we used in the film. We were rather crushed, but I secured Flaherty a room for himself. He expressed the warmest gratitude. At least for sleeping, he liked solitude.

'Flaherty was interested in the girl who looked after the bar and the bedrooms, one of those strapping Devon wenches, tall with a fine figure, splendid vital statistics, dark flashing eyes, black hair and a heightened colour. Flaherty, in an entirely aesthetic way, was fascinated by her "foreignness"; and when I, or someone else in the unit, brought up the old story of the ship-wrecked mariners from the Spanish Armada mingling with the local population, his imagination got to work with a flood of ideas on which, solemn young documentarist that I was, I tried to put a curb.

'What I remember most vividly is the soft, careful and tactful manner in which, over a number of days shooting, he (as it were) lent me his wonderful eyes. He never said, "Look, how wonderful! You must shoot that." Almost as in passing, he commented on the play of light on fields and woods and distant landscape, or on certain movements of horses or cattle, or even on the way a lane twisted between hedges to reveal the half-seen gable of a house. It's almost impossible to explain his way of seeing things in this manner, and how he, often in an undertone, conveyed it to you. I certainly would say that in those few days he enriched my understanding of looking at things

ACOMA INDIANS FILM — 1928
(*unfinished*)

'Beyond the smoke beautiful things are being made'

INDUSTRIAL BRITAIN — 1931

'The human factor remains the final factor'

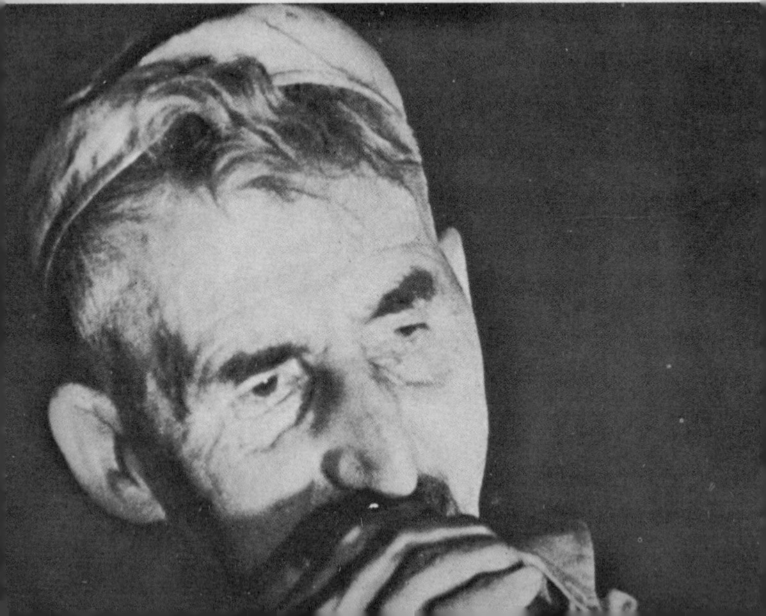

Maggie Dirrane

MAN OF ARAN — 1932–34

Tiger King

Seaweed

Mikeleen

Tiger King

The Aran Islanders make Broadway, October 18, 1934

and people in terms of movie in a way that ten million dollars would not buy. Incidentally when I was actually shooting, he went as far away as possible. He never advised or interfered. But he opened up for me a new field of revelation every day.'

Back in London, Flaherty found that Grierson had engaged as his production manager, J. P. R. Golightly, an estate manager from the West of England who had had no previous experience of film-making. With Golightly at the wheel of an old Austin and in the back a Newman-Sinclair camera and, for an E.M.B. film, a generous amount of film stock, they set out for Devon to film the steel bridge at Saltash near Plymouth.

Nothing was heard for some days.

Then one morning, when the E.M.B.'s various rushes were being screened in the projection-theatre, there came on the screen several reels of shipping and unloading scenes at an unidentifiable dock or docks. There was no indication on the cans of the production or the director. There followed a series of shots taken apparently from a railway carriage, but unusable because of the train vibration. Finally, there were some very fine shots of Saltash Bridge. This must be the Flaherty material.

Grierson was distraught. Hundreds of feet of precious film had been wasted on things which could not possibly relate to Industrial Britain. He immediately put through a personal call to Flaherty. 'I've seen your rushes, Bob,' he said. 'You can't go blazing away like that.'

'My dear John,' Flaherty said. 'Those weren't *rushes*. They were just *tests*, so I could get the feel of things.'

Before the production had started, Grierson had explained to Flaherty that 'someone down in Whitehall' (meaning Sir Stephen Tallents or his administrators) would want to see a script.

'That's impossible,' Flaherty said. 'I've never written a script before and I'm damned if I'm going to start now for some civil servant in Whitehall.'

'I'm sorry, Bob, you've got to,' Grierson said. 'It doesn't have to be too detailed.'

Flaherty retired to the York Hotel for several days and was seen by no one. Then he came round to Oxford Street with a large envelope in which was a fine new folder, containing four sheets of hand-laid paper, the first and fourth were blank. On the second in Flaherty's heavy hand was written —[1]

INDUSTRIAL BRITAIN
a film about craftsmen
by Robert J. Flaherty

On the next page were the words

A SCENARIO
Scenes of Industrial Britain

Flaherty had won; if Sir Stephen Tallents read a scenario of *Industrial Britain*, it was not by Flaherty.[2]

Golightly had been warned by Grierson of Flaherty's extravagance and he was not inhibited by awe of the great man, whom he'd never heard of before. But he could not protest, when Flaherty would glimpse a string of electric pylons and insist on making a detour to film them; nor could he point out that the windmill at which Flaherty quixotically tilted his camera wasn't in the script since there was no script for it to be in.

When they returned to London, preparatory to visiting the Midlands, there was, at least reputedly, a stormy meeting between Flaherty and Grierson.

How the end came to Flaherty's association with *Industrial Britain* is shrouded in legend. Exactly what happened doesn't matter to anyone except the immediate participants. The important thing was that while Flaherty was filming, he brought to the British scene his Eskimo eye, that wonderfully humble exploration of human skills. Perhaps, most of all, this was exemplified in the pottery sequence in which because Flaherty was so engaged not merely in the process of making pots but in the mind and body of the potter that the camera was in a way governed by what was happening inside the potter himself, the camera did not follow his movements. It anticipated them.

[1] Flaherty, who was left-handed, wrote in a strange way with pen between first and second fingers. See Illustration.

[2] I tell this as an example of the sort of anecdote which accumulated round this period of Flaherty's life. I have had at least one different version from everyone who told me this story and from one of them I have heard three different versions. Since these anecdotes throw more light on their narrators than on Flaherty, I have used them sparingly. A.C.-M.

This was the vision of *Nanook* and *Moana* brought right home in Stoke-on-Trent, the beauty of a craftsman intent on his craft. It was the legacy which Flaherty left with British documentary directors, the beauty of men working skilfully.

The lesson has been learnt so well both by film-makers and by the public that today it appears absurd to emphasize it. But in the class-ridden society of the thirties it was a revolutionary thing. A potter was a potter; his pots might be admired as beautiful; but to Flaherty what was far more beautiful than the finished pot was the making of it.

It was this ocular equipment which enabled, for example, Basil Wright to go to Ceylon and within a short time to make a film of lasting beauty in *Song of Ceylon*. *Nanook* and *Moana* were exotic and remote. The same eye innocently roving over Industrial Britain taught the lesson more immediately. It was like the modern teaching of geography, compared with the ancient. If one understands one's own city and the complexity of the country within its watershed, one has learnt the grammar of geography. Any other city in the world is easy to understand. Flaherty in the same way had taught the grammar of sight and this, as Grierson recognized, was far more important than completing a picture.

In that early makeshift of Grierson's unit, what happened after Flaherty stopped shooting was that Basil Wright was sent off to shoot footage on waterways and flying-boats and Elton was sent down a coal-mine. Edgar Anstey was made assistant editor and all the material was removed to Grierson's house in Merrick Square, south of the Thames, which had been fixed up with primitive editing equipment and a hand-turned projector.

Anstey had no script from which to work; but Grierson knew what he wanted to say. Even when he was confined to his bed with illness he continued to supervise the editing by eye. The whole future of Grierson and his unit depended on the Flaherty gamble succeeding. That was probably the reason why at no time during the editing did Anstey see Flaherty himself or Flaherty see the film.[1]

The film lay fallow during the whole of the next year, 1932. Grierson

[1] Anstey, however, in the trip he made in 1932 to Labrador on H.M.S. *Challenger* during which he filmed *Eskimo Village* considers that he owes a debt to Flaherty both for subject matter and film approach.

on his smaller scale found himself up against the same distribution problems which Flaherty had encountered with *Nanook* and *Moana*, A single picture was more difficult to sell than a group. So Grierson stockpiled half a dozen two-reel documentaries, which he was able to sell to Gaumont-British Distributors in a package deal as 'The Imperial Six'. Part of the deal was that Gaumont British should supply facilities for recording music and commentaries.

Flaherty had nothing to do with the commentary of *Industrial Britain*. His vision made a direct contribution to the main sequences and an indirect one to the sequences shot as supplementaries by other directors. But the idiom of the Commentary was Griersonian. 'The Human Factor remains the Final Factor.' 'Behind the smoke beautiful things are being made.' 'The keen eye of the individual.' 'The process may change but the man doesn't.'

This last theme, with its desire to carry over into mass-production the sort of prides which belonged to craftsmanship, was the sort of thing which Grierson could say, hoping that if he said it heartily enough at least some of that pride would come through. Flaherty couldn't have said it, because he knew that the process of working was so different that even the most devoted of craftsmen would have changed in relation to his work and so changed in himself. It was the sort of creative lie imperative to the industrial midwifery of Grierson which Flaherty could never tell; just as Flaherty's poetic over-simplification was the sort of falsity which Grierson could never allow himself.

One sees at this single point at which their work crossed the fundamental division between the two men, Flaherty's individual quest for the long truth and Grierson's with the brief progressive one. Grierson had an articulate social philosophy. Flaherty had an inarticulate human love. The two met in the potter's hand and face, but began to diverge in what was made of them.

Industrial Britain was a landmark in British documentary. It was still being shown by the British Information Services abroad after the Second World War; and Grierson tells of various other pictures made from Flaherty's footage.

But it wasn't very important in Flaherty's own career. It was a stop-gap job, which enabled him with Grierson's aid to set up a picture nearer to his heart.

12 SHOOTING *MAN OF ARAN*

On the boat coming over from the States to Europe, the talk had turned on the Wall Street crash and the depression looming over Europe. A young Irishman had broken in impatiently. He knew an island off the West Coast of Ireland, he said, where life was so primitive that the islanders had to make soil by hauling seaweed up the cliffs and mixing it with sand to join a top-soil in which to grow their potatoes; where the curraghs which they used were little better than the coracles of the ancient Britons and the struggle for bare subsistence made booms and slumps look silly.

This impressed nobody except Flaherty. After all, these people were only peasants, a genus one stage lower than pheasants. But this was the obvious location for the film of Man against the Sea, which Flaherty had hoped to make in Samoa. 'Where is this place? What's it called?'

'The Aran Islands,' the young man said.

When Flaherty came over to work on *Industrial Britain*, he had the *arrière pensée* that this might be the chance of mounting a Man against the Sea feature.

At the York Hotel, Flaherty talked with Grierson about this project.

Grierson pointed out that the Aran Islands were not entirely unknown and gave him J. M. Synge's *Riders to the Sea* and *The Aran Islanders.* They heightened Flaherty's enthusiasm and deepened his knowledge, while he was working on *Industrial Britain.*

Meanwhile pressure on the British commercial film industry had been built up. Film critics complained that British films were flaccid imitations of Hollywood. To the perennial bleat that there was no creative talent Cedric Belfrage, hard-punching critic of the *Sunday Express,*[1] answered that in London there was a movie genius named Robert Flaherty needing work.

At the same time, Grierson got in touch with Angus McPhail, head of the story-department of Gaumont-British, the biggest single organization in the British film industry, with two studios and a distribution company serving several hundred important cinemas.

Luncheon was arranged at the Savoy for Flaherty to meet Michael Balcon, production chief of G.-B., Angus McPhail and Hugh Findlay, who was in charge of publicity.

Flaherty outlined the film he intended to make about the Aran Islands. He was eloquent and he provided, from a publicity point of view, an answer to the critics' demand for a naturalistic school of acting.

In July 1932, there was a harassing attack by C. A. Lejeune (*The Observer*) and William Foss (*Morning Post*) against Michael Balcon on the B.B.C. for the artificiality of British film production. Balcon countered by saying 'In our view, Flaherty's doing that for us in Aran. Training the islanders to take part in this film.'

Man of Aran was a sop to Cerberus. To make nineteen pictures, Balcon was given a million pounds, through G.-B. and Gainsborough. Ten were musicals, five comedies, two melodramas, one an unknown quantity and the nineteenth a real-life drama. This was *Man of Aran* and for its production as a sound picture was allotted £10,000, less than the cost of the silent film *Nanook,* ten years before.

It was rumoured that G.-B. backed Flaherty to prove the critics wrong economically and aesthetically. For the Osters who owned G.-B. it might be worth £10,000 to exorcise this individual product.

This was certainly not true of Michael Balcon, a fine producer

[1] Cedric Belfrage in the *Sunday Express,* June 19, 1932.

prepared to let Flaherty have his head without a script. In the autumn of 1931, he arranged for Bob and Frances Flaherty to go to Ireland to make their investigation. They were accompanied by J. N. G. Davidson of the E.M.B. Film Unit, who was familiar with the Aran Islands.

Davidson took them to the Gresham Hotel, the best in Dublin. Flaherty looked at it. 'Young man,' he said, 'never again bring me to an American-style hotel', and removed forthwith to the Hibernian, from which he sallied to meet Lennox Robinson and others, while Davidson chafed with impatience to get him to the Aran Islands. But he was uncertain. One could never be sure whether Flaherty was 'drinking in' the atmosphere or just 'drinking' in it.

From Dublin, the Flahertys moved to Achill Island off the Mayo Coast. There Flaherty found a fishing hotel where he mooched around, while Frances Flaherty went clicking away with her Leica and Davidson kept saying wasn't it time to get a move on? 'I've got a sort of mental hook-worm,' Flaherty answered.

One afternoon Frances Flaherty spoiled a whole roll of film. After a fearful row, she locked herself in their bedroom in which they did the developing. Flaherty sat on the stairs outside and pleaded with her. Frances refused to come downstairs for tea and Bob refused to go down if she didn't. So Davidson ate three teas, jam, cake and buttered potato-bread.

Davidson kept telling Flaherty what he knew of the Aran Islands, but the old man talked of making the film in Achill Island, using a 16-mm. camera and having the film blown up to 35 mm.

This 'mental hook-worm' image didn't mean much to Davidson, who had never seen anyone suffering from physical hook-worm, the anæmia, the debilitation, the loss of energy. But Flaherty had seen hook-worm victims in Polynesia, the paralysis of effort it caused.

Flaherty was nervous. He had made *Nanook* from the depth of his being. He had made *Moana* sincerely but from a more superficial level of experience. Everything since then had been either downright failure or imperfect. The Aran Island film was to be his test.

The stay in Dublin, I think, was prompted by the desire to confirm his belief, weakened by Grierson, that film shot with natural actors

[1] J. N. G. Davidson's notes to Paul Rotha. July, 1959.

should be used for poetic and not socio-political ends; and the stay in Achill Island was a period of preparation. He wanted to get the feel of the western islanders, knowing that from the moment he landed on the Aran Islands, he and his party would be sharply scrutinized.

A day came in the late autumn when Flaherty said that he wanted to see the Aran Islands. Davidson's car was open and Flaherty sat in the 'dickey' or 'rumble seat' and to keep himself warm took a bottle of Irish whisky. Mrs. Flaherty sat in front with Davidson, disapproving; and even more disapproving when they had to stop for another bottle or the relief of nature.

They reached Galway and spent some days there sight-seeing waiting for the *Dun-Aengus*, the steamer plying to the islands. Even the sight of Galway had banished all thoughts of using Achill Island. Flaherty started to ask questions about the Aran Islands. 'Get a bottle of whisky to give the priest,' Flaherty said.

'That wouldn't be diplomatic,' Norris Davidson said.

'Buy it all the same,' Flaherty said. 'It'll come in useful.' It did, but not with the priest.

When they reached Kilronan harbour, the first man Flaherty spotted was Pat Mullen's father. 'The dignity of a dook!' Flaherty said. Frances recorded it with her observant Leica.

Pat Mullen himself had been back from the States seven or eight years. He was known as The Socialist and the islanders who had not been away thought it bad of Davidson to have The Socialist drive the Flahertys around.

Davidson tried without success to interest Flaherty in a village where he had stayed earlier. But when Davidson introduced him to Mikeleen Dillane, one of two little boys who had brought water, fish and letters to his tent the year before, Flaherty spotted him as the boy he wanted as his main human character.

The central theme, he had already decided, was the natural force of the sea against which human beings appear as dwarfed as mortality against eternity.

Flaherty had seen enough for his first view. He returned to Inishmore in January 1932, with his wife and children and the seventeen-year-old

John Taylor, whose job was ostensibly film-processing and extra camera-work, but proved to involve accountancy as well.

They settled in to the best house in the island, owned by a Mrs. Sharman living in London. There were two freshwater springs near an old stone wharf-house, which was to serve as laboratory. As the main house was only large enough for living quarters, another was built from hard grey limestone as a studio, with a turf-covered roof thatched with straw. Pat Mullen engaged the labour and while the studio was a-building, he drove the Flahertys around, looking for possible film types and incidents which might be built into a film about the typical Flaherty film family.[1]

'Every other person in the Aran Islands,' Flaherty said, 'has the name Flaherty or O'Flaherty, including Liam O'Flaherty, who was born there. There were some who were quite sure we had assumed the name in order to gain their confidence.'

It did not win the confidence of Mikeleen Dillane's parents. Though they were as poor as peat, the boy's mother wouldn't let the boy leave Killeany to work for Flaherty in Kilmurvy. Pat Mullen pleaded in vain. Mrs. Flaherty pleaded in vain, though the money offered was a little fortune to the Dillanes. But the tests Flaherty had shot of Mikeleen were so good that he persisted in going to Father Egan, the priest of the island. A donation to the Church persuaded Father Egan to visit Mother Dillane and the boy was Flaherty's.

What had held back the mother was that during the potato famine a hundred years before, Protestant evangelists had invaded Ireland promising soup to all who would become Protestants. Mrs. Dillane feared that Flaherty wanted to make her lad a 'souper'.

The petty stupidities which Flaherty encountered in Samoa cropped up again. If Flaherty was going round with Pat Mullen, he must be a socialist; and though nobody knew what socialism was, all were convinced that it was a policy of the Devil. Then there was the story that the studio building was really an orphanage to convert the parentless to Protestantism.

The first member of the cast to be recruited was Mikeleen. While

[1] In *Man of Aran* (E. P. Dutton, 1935), Pat Mullen has a full acount of the making of the picture. We have drawn from it, but even more from Flaherty's own account, unused except in a B.B.C. Talk, 1st October, 1949.

Flaherty was searching for other natural actors, he was consciously binding the boy more and more to himself, so that he would not be self-conscious in front of the camera. With each of his successive films – with the exception of *The Land*, which had no family story – Flaherty's interest shifted more and more from the father of the family to the son.

There has been the suggestion that Flaherty's boy heroes were due to disappointment because he had produced only daughters. Certainly if John Taylor is to be believed, while they were shooting *Man of Aran*, Flaherty proposed adopting him (John Taylor) as his son. Taylor replied that he had two satisfactory parents of his own. Flaherty clearly would have felt more fulfilled paternally if he had had a boy. But I do not think it is accurate to talk of his boy-children purely and simply as son-compensations.

To Flaherty it was natural that the hero of *Nanook* should be a father-figure. On the father depended the survival of the Eskimo family. And Flaherty in the North looked up to the father-figure. His own father had taken him in childhood to the enchanted North; and in all his travels there, he was protected by people like Nero. The Eskimo who saved his life, lit his cigarettes and rescued him from countless dangers were father-figures.

But the boy in *Moana*, having to undergo the obsolescent tattooing, was a fantasy of Flaherty himself. In the South Seas he was re-enacting his own initiation into courage. And the older he grew in a world which he felt was steadily growing less heroic, the more he identified himself with the boy. This less was a hankering for a son, than a re-creation of his own childhood. The only way in which it would be true to say that his art would have been different, if he had had a son, is that he might then have identified himself with the father figures and expressed his love towards a boy who was the symbol of his son, rather than of himself in youth.

There is another aspect. That innocent eye of Flaherty's caught box-office takings in a sidelong glance. A beautiful boy, like a beautiful dog, went straight to the heart of a very large public. It provided a way of avoiding in his sort of picture the conventional love interest which the exhibitors wanted.

For one of his subordinate roles, Flaherty chose Patch Ruadh, an old man who had been working on the studio, and who had a very dramatic beard. He was very willing, but he would disappear at times, to be discovered behind a boulder near the shore, where in front of a little mirror he was combing his beard 'to keep the drama in it.'

The 'mother', Maggie Dirrane, was seen by Flaherty in the doorway of her cottage with a baby on her arm. The first tests were bad, but a second test convinced Flaherty she was the woman he needed. Maggie was terribly poor; her husband had crippled himself carrying seaweed up from the sea. Maggie had no milk for children; so the unit presented her with a cow. Maggie came over with tears in her eyes. 'Why are you crying?' Frances asked. 'Nothing wrong with the cow?'

'Oh, it's wonderful,' Maggie said, 'but what if the children get used to milk and then the cow died?'

Maggie's three children were all dressed as girls, though one in fact was a boy, the reason being according to Flaherty that 'fairies don't steal girls'.[1]

The most difficult character, not to find but to catch, was Tiger King, whom Flaherty wanted as the father, the Nanook of his picture. Flaherty was not a Roman Catholic, for all his German mother's devotion, and wild rumours about him circulated among the islanders. He carried a bottle of water, the rumour went, with which he would sprinkle children and turn them into Protestants. And since the unit landed a flower had started to grow, which if it spread would lead the people to damnation.

Tiger King believed these stories. He refused every invitation to meet Flaherty and if he had to pass his house, he rode at a gallop. But Pat Mullen finally collared him at a wedding and captured him half-seas-over to make a film test. Meeting Flaherty at last, Tiger King was captivated by the old man's charm.

[1] According to John Taylor, Maggie wasn't the dimwit Flaherty made her out to be. She had worked ten years in Dublin and was one of the few islanders, male or female, who could swim. As well as taking a leading role in the film, she did all the housekeeping for the Flahertys. The film did not make Maggie's fortune, because three months after the unit left she handed all her earnings over to a missionary-father from the mainland.

According to Newton Rowe, who at Flaherty's invitation stayed some months on Aran trying to write a novel, Maggie was in the habit of taking the slops out in a bucket and, having emptied it, coming back with it full of well-water. Frances put a stop to this, as soon as Rowe pointed it out. But thereafter, Bob would temper his love of the Irish with qualifications.

At last he had his characters. The theme of his story was the sea, a sea he made more fabulous and inimical even than the great seas off Ungava. This is how Flaherty saw that sea.

> The Aran Islander in order to survive has to fight the sea. The sea around Aran is one of the most dangerous in the world. The craft he uses is a curragh – one of the oldest and most primitive craft that man anywhere has devised. In the old days it was a framework of ribs of thin wood covered with hides and it was propelled with long thin oars, with an extremely narrow blade so as not to 'trip' in the heavy seas. But the curraghs used in Aran today are covered with tarred canvas. It is wonderful the way they can manœuvre them in the big seas. If they are heading into a very large sea which is too big to take head-on, they will sidle over it in much the same way as a gull rides the water.
>
> There was one instance of a crew in a curragh trying to get in to land. The following waves were so overwhelming that when a wave larger than the rest towered behind them, they had to swing round and face it, and then sidle over it, and then turn and run until the next wave came on and then the performance had to be gone through over again. That day the seas were so high that they couldn't make a landing on the island at all but had to keep on and on and finally landed at the head of Galway Bay some thirty miles away. I have never anywhere in the world seen men so brave who would undertake such risks with the sea. Yet the Aran Islander can't swim a stroke. If he touches the water, he gives up and goes down like a stone.
>
> We lived one and a half winters on Aran, and during the second winter the storms were incredible. On the seaward side of the island was a cliff-face that in its highest parts was over 300 feet, high. Often after a storm, walking along the top of these cliffs we picked up pebbles and seaweed thrown right up there by the fury of the sea. In one of the culminating scenes of our film, the sea soars up against one of these cliffs and not only rises up to its head but keeps on rising until it reaches a height of some 450 feet from water-level . . . a towering white wall of wrack and spume, which then slowly bends in like a wraith or ghost over the island itself.

He was never a man to film someone else's plot. He had to evolve not a story but a pattern from what he and the camera found. The hard everyday life of the island formed part of this and the terrific storms another part. These were actual conditions of life on the Aran Islands at the time. But Flaherty wasn't interested in them for that reason, but because they were the symbols which he wanted for a film poem of man against the sea.

But there was something lacking film-poetically. Summer was just boringly hard work. If he had been a social realist of the documentary school, he would have concentrated on making that boring, hard work significant. But he did not want to produce a film White Paper on life in the Aran Islands. He had to find something which in summer was as hazardous as the storms of winter. He found it one day in April of their first year on Aran, when they caught sight of a strange creature swimming in the cove just below their house. Here were the sea monsters he had sought in vain in Samoa.

> It was enormous in size and had a black fin sticking up about a foot, maybe two feet, above the water. It was slowly swimming around in the clear green water. We got a curragh and rowed out to it. It didn't seem to be at all bothered by us. It came slowly alongside and passed by the curragh, not four feet away. Its huge mouth was open – like the mouth of a cavern, at least two feet in diameter. I asked Pat Mullen what it was. He said it was a sunfish.
>
> This puzzled me because the sunfish, as I knew it, was a different creature. This monster, judging by the length of the curragh which was 18 feet long, must have been at least 26 or 27 feet in length. Pat went on to tell me that soon there would be a lot of them there. They were to be seen every Spring, hundreds and hundreds of them, so that the sea 'would be filled with them'.
>
> Staying with us was my friend, Captain Munn, an explorer and hunter, who had been pretty well round the world. When he left to go back to London, I asked him to call at the National Library in Dublin and find out more about what Pat Mullen called a sunfish. He finally dug up a book written in 1848 by J. Wallop Brabazon. At the time it had been written, there were sunfish fisheries all along the West Coast of Ireland. The sunfish was known as the basking-shark and it was hunted for its liver which, as is common in sharks, was enormous. Out of the liver of one basking-shark could be rendered as much as 100 gallons of oil. This oil was used for illumination. It was poured into a small

shell with a rush for a wick. The shark was hunted with harpoons and lines, in the old way of hunting whales.

Sure enough, as Pat Mullen had foretold, the basking-sharks soon began to come in in schools. One Sunday we sailed through one of these schools in Galway Bay. The sharks averaged a length of about 27 feet, the tail being about 6 feet across. The school was four miles long. Looking down into the water, we could see that they were in layers – in tiers, tier after tier of them until we could see no deeper. There were thousands and thousands of them. They come every year to the west coast, approach the islands, and then pass farther up the coast to the Hebrides and the Faroes, up the coast of Norway and out beyond the Arctic Circle.

The Aran islanders no longer hunted basking-sharks. For fifty years they had used paraffin. But visually the hunting of sharks, especially in curraghs, was exactly the sort of poetic symbol Flaherty was seeking. The Aran Islanders didn't know how to do it – well, let them learn as Nanook had learnt to capture seal by a method he never used. Perhaps with these vast shoals of fish, he might revive an industry which would bring fortune to these poverty-stricken islands.[1] He set Pat Mullen looking for examples of the old harpoons, and had these copied by a Galway smith.

Flaherty hired a Brixham trawler during the summer of 1932 to pursue the sharks and give the crew practice in harpooning. As in the old days, look-outs were posted on high points. As soon as shark were spotted, the sentinel raced down to the boat and out it went. But the season had passed before the harpooners had learnt proficiency enough for filming; and the shooting schedule had to be extended until the summer of 1933.

To help with it, Flaherty called in his old friend, Captain Murray, now retired and living in Scotland. Murray had captained the whaler *Active* and could train the islanders in harpooning. He brought with him a harpoon-gun, made in 1840, which Tiger King seized upon eagerly.[2]

[1] The Aran Islanders did not revive a shark industry. But the Achill islanders catch them with nets for fish fertilizer. Flaherty had the liver oil analysed, hoping that, like cod and halibut liver oil, it would be rich in vitamins. But it wasn't.

[2] Captain Murray was very popular with everyone except Flaherty, who resented the old boy interrupting his stories, with protests that it didn't happen that way at all.

There are more reminiscences of working with Flaherty on *Man of Aran* than of any of the earlier pictures. Apart from Davidson and John Taylor, Grierson seconded another young man, Harry Watt from the E.M.B. Film Unit. There was an idea for a film to be made in Ceylon and Watt was being considered for running its field laboratory. In return for making himself generally useful, Watt might learn a lot from the Flaherty set-up.

John Taylor had been processing thousands of feet of film. In all Flaherty was to shoot over 200,000 feet of film for *Man of Aran*. On Christmas Eve, with Taylor loading, Flaherty shot 5,600 feet of film with two cameras between 10 a.m. and 3 p.m. But though in a sense this was wild over-shooting, it did not add greatly to the cost of the budget. The stock sent over by Gaumont-British was made up of 'short-ends'[1] and had already been paid for; while the cost of processing on Aran was a small fraction of what a London laboratory would have charged.

John Goldman, one of Balcon's university recruits to Gaumont-British, managed to wangle himself out to Aran and very soon settled down trying to sort the material which had been shot and assembled it in some very rough form. 'Much the worst of Flaherty's profligacy,' in Goldman's point of view, 'was his addiction to panning his camera. Perhaps the smoothness of the gyro-headed tripod had something to do with this, and touched a tactile nerve in him. One shot – quite pointless in itself – consisted of a complete magazine (200 feet) of an unbroken pan-shot ranging over the perpendicular walls of a cliff from the top – though never showing the skyline – down to the sea and back again until it finally lost itself. I think he was trying to establish by feeling it the height of the cliff. It was typical of him to try to do this by the camera rather than by cutting. His feeling was always for the camera. This wanting to do it all *in and through* the camera was one of the main causes of his great expenditure of film – so often he was trying to do what could *not* in fact be done.'

Everybody noted the change between the relaxed and jovial Flaherty of the Café Royal and the tense, violently irritable film-maker, living every minute of the twenty-four hours in his creation.

[1] Left-over negative from other productions, too short to be used for elaborate studio shooting.

'Bob on the job was not only bereft of all humour and wit,' says Goldman, 'but was utterly concentrated on the film. His being was, as it were, both wrapped around the subject and at the same time engulfed in the subject. The result was an atmosphere difficult to describe, if not experienced, heavy, thick and charged. There was tension everywhere, an unbearable tension, thunderous, black tension, a tension you could feel with your hand, smell and sweat in. It would swell and grow thicker and darker. Your very blood thickened into a sludge and life slowed down into profound depression, compressed, dangerous and explosive. The final explosion was like a volcano blowing its top. It had to be. The atmosphere then lightened, work started anew and grew into a furious pace until the tide ebbed again and the fog gathered round and the tension grew again and stretched and brooded. And there was no relief.'

He was an intolerable man to work for. In the course of eighteen months John Taylor was fired twice and quit once, but never stopped working. The members of the unit recognized that Flaherty was not an angry man; but he was one whose creative power was 'the tremendous power of a force of nature'. They were lucky as they could sneak away and sit on the cliff on a peaceful sunny day. 'But Flaherty could never escape from himself, from his brooding and passion. God! how that man suffered!'[1]

Goldman says there were times when Flaherty hated the film like 'a living monster with greater endurance and greater powers of evil than any human being possesses', and he pays tribute to Frances Flaherty's endurance and understanding. 'I can think of no other woman who could have lived through it. We others, after all, could come and we could go. But she stayed. She coped. With infinite patience and extraordinary courage, she endured and saw it through.'

The others could go. But they didn't. They were young men, gripped in a creative experience, which Goldman best expresses. 'There was a strange light in his eyes. He was as a man possessed. The smell of this possessedness pervaded and spread through the unit. We all felt it. We were all touched by it. There was nothing rational about it. There was nothing rational about making a film with Flaherty

[1] John Goldman notes to Paul Rotha. July – December, 1959.

from beginning to end. When I heard him talking of the making of his earlier films, I could recognize the same atmosphere, the same irrational forces at work. When he told us of his troubles during *Moana*, the accidents, the passions, the murders, I could understand them for they were the product of the tensions generated.'

The islanders felt it too. For people who astonishingly couldn't swim, they performed the most astonishing feats of bravery, perhaps led on by his unsparing energy. 'He'd see some spot in the distance where he would figure he should put up his camera,' Pat Mullen said.[1] 'Well, nothing could stop him getting there. He made a direct line and he'd bolt through a field of briars, you know, that would hold a bull – that sort of way. He had that fire in him.'

Looking back, Flaherty said: 'I should have been shot for what I asked these superb people to do for the film, for the enormous risks I exposed them to, and all for the sake of a keg of porter and £5 apiece. But they were so intensely proud of the fact that they had been chosen to act in a film that might be shown all over the world that there was nothing they wouldn't do to make it a success.'

One can understand why Flaherty's tensions were so great on *Man of Aran*. In *Nanook*, the Eskimos were always living on the brink of death. In *Moana*, he reintroduced the tattooing discipline which lent hardness to soft living. But in *Man of Aran*, he was gambling with the lives of people living at starvation level.

> 'We had picked three skilled men to be the crew of the curragh in the film. I am appalled at the dangers I asked them to run. There was one scene which took place so quietly in the finished film that most possibly it wasn't noticed. When the curragh is racing and trying to get to land, suddenly a jagged tooth of rock is revealed by the momentarily sagging waters and the curragh comes to within a foot of it. If it had struck that tooth of rock, the curragh would have been ripped from bow to stern and the three men would have been drowned before our eyes.'

One result of that would have been that the film would have stopped production. The enthusiasm which Flaherty had commanded would

[1] *Film News* (New York). Vol. 13, No. 3, 1953.

have turned to hatred and his family been either lynched or driven from the island. It is even possible that Flaherty might have killed himself.

Though people had died indirectly as the result of his filming, he had never killed anyone. But throughout the eighteen months filming on Inishmore, where the sea might reach 300 feet up a cliff to pluck off some unfortunate, he was in constant terror that tragedy would strike. He was gambling with death and no wonder, if after a thick and sleepless night, he sometimes flung his breakfast across the room.

What was Flaherty trying to do in this hazardous picture, endangering the lives of Aran Islanders, harpooning basking-sharks, which normally they ignored, large plankton-eating fish which would have choked if they swallowed a sardine? Was it, as Grierson's documentary school believed, a crude bid for the commercial box-office?

I don't think so. I am quite sure that the islanders and the members of the unit would never have given their loyalty, if they had ever thought so. John Goldman's phrase 'both wrapped around the subject and at the same time engulfed in the subject', offers only a clue. Flaherty was never his own theorist. He would talk about making a picture. But he never discussed what he was really trying to do. In this respect, he was like most great creative artists. Doing was hard enough, he had no time left over to explain exactly what he *was* doing, nor was he interested in gathering round himself a group of evangelists or disciples.

Flaherty was a film poet. He used images out of real life. But it was the images with which he was concerned, not the social-economic situation. The actual making of the picture was in the true Greek sense a 'poiesis', a making, a creative act. *Man of Aran* was something which Flaherty, his unit, Maggie, Mikeleen, Tiger King, Pat Mullen and all the rest had done together. It was not a denunciation of social conditions. It had no remote association with the I.L.P., Lord Keynes, P.E.P., the London School of Economics or John Grierson. In fact, if there was an impure motive in it, it was to rub Grierson's nose in basking-sharks. They didn't fit in to the documentary pattern. But they symbolized superbly the sort of hazard which Flaherty had wanted to make his central theme.

It would be interesting to know what sort of reception Flaherty's picture would have got if called Man against the Sea, instead of *Man of Aran*.

Though Flaherty may have raged against Gaumont-British, he had in Michael Balcon a loyal producer. *Man of Aran* became known as 'Balcon's folly'; and back in London Balcon used to screen the seemingly endless storm scenes on Saturday afternoons in order to escape the caustic criticisms of his colleagues.

On one of these Saturday afternoons, Isidore Ostrer and his wife came into the projection-room. They had obviously been tipped off and they sat down without saying a word. When the lights went up, they were full of praise. 'After that life became a little more tolerable,' Balcon says.

But Flaherty was a man who would go on shooting until he ran out of money. He had already exceeded his £10,000 budget and Goldman, seeing that Flaherty was shooting the same material over and over again, suggested Balcon should stop production.

Flaherty made no demur. He had probably been waiting for the decision to be made for him and was glad to be relieved of the compulsion.

Of all his previous films, apart from episodic shooting such as *Industrial Britain*, Flaherty had been his own editor, with help from Frances and a junior assistant. Now in John Goldman, he had a professional editor.

Goldman, like most editors, believed that the real work of a film started on the cutting bench. Flaherty, as Goldman rightly pointed out, tried to make the film in the camera. Balcon, knowing that Goldman had come back from the Soviet Union with pronounced views about editing, left Flaherty and Goldman to work it out between them.

He knew that Goldman had a great admiration for Flaherty, as well as an aesthetic sympathy which wasn't bound by doctrinaire principles. He was far too busy a man to act as arbiter between director and editor; and he thought that Goldman would learn something valuable from working with Flaherty.

In the editing of *Man of Aran*, one sees the first major encounter between Flaherty's Eskimo way of film-making, fumbling, intuitive and exploratory, treating the material as if it contained some inner nature which needed to be understood and the American or European attitude which from the start tried to visualize what would appear on the screen in its totality.

Whether studio or documentary, whether designed to make money as Hollywood and other commercial pictures, or to alter ideological attitudes as in the U.S.S.R., the basic technical process was very similar. There was a story idea, a full treatment of the story, a break-down into a shooting-script, with visuals, synchronized dialogue and then the real business of film-making began in the cutting-room. The projection-theatre in this scheme was only used so that the film-makers, producer, director, editor, etc., could see how the film was coming along.

Inevitably in such a process, there were continual changes, as ideas which had appeared good proved wrong and new values were discovered in the material at each stage. But from the start, everybody's eyes and ears were concentrated on the final picture, including music, sound-effects and the dramatic use of silence.

This method was as different from Flaherty's as Sir Christopher Wren's building St. Paul's from Christopher Columbus' discovering America.

Flaherty said he 'photographed what the camera wanted to photograph'. If Goldman explained he wanted a link shot say between a man leaving a cottage and arriving at the seashore, Flaherty would say, 'No, the camera doesn't want to shoot it . . . the camera doesn't see a shot like that.'

Flaherty was ever looking at the film through the camera. Goldman was thinking of what would be on the screen. 'Cut away to something else,' Flaherty would say, but if there was nothing to cut away to, Flaherty would reluctantly agree to shoot a link.[1]

[1] In *Nanook* and *Moana*, silent pictures, visual continuity did not arise, because sub-titles filled in the gaps. Flaherty did not realize at this time what a difference sound (or rather absence of titles) made to the visual narrative.

Goldman noticed that if a particular shot was praised for its composition or photographic quality, Flaherty told him to drop the shot. 'Too self-conscious.' Goldman reached the conclusion that this was because Flaherty didn't want to impose his personality on the subject; he wanted it to emerge. Flaherty had a very sensitive feeling for rhythm in the people and things he photographed. No cinematographer has moved his camera better. But he had, thinks Goldman, no sense of 'the rhythm of film'; his delight was in the shot *per se*, not in the cumulative effect of shots arranged in a particular way.

And yet, as will be seen in the following chapter, the process was not nearly as simple as that. It was a matter not of intellect or of film-theory, but of intuitive awareness.

13 STORMS OVER ARAN

People who make films are not dedicated to verbal precision. This applies first and foremost to Flaherty himself, but also to all the people with whom he mixed and worked. It is a work of verbal impressionism at its best and at its vulgarest verbal showmanship.

I have in the last chapter quoted John Goldman as saying that Flaherty had no knowledge of the 'rhythm of film' as opposed to the rhythm of movement within single shots. I would now like to quote from Goldman's retrospective account of the editing of *Man of Aran*. It was written to Rotha in 1959, over a quarter of a century after the events, and the reader will detect in it a rhetorical dramatization which belongs more to the personality of Goldman than to that of Flaherty himself. Both these factors have to be discounted, the distortion of time and the distortion of personality; but if I tried myself to correct them, I would only add a further distortion. I have however taken the liberty to condense his lengthy document.

> To make such a film as *Man of Aran* requires an extreme awareness, an openness to reception which in my experience is very rare among people. This freedom to be aware was Flaherty's

great gift. All the time I was on Aran I never saw Flaherty deliberately pose his camera. The camera was set-up and he peered through it. Either what he saw through it was right, or absolutely wrong. Either what he saw had its own life and existence, or it was dead and lifeless, meaningless in its own terms.

When seeing rushes, it is easy to see and reject the shots which are failures, which are lifeless. And Flaherty had a very high proportion of such failures. These having been rejected, the second stage of selection came, and here the difficulties began. During these viewings nothing existed for Flaherty except what was on the screen. Gone was the moment when he took the shot. Gone was any preconceived idea of what he wanted for the film. Gone were any notions of good photography or of focus or exposure. In the theatre, he would sit for hour after hour, smoking cigarette after cigarette, heaving with his peculiarly laboured breathing, concentrating wholly on the screen.

Flaherty's actual film-making took place not in the camera, not on the cutting-bench, but in the projection-room. Here he would sit running through reel after reel over and over again, panning for the gold nugget, and the only criterion for the recognition of this nugget was his own bare awareness.

During this long, tedious process there was no shape to the film, no beginning, no end. Imperceptibly shots would start to sort themselves, migrating from film-can to film-can and gathering like molecules round a nucleus. But there was no conscious thought directing it.

Then one day, months after the start, Flaherty would suddenly realize that he was looking at a sequence. It was a peculiar sensation. One day a mere collection of shots joined up together; the next, a perceptible semblance of a sequence, seemingly self-generated, organic, belonging. And that, so far as that sequence was concerned, was the end of the second stage in making the film.

The third stage began, similar to the second, but more demanding in patience and perception. Again the projectionists would work day and night. They would have endless strips of paper which they would insert in the reel of film on the projector when Flaherty pressed the buzzer in the theatre. 'Cut that shot in half' ... 'Take out that long-shot, it's dead!' From the first germ of life, the sequence would start to grow up. First, the internal life in the individual shot, then the internal life in the sequence. I recall one sequence growing this way into life and then it seemed to wilt and die, stillborn. 'We've been preconceiving,' Flaherty said. And so every shot had to be broken down and shuffled up and the reel put back again into rushes.

Then individual sequences would be linked. Disaster. Whole sequences built up and grown after long months of loving care and fatigue would have to go. But never for one instant did Flaherty himself intrude on the film. Always he allowed it to grow from within.

Just as Flaherty was never concerned with the conscious composition of a shot, so you found the same attitude towards rhythm. The complex of shots, the sequence of shots grew from within and conformed to no preconceptions about rhythm and flow. The rhythm in the film flowed from life, not life from rhythm. If disjointed and jerky, maybe that's the way it was; you can't change it because it is not pretty and smooth.

There are two kinds of creative people. Those who create by inspiration and those who create by revelation. Flaherty did not work by inspiration but by revelation. And the way is long, laborious and frustrating, requiring fantastic patience and a degree of sustained awareness and perception that is exceedingly rare. Flaherty possessed these qualities *in excelsis*.

Having written of Flaherty's method of allowing a film to grow organically out of its material and the material out of what he called his 'tests', there remains the other side . . . the stylistic and grammatical idiosyncrasies particular and individual to him. However much he may not have wished it, these were in fact imposed upon his work. What had begun as an almost imperceptible style in *Nanook* had become an exploited habit by the time of *Man of Aran*.

He had definite ideas of what he meant by drama. As a dramatic film director, I found his grammar and vocabulary, using those terms in a film sense, curiously limited. His drama was based solely on suspense and since this was the one weapon in his armoury, so to speak, he used it increasingly hard and extended it to a degree that could be said to be monotonous. On the other hand, this suspense drama was ideally suited to his needs. Suspense was always based on revelation, and the revelation delayed until the last possible moment.[1] He was very careful about this exact moment of the resolution of the suspense. This had to be cut as short as possible. He was afraid of anti-climax. One of his maxims was 'Never reveal anything'. In close-ups of people, he hated full-face shots. He preferred three-quarter profiles, heads shot from behind, anything which did not reveal the full-face. The full-face showed too much. He disliked medium and mid-long shots because they revealed without hiding. In all his films after *Nanook*, he proceeds from close-ups eventually to a long-shot as a pay-off. 'If they want to know more,' he would say, 'you know you have got them.'

He also believed that it is not the task of a film to do all the work. The audience must meet the film, at least half-way. This relationship between the film and audience was never absent from his mind.

The bigger the thing he had finally to reveal, the longer he could keep the audience in suspense. The shark sequence in *Man of Aran* is an example. The whole sequence is built up on this method, from the moment of Mikeleen seeing something, we are not shown what, while he is fishing on the cliff-top to the launching of the boats, to the first sight of something indefinable in the sea,[2] to the harpooning, the fish being twice lost, until finally the revelation of the basking-shark in all its length and turbulence.

The last sequence of the film, the great storm sequence, appears to me to be quite different from anything else in Flaherty's work. In this sequence Flaherty hinted at and started to develop an entirely new breadth and splendour of expression. Here was something that was new and deeper than anything he had previously attempted. Technically, too, it was different because no tricks, none of his stylistic habits, play any part in its construction. And the sustained power and drama owe nothing to his previous ideas of suspense and revelation.

It stems, of course, from the final sequence of *Nanook*, where the blizzard howls round the igloo and the dogs get covered in

[1] Nanook fishing in a hole in the ice without the audience knowing what he is fishing for; the little boy searching for the crab in *Moana*; and many similar examples in *Louisiana Story*.

[2] The one illegitimate element of the suspense build-up is the look of terror on Mikeleen's face on seeing the indefinable monster. The basking-shark is a plankton-feeder not a man-eater. Sight of it would inspire not terror, but joy that the oil-yielding sharks have at last arrived.

snow, but in *Man of Aran* the storm is utterly transformed. It rears up as a gigantic piece of nature, majestic and profound where human beings are as fragile and pathetic as mosquitoes in a summer storm. Here is the force of eternity bursting upon us; and all that frail human beings have to pit against it is their human spirit, their courage which proves eternal and enduring as the prodigious cataclysm of the Universe. This is a spectacle beyond spectacle. This is a grandeur of conception that I have not seen equalled on the screen, Lear-like in its force and expression and, I have always felt, fully realized.

Granted that the storms we saw that winter on Aran were stupendous and breathtaking. Granted the superlative use Flaherty made of every change in light to photograph them, yet there is something beyond all this in the dark poetry of the scenes as they flow before us and produce on us a new and unique experience. This storm sequence was profoundly Flaherty's work. Yet there are aspects of it which I believe came about through a unique collaboration between us and through a deep sympathy and understanding which merged us.

Perhaps what I did was to suggest a way of editing the material that was different from the way he had approached construction before. My natural approach was not by drama of suspense but by the drama of overwhelming emotional experience. I remember that after many attempts, I had got the sequence into four reels, built on my method of construction. I screened it to Flaherty who sat through it in silence, lighting one cigarette from another. As I threaded up the last reel, he said, 'What, is there another reel?' At the end he said nothing for a while. Then he said, 'Patsy must see this.' So Frances was fetched and the four reels were run again.

It never occurred to him that there was a new way of editing a film. He had grasped and felt the essential element of monumental building that was in any event implicit in the material. Here was no violation of his own fundamental approach to the material. It was following its own logic, developing its own life. Throughout that whole sequence we worked in complete harmony, except for my minor irritations when some inner rhythms were upset by his changes. The only problem lay in reducing the four reels to one. Flaherty never made any attempt to alter the fundamental style. On the contrary, the style became his and it

> was under his direction and guidance that the final version took life and breathed remarkable fire. He never suggested incorporating any of his favourite suspense drama. I have always thought that this showed the real greatness of the man as a film-maker, that he could grasp and master a new method and bring it to perfection as I believe he did with this sequence.

When the silent picture had been more or less completed, there remained to compile a sound track. Flaherty insisted on retaining some sub-titles, though these were considered obsolete by 1934. Pat Mullen, Tiger King, Maggie, Mikeleen and others were brought over to the studios to record snatches of dialogue which could be added to a sound-effects track. What they said was dictated largely by their exclamations as they watched the silent film. But the recording of these exclamations was made indoors and produced an artificial effect when added to visuals shot out of doors.

The visit of these Aran Islanders was, with Flaherty's full approval, exploited to the uttermost by Gaumont Publicity. Dressed in their island clothes they were met at Euston by the Flahertys, John Goldman and Hugh Findlay, G.-B. publicity chief, for a Guinness party, in which Press-men and photographers joined. And for the nine weeks of their stay, there was a steady output of newspaper stories, genuine and phoney.

This advance publicity built up expectation for the film. But it was also to produce a false impression which has still not been effaced. These were the genuine Aran Islanders as large as life; and the film was represented as a description of their day-to-day lives. Flaherty did not give a Press conference and say, 'These are the people whom I used for a poetic presentation of the age-long struggle of Man against the Sea. The reality which I attempted was poetic and *Man of Aran* is not intended to be an actual presentation of everyday life on the Aran Islands.' On the contrary, *Man of Aran* was presented as a true film of real life.

There was some difficulty with the British Board of Film Censors. Brooke Wilkinson, secretary of the Board, told Goldman 'it is not the policy of the Board to let films show poverty on the screen'.[1]

[1] This was taken at the time to show how reactionary the British Board of Film Censors was. Perhaps that was the intention of the Board. But the effect was opposite. The sight

On 25th April, 1934, *Man of Aran* had its première at the New Gallery, London, with the Irish Guards playing folk-music, the audience wearing evening dress and the actors home-spuns. No publicity angle had been neglected. A basking-shark had been brought over to be stuffed by a North London taxidermist and placed in the display window of G.-B. Film House, Wardour Street.

Flaherty was wild when he heard a bit had been cut from the middle so that the shark would fit the window. Whether this was because he felt it was cruelty to stuffed sharks, because he thought the shark should have been shorter or the window longer was never clear.[1]

New Gallery presentation, at that time, was very good. Only exceptional films were shown there. It commended the film to a critical London audience. But it also prejudiced it with nation-wide exhibitors who preferred, to exceptional films, sure-fire Westerns, Comedies, Horrors or Gangster pictures.

Flaherty knew this problem in advance and he tried his *Moana* technique to give the film special promotion. Gaumont-British backed him. With Hugh Findlay and two of the cast, special presentations were arranged in six British cities on the *Moana* model, Manchester, Birmingham, Wigan, Sheffield, Liverpool and Leicester. Flaherty and Goldman went too. But there was one essential of specialized promotion lacking, the praise of respected critics.

C. A. Lejeune of the *Observer* wrote, '*Man of Aran* is lovely to look at – sincere, virile and understanding. It has been made by a man who loves the place and the people, and his passion has been communicated in every shot. Everyone will go to see it – everyone should go to see it – for Flaherty has not his like in the film-making world. But it is not a great picture, in the sense that *Nanook* was great . . . *Man of Aran* has no story, not even the trace of a story that was to be found in *Moana* and *Tabu*. It barely recounts the movements of a nameless

[1] Today such a truncated basking-shark would find its spiritual home immediately at a Butlin camp. Then it went back to the taxidermist who charged £2 10*s*. a week for its lodging until Hugh Findlay hit on the idea of passing the shark to the Brighton Aquarium, presented by the starlet Anna Lee.

---

of extreme poverty reconciled the poor to their less extreme poverty. The most revolutionary pictures ever shown on the screen were the super-glossies of Hollywood, London and Neubabelsberg High Life which created an envy far more powerful than the dynamic Soviet or Documentary propaganda.

father, mother and son through their daily life of fishing, seaweed-gathering, the planting of potatoes, the harpooning of sharks. . . . *Man of Aran* is a sealed document, the key to which is still in Flaherty's mind.'[1]

This provoked a protest from Huntley Carter, author of several books about the theatre, especially the Soviet theatre, protesting that Miss Lejeune had missed the 'soul' of the picture. 'If there had been a better picture of a little community fashioned and impassioned by constant and close contact with Nature, I have never seen it.'[2]

Miss Lejeune, who had talked with Flaherty about the economic conditions on the Aran Islands, immediately retorted that there was a far finer story on the Aran Islands, but Flaherty hadn't told it on the screen. 'The real story of Aran, as he sees and tells it, is the fight to hold the land against eviction – the women and children gathering, on the cliffs, with their heaped stones and missiles, the police rowing out through the storm in open boats, with orders to pull the roofs from the cottages. . . . He calls the present picture "an idealized cross-section of life on the island" and says frankly that it is designed "to pique the curiosity of the audience and make them want to know more." [3]

'In that sense, as a kind of "trailer" to a bigger picture, I agree that *Man of Aran* is a brilliant, if overlong essay. . . But if *Man of Aran* is, as experience teaches us to expect, the final account of Western Ireland so far as the screen is concerned, I shall continue to feel that seaweed is a poor substitute for story. . . .'

If Flaherty had had as publicity adviser someone as verbally agile as Grierson, he would have made it publicly plain that *Man of Aran* was not a 'document', but an 'eclogue', a pastoral and marine poem. As it was, he took the brunt of C. A. Lejeune's new-found dislike of 'documentary' in the Griersonian sense.

Charles Davy in the *Spectator* complained that in order to discover what life on the island was really like, he had to turn to the synopsis and Graham Greene remarked: 'Photography by itself cannot make

[1] *The Observer*, 29th April, 1934.

[2] *The Observer*, 6th May, 1934.

[3] Ibsen before writing a social play would write a poem. Flaherty's films were the equivalent of Ibsen's poems, but the nearest he got to Ibsen's play, as the second stage, was what he said he wanted *Tabu* to be.

poetic drama. By itself, it can only make arty cinema. *Man of Aran* was a glaring example of this; how affected and wearisome were those figures against the skyline, how meaningless that magnificent photography of storm after storm. *Man of Aran* did not even attempt to describe truthfully a way of life. The inhabitants had to be taught shark-hunting in order to supply Mr. Flaherty with a dramatic sequence.'[1]

It must be remembered that in 1934, Europe and the United States were plunged into an economic depression which made films of childhood poetry, such as Flaherty's always tended to be, almost as outrageous as J. M. Barrie's *Peter Pan* or Maeterlinck's *The Blue Bird.* Though photographically superb, ideologically Flaherty's filming appeared old hat. And Ralph Bond, a Communist party stalwart, made a united front with Graham Greene. 'Two storms and a shark-hunt do not make a picture and we are more concerned with what Flaherty has left out than what he has put in. . . . *Man of Aran* is escapist in tendency,[2] more so probably than any other previous Flaherty production. Flaherty would have us believe that there is no class-struggle on Aran.'

There was also on the Aran Islands a religious struggle as well as a class one. Both were ignored. If he had included them, Flaherty might have made a far better film. But today we are concerned with the film he made and wanted to make, rather than what he could and perhaps ought to have made.

But before considering that, we must look at one further contemporary view, that of Grierson and the documentary movement which he had founded. As Rotha said, thanks to Grierson, 'Here was the father of documentary with an honest break to do something big in a manner after his own heart. Two long years in the making, month after month of waiting for us poor folk who knock out a living at back-door documentary, and the film is here to give us more or less what we expected and something else beyond . . .

'There are moments in the film when the instinctive caressing of the camera over the movements of a boy fishing or of men against the

[1] *Footnotes to the Film*, ed. C. Davy, Oxford, 1937, pp. 61-62.

[2] In the 'smearology' of that time, escapism was only one stage better than Trotskyism – which twenty years later became Stalinism.

horizon brings a flutter to your senses; so beautiful in feeling and so perfect in realization that their image is indelible. And again there are softer passages when you have to collect your thoughts and wonder if the sequence construction is built up quite so firmly as documentary of any kind demands; and whether dawdling over a woman carrying wet seaweed across the shore, beautiful in itself to behold, does not tend to weaken the main shape of the picture. It might be that two minds have disagreed, each seeking the major issue of the theme and each finding a different answer. Either the dramatic grandeur of the sea or the thrill of the sharks must take precedence, but they disturbingly share the peak between them. So great is Flaherty's shooting of the sea . . . and so overwhelming the sweep of the Atlantic that the sharks, I feel, are commonplace. . . . Here is the living scene *as it appeared* to Flaherty, recreated in terms of the living cinema . . . His approach is wholly impersonal. What really happens on Inishmore is not his or our concern in this conception. . . .'[1]

In those last three sentences, Rotha with characteristic sensitivity went to the heart of the matter. He perceived what Flaherty was attempting to do. But earlier he was applying to the 'father of documentary',[2] standards which had been evolved by Grierson for a totally different type of film with a totally different aim.

The attack on Flaherty from almost all sides in Britain was countered at Venice by the award of the Grand Prix at the Second Festival. This was a slap in several eyes. *Man of Aran* hadn't been selected by the British Film Industry for submission. It was requested by the Italians. And the British documentarians would certainly not have chosen it either. The Venice Gold Prize was discounted as Mussolini's Gilt Medal in praise of a reactionary film which bolstered Fascism.

This may in retrospect appear absurd. But arising from the Wall Street crash and the world depression (to which it should be remembered *Man of Aran* was Flaherty's unconscious reaction as *Nanook* had been his reaction to the First World War), there arose among the more recently engaged a storm of indignation against the older man who chose to make epic stories in modern settings.

Flaherty wasn't a fool. The father, mother and son were not given

[1] *Sight and Sound*, Summer, 1934.

[2] In fact, the putative grandfather of documentary. Grierson was the father. A.C–M.

names or personalities in *Man of Aran* because he did not want to focus on some remote islands off the west coast of Ireland. He was inventing a myth of a folk way of life which would apply to people all over the world. He was saying something terribly unpopular; that the world was an untamed place and that to tame it all human creatures should work together. He was addressing the whole of humanity.

His critics were concerned with the Aran Islands. Here was a perfect example of absentee landlordism, eviction, the class struggle, the sort of sorrow caused by people so near to death that potheen was the short cut to paradise.

Flaherty had his tribute as soon as he got away from British critics. In the *New York Herald Tribune*, Richard Watts, Jnr., nominated the film as the best of the year while James Shelley Hamilton in the National Board of Review Magazine, in a long rave notice, wrote: 'The whole effect is a heartening, thrilling effect of a unit of life – man, woman and child, the continuing link in the human race winning survival in an unending war with the grim impersonality of the elements.'

But Richard Griffith, later to become Flaherty's staunchest champion in the United States, wrote in 1935: '*Man of Aran* finally arrived and was the most disappointing film I can remember. . . . The characters were non-existent as personalities. One knew that they were human beings because of their form, but nothing more. There was nothing to distinguish them as Aranese, or as members of any nationality. That was what first amazed me. The second was the utter failure to dramatize the conflict between man and the sea. With all the marvellous material at hand, that conflict came through more because of the subtitles than the cutting. I can find no explanation for it save that Flaherty is so in love with primitive man because he *is* primitive that he feared to deflower the virgin freshness of Aran by intruding a civilized editorial point of view. But a film must take an attitude; otherwise it is a soulless record.'[1]

The most violent public attack came from David Schrire in *Cinema Quarterly* [2] in the course of which he said, 'Man's struggle with

[1] Letter to Paul Rotha, 5th February, 1935.

[2] Vol. 3, No. 1, Autumn 1934.

nature to wrest from her his means of subsistence has lost importance today. It is his struggle for the right to divert what he has produced to the interests of humanity that is the vital question. And it is there that documentary has its justification, in truthfully depicting modern relationships, in rendering audiences conscious of their interests, of the economic claims, aware of their remedy. . . .

'Flaherty is an institution. He rushes to the bucolic present for material to fashion into his exquisitely finished product. Our economic system breeds such types . . . But let us now realize, clearly and finally, that the pictures of Flaherty are hindrances to the growth of documentary; that not only must we withdraw all support, not only cease damning with faint praise, but the time is over-ripe to attack evasive documentary for the menace it really is.'

Grierson immediately came to the defence of Flaherty. While *Man of Aran* was being shot, he had the hope that 'the Neo-Rousseauism implicit in Flaherty's work dies with his exceptional self', but he was not prepared to stand by and see a great artist attacked for not doing what he did not want to do.

'One may not – whatever one's difference in theory –' he wrote in the same number of *Cinema Quarterly* as David Schrire, 'be disrespectful of a great artist and a great teacher. Flaherty taught documentary to create a theme out of natural observation. He brought to it for the first time a colossal patience in the assembly of effects. And this was necessary before the discursive travelogue could become a dramatic – or dialectical – analysis of event.

'It is of course reasonable for a later generation of film-makers to want a documentary tougher, more complex, colder and more classical, than the romantic documentary of Flaherty. . . . But there are considerations one must watch carefully. The first one is that Flaherty was born an explorer, and that is where his talent is: to be accepted on its own ground. It would be foolish, as Professor Saintsbury once remarked, to complain of a pear that it lacks the virtue of a pomegranate.

'I call it futile, too, to ask of Flaherty an article which cannot under commercial conditions be possible. Some of us can make do with a thousand pounds on a production, and we buy our independence accordingly. Flaherty's method involves the larger backing of the commercial cinema. He has of necessity to obey its rules. These rules are not always articulated but they are understood. . . .

'Rather than complain of the result, I wonder that so much was done within commercial limitations. . . .

'*Man of Aran* has been blamed for distorting the life of the islanders, for going back into time for its shark-hunting and its dangers, for telling a false story. But is it unreasonable for the artist to distil life over a period of time and deliver only the essence of it? Seen as the story of mankind over a thousand years, the story of Aran is this story of man against the sea and woman against the skyline. It is a simple story, but it is an essential story, for nothing emerges out of time except bravery. If I part company with Flaherty at that point, it is because I like my braveries to emerge otherwise than from the sea, and stand otherwise than against the sky. I imagine they shine as bravely in the pursuit of Irish landlords as in the pursuit of Irish sharks.'

This was a most skilful exercise in the art of defending an old friend without alienating followers. As a practical politician, working within his own disciplines, accepted though stretched to the limit, Grierson knew perfectly well that his low budget 'independence' would not have allowed him to make at that time any film denouncing landlords. *Man of Aran* however gave him the chance of beginning the propaganda which later made possible the sponsorship of *Housing Problems* by the Gas Industry.

There was between Grierson and Flaherty a most interesting love-hate relation. Grierson admired Flaherty's genius, the innocence of his camera-eye which could see anything with utter freshness, but with a Calvinistic rub-your-nose-in-the-truth, he hated the ignorance-of-what-was-going-on, which was the corollary of that innocence. Both had greatness, but Flaherty's was the greatness of a poet, Grierson's of a propagandist. They met however on certain common ground, an enormous gusto, a love of good food and drink and good talk. The number of occasions on which Grierson and Flaherty had afternoon tea and morning coffee together has not been recorded; the number of occasions on which they drank together couldn't be. Immediately they had a great deal in common and ultimately they were at loggerheads. They were in rivalry with one another throughout what

Grierson called a 'dialectical pub-crawl across half the world'. There were frequent explosions. One was during a visit by the Flahertys to the Blackheath Studio to see what Grierson was doing with his film unit, now under the aegis of the G.P.O.

Grierson was using public money not merely for documentary experiments such as *Night Mail*, using Cavalcanti, Wright, Watt, Britton and Auden for making a commonplace theme exciting,[1] but also for encouraging non-documentary *avant-gardistes* such as Len Lye.

Flaherty had heard that Alistair Cooke was going to give a film talk on the B.B.C., in which *Man of Aran* was to be discussed. He insisted that the tour of the studio should be so timed that he and Frances could listen to it.

This was arranged; and I've no doubt that Grierson provided suitable refreshment. Flaherty, a big as well as a great man, sat listening to that clear, warm, judicial voice that has come through the years to be so authoritative.

Cooke spoke of *Man of Aran* as documentary. He compared the escapism of Flaherty unfavourably with the progressive work of the G.P.O. Film Unit.

Flaherty thumped his fist. 'Goddam it, John! You fixed this!'[2]

Grierson grinned. 'I didn't know a word about it, Bob.' It was true. He hadn't fixed it. But in another deeper sense he had. He had called *Moana* 'documentary' and then he had evolved his own theory of documentary by which any Flaherty picture would fail as surely as Lewis Carroll failed to be a true surrealist.

That coolness between Grierson and Flaherty lasted rather longer than most. Today Grierson still thinks that *Man of Aran* was sensationalized in order to get the box-office success, which Flaherty wanted passionately.

There is no need for discrimination here. 'Box-office success' in relation to a film studio means return on the money expended. *Man of Aran* cost about £30,000 to produce and grossed during the first

[1] *Night Mail* might be called the Wordsworthian romanticism, compared with the Coleridgean romanticism of Flaherty.

[2] Told by John Grierson, 13th January, 1960.

six months about £50,000. In terms of money-making, this wasn't very important. Lots of films earned several times more than their production cost. But it brought Gaumont-British prestige, that invisible asset which accountants cannot assess.

Man of Aran may have been escapist nonsense when Hitler was grabbing power in Germany, Mussolini was bombing Abyssinians, Spain was ravaged by an international civil war and millions of the unemployed either side of the Atlantic were near starvation, but this situation was totally changed by the outbreak of the Second World War.

Richard Griffith in a Biblically phrased confession says: 'The scales fell from my eyes on a day when I was ushering at the Little Theatre of the New York World's Fair in 1940 and was thus *forced* to see *Man of Aran* again. I sat through every performance for the rest of the week.'[1]

Griffith exemplifies the peculiar change in taste which time brings in different places. The United States was at peace and booming in 1940, but in Europe *Man of Aran* would have appeared, either side of the lines, utterly remote. Yet by the end of the Second World War with rationing and privation, it would have seemed as heartening as Flaherty had hoped it would be at the time of the World depression.

[1] In a letter to Paul Rotha, 29th November, 1959.

14 FLAHERTY OF THE ELEPHANTS

On 16th February, 1934, Robert J. Flaherty entered his fifties. At such an age the pattern of a man's life is established. His ways are set and there is little likelihood of change, except that the grooves with the revolution of the years will grow deeper.

It is worthwhile examining him at leisure, while he, still on the Gaumont-British pay-roll, was touring Britain and the United States, promoting the distribution of *Man of Aran*. His character is as rewarding as some ancient city is to the loving archaeologist, who discovers not one but many cities built on the same site.

Buried out of sight was the 9-year-old boy who had watched the miners advance upon his father's office. That was a dark memory not to be resurrected till later. But the youth and young manhood in the North, all those years in Hudson Bay, Ungava and Baffin Island, became with each year more vivid. Then it was joy to be alive. And with each re-living it became more joyful. This was the purity of living, the explorer finding himself.

On top of that was the delight of making *Nanook*, of discovering creation through the camera, a form of exploration which in a curious way repeated his early romantic thrill of seeing for the first time what no white man had ever seen before. His eye was innocent in the sense that it saw no evil. It was also exploring, in that it saw things that others had failed to see.

He still had that eye, though his sight was no longer so keen. The prospect of the future was less enthralling than the rich retrospect.

Film-making was agony and bloody sweat. Holding forth to a private audience with a full glass was easier and more enjoyable. He was a natural artist of the anecdote, a narrative spell-binder.

But these two different artists in him, the film-maker and the story-teller, were never united. As I have said, his early diaries showed that Flaherty was a natural stylist. The books written with the assistance of his wife lack the original freshness. Writing for publication inhibited him. In the intervals between films, he did not express his narrative gifts in writing, but in talking. He was one of the great anecdotalists of his generation.

As such, he would have been welcomed in any social gathering where this gift, as opposed to conversation, argument or the exchange of wit, is prized. If he had been an Arab, he could have made his living telling stories in the bazaar.

He was a great film-maker, commanding the awe of an Eisenstein, Pabst, Pudovkin. He was great in body and spirit; but he wasn't always great in fortune.

The idea that he should 'sing for his supper', that his company was good enough to pay for his drinks, or that he should hog the conversation without paying for the drinks of all his audience never occurred to him.[1]

The dialectic of Flaherty's life was that he liked to drink and talk and entertain all and sundry on the one hand and he liked to make films on the other. Grierson, the shrewd Scot, liked precisely the same thing. But he observed his budgets, filmic and personal.

As Flaherty entered his fifties, he had acquired the tastes of a highly paid commercial film director, but he had not learnt the disciplines of the industry. He had never made two films for the same company.

[1] It is very possible that if broadcasting had come twenty years earlier, Flaherty would have been paid to entertain millions, instead of entertaining hundreds at his own expense. As it was, in 1949, when Michael Bell tried recording his stories for the B.B.C., he experienced appalling difficulty. The sight of the microphone inhibited Flaherty. The spontaneous flow dried up.

He was a prestige director. Just as a young man, coming of age, was given a gold watch, so a film company was given a film by Flaherty. It was a status-symbol, meant to last a lifetime.

There is some truth in the saying that if you are broke, the only way to get a job is to look as if you don't want one. Flaherty would have believed it, even if it wasn't true. He considered the lilies of the field and entertained all and sundry at the Café Royal. He no longer patronized Grierson's documentary pubs. Epstein, Hayter Preston, Augustus John, James Agate and Liam O'Flaherty belonged more in his age group than Arthur Elton, John Taylor, Edgar Anstey, Paul Rotha and Basil Wright. But if any of them had walked in to the Brasserie, they'd have been waved in to the group. 'You must listen to this,' and he'd have gone back to the beginning of the story and ten to one, if he observed the attention of the others flagging, he would think up a fresh detail to refresh the story for them. And if it was an effective detail, it would be incorporated in the saga.

But these were Flaherty's public personalities, even more in conflict with his private personality than they were with one another. His wife, Frances, ran through the texture of his life like the warp through the weft. It was her money which had supported them in the lean years. It was her money paying for the education of the girls, now at the progressive co-educational Dartington Hall. It was her drive keeping the home together and her faith in Flaherty's film genius and her scepticism about his business competence on which he would have relied totally, if she hadn't disapproved so strongly of his paying for everybody's drinks as well as his own.

One mustn't overstate these things. Flaherty was obviously an infuriating and extravagant husband; and perhaps when Frances had to listen for the hundred and fiftieth time to an anecdote, worn as smooth as a walrus-tusk carving, a bit of a bore, conjugally speaking. But compared with most husbands after twenty years, he was exciting. Any woman, given total security, will like Bluebeard's wife discover the fascination of danger. Frances Flaherty, in obverse, must have yearned for security in the bleak periods. But she certainly loved the excitement of the grandeurs. And she welcomed the next prestige invitation to Flaherty.

. . . . .

While they were making the Acoma Indian picture, Flaherty had gone down to Mexico to find a suitable boy star. He found instead a story which had appealed to him; a bull during a fight had been reprieved by the acclaim of the spectators. He had written it up as *Bonito the Bull*, a short story of the friendship of a boy and a bull which he hoped to sell to Hollywood. When he went to Europe, this same idea was furbished up as a Spanish picture. Then at some unspecified time, either in Berlin or in London, the bull was turned into an elephant. As Mrs. Flaherty explained, to find a bull, bred for the ring, who would prove really affectionate to a boy might be difficult. Elephants were gentler – and much bigger.

This idea was one of those which Flaherty placed in the hands of T. Hayes Hunter of Film Rights Ltd., an agent to whom he now entrusted his film affairs.

Since the world-success of *The Private Life of Henry the Eighth* (1933), a modest budget picture which made a fortune, Alexander Korda had become the great white hope of the British film industry. With the backing of the Prudential, Korda built costly studios at Denham and gathered a glittering series of star directors and actors around him.

Korda and Flaherty had met in Hollywood in 1929, when both of them were written off as failures; and Flaherty felt perhaps that his own fortunes would be changed by the magic of Korda's success. When Flaherty was summoned to Korda's presence, Hayes Hunter said, 'For God's sake, when it comes to contracts and terms, leave it to me.' 'Of course,' said Flaherty.

But when the great Irish-American charmer was leaving the great Hungarian charmer, the latter gripped his right hand firmly and patted his elbow with his left hand. 'We're both artists, Bob,' he said. 'We understand each other. Leave the contract side of our friendship in my hands.'[1]

Flaherty agreed without a murmur to a contract which gave Korda overriding supervisory powers. With the enthusiasm generated by every big money venture, he believed that this time he had really found the producer to understand him. Lasky, Fox and Thalberg had betrayed him in Hollywood and in London the Ostrer Brothers and

[1] John Goldman is the authority for this story.

Michael Balcon had done the same. But Korda really understood his documentary conception.

The truth is that *Elephant Boy*, as the Korda film was called, was Flaherty's one sustained effort to make a box-office feature picture. He had resigned from *White Shadows in the South Seas*. He had dug his toes in on the Acoma Indians film and the production had been shelved. He had withdrawn from *Tabu*.

His other three pictures, *Nanook*, *Moana* and *Man of Aran* had all engaged him more or less to the depths.

But *Elephant Boy* sprang from Flaherty's profound need to make a lot of money; and Korda, instead of thinking of a modest budget prestige picture, planned to make a large scale production, based on Kipling's *Toomai of the Elephants*. Flaherty thought he could get the best out of Korda, while Korda thought he could get the best out of him; but their methods were so incompatible that they brought out the worst in each other.

Flaherty found himself involved in long script conferences with Lajos Biro, the old Hungarian writer friend of Korda's, who acted as Script Editor. Biro had a distinguished presence and a diplomatic imprecision of utterance, which made for good relations in the early stages of a film; and when productions ran into trouble, they had reached a stage when the script had been forgotten.

While these conferences went on, David Flaherty and a production manager went ahead to Bombay to prepare the ground. Flaherty with his eldest daughter Barbara left at the end of February 1935; and Frances was to follow on six weeks later. Instead of acting as cameraman-director, Flaherty was to be director with Osmond H. Borradaile ('Bordie') as his cameraman.[1]

But even if the original unit going out resembled the usual Flaherty documentary unit, its style was different. The publicity boys had blazed the trail. Flaherty dined with the Viceroy, Lord Willingdon. His Excellency, ran the story, had been most cordial and suggested that he might play the part of Petersen Sahib! Flaherty accepted an invitation to make his picture in Mysore, the Dewan of the Maharajah

[1] Borradaile had spent ten years with Jesse Lasky at Paramount, as lab-technician, assistant and operating cameraman, before coming to England to shoot exteriors for Alexander Korda's *Private Life of Henry Eighth* and Zoltan Korda's *Sanders of the River*. He later shot Harry Watt's *The Overlanders* and Charles Frend's *Scott of the Antarctic*.

placing at his disposal the animals of the Royal Zoo and as living quarters the Chittaranjan Mahal, a disused palace which was cleared of cobras to make room for the unit and their equipment. The old servants' quarters were converted into a laboratory, where in shallow tanks on 200-feet racks all film except the sound-tracks [1] was developed.

Mrs. Flaherty has given her own story of the making of *Elephant Boy* in a book which consists chiefly of letters written to her two youngest daughters, Frances and Monica at Dartington Hall.[2] From this it is quite plain that a strange amalgamation of two conflicting methods took place. The unit arrived in India with a story-outline, *Toomai of the Elephants*, but Flaherty and his unit went through all the motions of observing the people and evolving a new script.

'I wish you could see us here; you who saw us in Aran!' wrote Frances to her girls. 'How you would open your eyes! It is so different that we hardly know what to do about it – so many people about, doing for us all the things we usually had to do ourselves – a fleet of cars flying here and there, a lorry as full of people as a Sunday-school picnic plying daily from town (two miles) to our "bungalow"; thousands of cameras [*sic!*]; thousands of racks bristling with tripods; a stills department with two assistants and I don't know how many still-cameras; thousands [*sic!*] of carpenters, electricians, tailors, bearers, coolies, sweepers, *mahouts*, animal-trainers, clerks, accountants, interpreters – you would think we were a b . . . y factory!'

From this proliferation of thousands, one might expect some film. But according to Korda,[3] after Flaherty left for India, 'For months I heard absolutely nothing. Of course, I heard from the business-manager . . . and money had to be sent to India, but still we had optimism, but . . . you know, when you spend money for eight, nine months and no film comes back, you start to get worried.'

Sir Alexander Korda was talking seventeen years later without having checked his exact dates. A letter is quoted below dated 28th September, 1935, which is *seven* months after Flaherty's departure by boat for India.

Flaherty was a slow worker. He worked through intuition, not

[1] Sound-tracks were sent to Bombay. Borradaile says that much of the footage shot in India consisted of tests for the labs.

[2] *Elephant Dance*, Scribner, 1937.

[3] *Portrait of Robert Flaherty*, 19th July, 1952, B.B.C.

intellect. He took in facts through his eyes and his sensibilities rather than his brain. India was a new continent and there were two worlds to master, that of the elephants in the jungle and that of the elephants in the stables. He had to find his elephant boy and having found him he had to bind the boy to him with a chain of devotion.

There was a genuine Flaherty theme in the oneness of created life, the love of boy and elephant. But apart from the general theme, if he was going to film an elephant-boy story, there was a great deal of rehearsal. The love had to be built up. The elephant had to be taught how to act, to pick Sabu up and place him on head or back according to the script. Even the blondest film-actress from Scandinavia can learn faster than an elephant.

Flaherty arrived in India in March. In June the monsoons broke and continued throughout July, August and early September. For Korda to expect much film during that period was not as reasonable as it may have appeared in Denham. On 28th September, 1935, Flaherty wrote Korda, 'Since calling you last Sunday we have been shooting continuously with perfect weather and good results. The monsoon has at last passed away, and I expect no hold-up from weather from now on.'

In the same letter, he told about an incident he had dreaded.

> Mr. Biro ever since we first started the story has been nursing a pet scene which I was rather reluctant to undertake. The scene in question is one in which, while Little Toomai is proceeding through a crowded street on his elephant, the elephant inadvertently walks over a baby.
>
> We tackled the scene last week.
>
> Having secured the mother's consent, we placed the baby in the street and called on Sabu, and his elephant. There were hundreds of people about, all intensely curious. We started our cameras. Irawatha, looking like a walking mountain, approached. The tip of his trunk went down and momentarily sniffed at the baby. Then on he came. Each of his feet was thicker than the baby was long. Slowly he lifted them over, the baby looking up at him, too young to understand.
>
> Then the elephant's hind feet came on. The first one he lifted over slowly and carefully; but the second foot came down on the baby's ankles.

> I never heard such a yell in my life as that which came up from the hundreds of staring native onlookers. Someone swept the baby up, while our camera-crew made a circle round it to keep the crowd back, jammed it with its mother into a motor-car and raced off to hospital.
>
> I thought there would be a riot. But fortunately nothing happened; and before we had the cameras struck, the car came racing back from hospital. The baby was smiling and the mother was smiling.
>
> When we ran the picture that night, we could see that the elephant, as soon as he had felt the touch of the child's feet, had thrown all his weight on the outer rim of his foot.[1]

Flaherty added a request not to mention this to the Press, as he had already been accused of trying to drown a boat-load of wild Irishmen on Aran.

Borradaile says that Flaherty himself was fearless but hated to place others in danger. 'He nearly went frantic watching Sabu riding his swimming elephant across a flood-swollen river.'

By Flaherty standards production was advancing rapidly. But it was not rapid enough for Korda who had already safeguarded himself against Flaherty's dilatoriness. By the time that Flaherty had moved to his jungle location, Korda decided that he needed further assistance. He first sent out Monta Bell, a Hollywood film director whose credits included *West Point of the Air* and *The Worst Woman in Paris*.

Korda's personal assistant, David Cunynghame (later the 11th Baronet), says that Korda thought Flaherty was finding it hard to cope with the difficult conditions of the jungle. Borradaile, on the other hand, says that Bell told Korda about a book just published in New York, called *Siamese White*, about a ghost elephant. Korda liked this idea and sent Bell out to incorporate the ghost in the script. 'If it had not been such a tragic mistake, the whole affair would have been comic. Monta Bell didn't like the jungle and wanted to return to the bright lights as soon as possible. But he didn't get away before Flaherty received and read a copy of *Siamese White*, which turned out to be a story of a man named White, who lived in Siam – a bit embarrassing because an elephant had actually been white-washed to play the ghost.

[1] Reproduced in *The World of Robert Flaherty*.

All the footage shot on this blunder – and a good chunk it was – went into the ash-can.'

Korda's brother, Zoltan, followed ostensibly to keep an eye on Monta Bell or Flaherty or both. And in the spring of 1936 there was a steady build-up of Denham technicians, cameramen and production staff, until at the end there were according to David Flaherty three different units shooting madly to three different scripts.

But to Mrs. Flaherty, at least in the book modelled on her letters to her younger daughters, everything went with divine ease. The kheddahing of wild elephants with a stockade made of 10,000 pieces of timber and 9 tons of rope was a failure film-wise. The elephants did not pay due attention to the cameras. Eighty were captured but they were far easier to film leaving the kheddah than entering it.

'When we saw the rushes,' Mrs. Flaherty wrote the girls, 'a miracle appeared on the screen – no semblance of a drive but instead these most extraordinary creatures, as if in the heart of their mysterious jungle, "going places". Where were they going? Why, to the Elephant Dance of course, just as it is in Kipling's story. So we re-wove our story all round this elephant dance. All we need to complete the illusion is their feet in action. All our camp of twenty-five elephants has gone into training like a ballet chorus – to learn to dance. Isn't it a quaint life?'[1]

After all the units were recalled in June 1936, life was to become even quainter with the model men at Denham making good the deficiencies of the tame elephant ballet chorus with dummy elephant feet.

To Frances Flaherty, brought up in Boston and educated at Bryn Mawr, *Elephant Boy* was a wonderful experience, with the visit from Sir Mahomed Zafrulla Khan of the Viceroy's Council accompanied by the Maharajah of Mysore's Prime Minister, Sir Mirza Ismail, with the constant supplies of superfluous native labour and the apparatus of, at last, a 'major production'.

This is exactly what one would expect the old Flaherty of *Nanook*, *Moana*, *White Shadows in the South Seas*, *Tabu*, and even *Man of Aran* to find nauseating. To have not one but two co-directors sent out to shoot film in contradiction to his would have infuriated him, if he had really believed in the picture.

[1] *Elephant Dance.*

But he didn't. He was just a man with a knack, expensive tastes and a high salary. This was a repeat of the situation in which he had found himself on *White Shadows*. But this time he did not resign.

When they sailed for England in June 1936, they had shot 300,000 feet, plus synchronized sound and dialogue scenes, which was a Flaherty record. Remembering the stuffed basking-shark, Flaherty suggested to Korda that they should bring an elephant with them as well as Sabu.

A great showman, Korda might have agreed if his fortunes had not changed meanwhile. The brilliance of the cheap success of *The Private Life of Henry the Eighth* had been dulled by many costlier failures. The current need was to turn the Flaherty prestige liability into a commercial asset as soon as possible.

John Collier, author of that brilliant satire, *His Monkey Wife or Married to a Chimp*, was called in to rescue Toomai and the Elephants. It was, film-wise, a logical choice. It kept the Zoo tone. Flaherty 'had shot some marvellous backgrounds and we ran 17,000 feet of them. The absence of a story was noticeable. It was suggested that a very simple story should be devised, such as could be shot (in the studio and on the lot) in about 5,000 feet of screen-time and that this should be grafted into an equal amount of Bob's material. Korda declared that this involved twenty-nine impossibilities; however it was done.'[1]

At Denham, Zoltan Korda shot some studio sequences. The part of Petersen Sahib played on location by Captain Fremlin was replayed in the studio by Walter Hudd. Tame elephants were hired from Whipsnade Zoo. Model shots for the 'elephant dance' were mocked up. Charles Crichton, then a studio editor, tackled the thousands of feet of Indian material. London cafés were combed for dark-skinned men to act tropical Indian scenes on the misty banks of the River Colne. Sabu's English was polished up. 'The studio went wild about him,' wrote Mrs. Flaherty. 'His acting amazed them. They insured his life for £50,000 and set their best writers to work writing for him the story of another film.'[2]

[1] Letter to Paul Rotha, 10th September, 1959.

[2] Op. cit., p. 138. After *Elephant Boy*, Sabu starred in *The Drum* by Zoltan Korda and later went to Hollywood.

Flaherty stuck with the film till the bitter end, even lending the assistance of the bottle of whisky in his pocket to the shivering technicians shooting night shots in Denham Woods. It may be that he had a semi-paternal interest in seeing that the boy he had translated from the Maharajah's stables to the mad world of films came to no harm. But it was also the knowledge that with Korda he had come to the end of the film possibilities available in Britain. He had no future in Hollywood. With Hitler in power, the chance of making films in Germany, or in the U.S.S.R. with German finance, had disappeared. The future looked bleak. To resign his weekly cheque would be quixotic. He hung on just as long as he could, even taking part in the promotion.

Released through United Artists, *Elephant Boy* was shown in London and New York in April, 1937. Flaherty attended the London première and later went, with Sabu and Mr. and Mrs. Borradaille, to Paris for its opening at the Colisée Theatre. Though it was submitted as one of that year's official British entries at the Venice Film Festival (where astonishingly it gained an award for Best Direction), *Elephant Boy* had as equivocal a Press as *Man of Aran*. But there was this difference. *Man of Aran* was a Flaherty picture. *Elephant Boy* was a Korda picture which contained some Flaherty sequences: Toomai's prayer to the Jain statue, the building of the *kheddah*, the scenes with Toomai and the elephant Kala Nag, the climactic drive of the elephants into the *kheddah* and some magnificent back-lit shots of the massed and massive elephants charging into the river under the dark trees. But apart from this there was nothing genuine.

Graham Greene epitomized the attack. 'Mr. Robert Flaherty is said to have spent more than a year in India gathering material for this picture; a scene of elephants washed in a river, a few shots of markets and idols and forest, and that is all. It cannot be compared in quantity or quality with what Mr. Basil Wright brought back from Ceylon after a stay of a few weeks.[1] *Elephant Boy* has gone the same way as *Man of Aran*: an enormous advance publicity, director out of touch with the Press for months, rumours of great epics sealed in tins, and then the disappointing achievement.'

Greene's review appeared in *The Spectator*, 16th April, 1937. The

[1] In fact it was four months. B.W.

following week Basil Wright wrote defending Flaherty and laying the blame for the picture's faults on the Kordas.

But Greene was non-repentant. Flaherty hadn't 'delivered the goods'. And it was no good blaming a producer in Denham for the failure of the director in India.

Greene, without loyalties to any school of documentary, was in the right. Flaherty's original weakness of continuity had been covered in silent-film days by the sub-title, which provided an optical break and logical join between one sequence and the next. He had clung to the old silent technique even in *Man of Aran*; sound was an after-thought, a form of fashionable ornamentation rather than part of the structure of the film. And *Elephant Boy*, as conceived by Flaherty, remained a silent picture. Supposing that Flaherty had conceived his picture in audio-visual terms, I think that it is possible that Korda would have given him his head. But, like Charles Chaplin at that time, Flaherty regarded sound rather as an enemy than as another instrument of communication; and unlike Chaplin, Flaherty wasn't the past master of silent communication. He remained an amateur of genius.

Grierson, that foul-weather friend, aware that Flaherty was at the end of his tether, came to his defence. Dismissing Capra as 'slick as the devil' and acknowledging Griffith, Eisenstein and Pudovkin as striking 'a gong in film history' and teaching 'us a new command of the medium', he paid homage to the old master. 'The greatest film directors provide us with a whole philosophy of cinema – a fresh vision which, glancing past all questions of skill and technique and even sometimes past success itself gives us an inspired insight of things. Of these is Flaherty. Vertov talks of the kino-eye, but Flaherty, who never talks of it, has it. Those who like myself have known him for a long time remain in this sense his students. We can whack him in theory and outdistance him in economics but the maestro has caught the eye of the gods.'[1]

Grierson went on to a half-hearted defence of *Elephant Boy*, using every sophistry of which his eloquence was capable, to prove that the badness of the film was due not to Flaherty but to Korda.

But that did little to sell Flaherty to another producer; because there wasn't another producer to sell him to.

[1] *World Film News*, March, 1937.

ELEPHANT BOY — 1935-37

Sabu before Jain

Kala Nag and Sabu

15 THE LAND

Under the shadow of a war,' wrote Stephen Spender, 'what can I do that matters?'

Flaherty could not believe that war was imminent. The positive things of life were so manifest that the madness of Nazism was as incredible and unintelligible as the vice and perversity of pre-Hitler Berlin.

Elephant Boy was over. There was no weekly cheque coming in. There was little prospect of any major film. Frances was writing *Elephant Dance* for Faber & Faber and Flaherty signed up to write a novel for Hodder & Stoughton, based upon his Eskimo stories. It was published in May 1938, under the title *The Captain's Chair, A Story of the North* and its dedication was 'To my wife and my brother David with whose great help this book was written'.

The dedication was correct. The natural writer who had penned the early travel diaries had become imprisoned by his anecdotage. The very perfection of his verbal narrative, the pause, the change of voice or of expression, the stopping to have a drink or light a cigarette, which had become the instinctive reaction to the mood of his audience, could not be recaptured in the written word.

The faults of *The Captain's Chair* reflect the limitations of Flaherty's film narration. There is the sustaining device of suspense. 'Who is the mysterious Captain Grant?'

The whole book is strung on this thread, like a necklace of amber beads picked from the sea-shore. To Flaherty, the beads were what mattered, stories of his travels in Hudson Bay and Ungava already told in early chapters of this book. They varied in vividness according to whether they came straight from his notebooks, obliquely through his anecdotes or from summary contrivance.

While writing *The Captain's Chair*, the Flahertys lived part of the time in a flat in Danvers Street, rented from the Alexander Flemings,[1] and part at Hurtmore Farm, a guest-house at Godalming, Surrey, run by the mother of Jack Holmes, the documentary film director. But after Munich, fearing a war, Mrs. Flaherty returned to the United States and took a lease on a farm at Brattleboro, Vermont.

Flaherty rented a studio in Chelsea. He still had his occasional Café Royal evenings, but as money grew tighter, he drank more often at the documentary film pub in Dean Street, The Highlander, and at the Star Club, run by Mr. Castano over his restaurant in Greek Street.

The British documentary movement had expanded meanwhile. The G.P.O. Film Unit was at 21 Soho Square. In the old E.M.B. offices at 37 Oxford Street was the Strand Film Company and a second offshoot of the movement was the Realist Film Unit, at 62 Oxford Street, initiated by Basil Wright. Flaherty became a director of Realist and remained one for the rest of his life. But this was just an act of grace: it brought him in no money. And he grew desperately in need of it.

Denis Johnston, the Irish playwright, who had met Flaherty in Aran adapted *The Captain's Chair* as a play for television, with John Laurie as Captain Grant and Flaherty himself as narrator. 'It was quite a small landmark in T.V. technique,' according to Johnston, 'and Bob's appearance was one of the highlights.' But it was a minuscule sop to the wolves constantly at the door of Flaherty's Chelsea studio.

He was desperately worried. His brother David was ill and needed a treatment at that time new and hazardous. His agent was pressing for the repayment of advances. *The Captain's Chair* had not earned the

[1] Sir Alexander Fleming, the discoverer of penicillin whose idealistic failure to patent his discovery forced chemists all over the world to pay royalties to the American patentees.

publisher's advance. Frances kept writing to urge him to join her in America; but though the dreaded war appeared to grow closer, he did not want to be swallowed in Vermont. In London, the chances of films were greater. He sold George Routledge the idea for another novel of the Canadian sub-arctic, *White Master*.

Olwen Vaughan, a British Film Institute employee who had met the Flaherty family over a showing she had given of *Nanook*, became his unpaid secretary, typing in the evenings what he had written during the day. 'He was so worried about David and money and the coming war,' she recalls, 'he couldn't have written a good novel, even if he had it in him.'

White Master was as clumsily constructed as *Wuthering Heights*, with A listening to B about what B heard from C. MacWhirter, the monomaniac white master, is as crude as any Jack London villain and the lovers are as flat as pasteboard. But within its old-fashioned idiom, it had a strange authenticity. It is at least a novel, as opposed to the travel botch-up, which was *The Captain's Chair*.

Forced down by debts, Flaherty took jobs he would have scorned. S. C. Leslie of the British Commercial Gas Association commissioned him to produce an idea for a story-film, dramatizing coal gas. Flaherty chose as his prism a small boy in Newcastle who stowed away on a coastal collier and after a series of adventures found himself in London. Cecil Day Lewis and Basil Wright worked the treatment up into a full-length dialogue script and after a series of tests a boy was chosen. But the imminence of war closed the project down.

Once or twice in this anxious contracting time, his world opened up. Olwen Vaughan gave a film-show for Jean Renoir, at which Renoir complained of the dubbing of his pictures. The reception afterwards was given at Flaherty's studio with something of the old lavishness; and in return the Renoirs and Olwen Vaughan arranged a showing in Paris of Flaherty pictures at the *Cinémathèque Française*. Jean and Marguerite Renoir felt an immediate sympathy with Flaherty, transcending the limitations of language.[1]

[1] In the highest echelons of art, this sympathy spreads from one art to another. In London, Augustus John and Jacob Epstein immediately recognized Flaherty as a fellow artist. The same was true in France of Pablo Picasso and Henri Matisse. Matisse, speaking in French, in the B.B.C. tribute to Flaherty, described the sympathy which leapt across the barriers of language.

But despite these interludes in the larger sanity, everything seemed to be closing in. The continent of Europe in which he had found himself in many ways more at home than in his native United States appeared to be blowing up.

Every day he would ring up Golightly and ask: 'Is there going to be a war?' and Golightly, with an optimism which was shared by the London *Daily Express* would answer 'No.'

But his two worlds were crumbling, the noble world of epic simplicities and the Maecenean world of hospitality. Money was scarce.

Borradaile remembers being called up by Flaherty in the spring of 1939. Flaherty explained that a payment which he'd expected had been delayed. Could he help out?

Borradaile said of course he could. He took round what Flaherty asked and they went to a pastrycook's to buy something for tea. On the way back they saw in a florist's a huge bowlful of hot-house sweet peas. Flaherty went in and buried his face in them. 'They are lovely,' he said, 'I'll take them.'

'How many?' asked the girl.

'The lot,' said Flaherty.

It was over five pounds. 'While enjoying tea and the scent of sweet peas,' said Borradaile, 'I hoped that the expected funds would arrive before the blooms faded and needed replacing.'

How irresponsible this was it is impossible to say without knowing exactly what remittances Flaherty was expecting. But it was certainly a gesture more characteristic of the highly paid film director which he had been, than of a novelist beating out a commissioned book.

So was the scale of his studio parties. 'Sometimes it was necessary to stay the night,' says Hayter Preston, 'which one did by sleeping on the floor. Next morning you would always find a new toothbrush and a box of fifty Balkan Sobranie cigarettes, placed beside you by the host.'

In the summer of 1939, Pare Lorentz cabled Flaherty asking him to come back to the United States to direct a film for the U.S. Film Service.

Lorentz had already made a name for himself with two Whitmanesque pictures, *The River* and *The Plow that Broke the Plains* shot with U.S. Government finance in furtherance of the New Deal. He had recently been appointed Head of the U.S. Film Service. Grierson, in New York *en route* for Australia where he was to make a film report for the Imperial Relations Trust, met Mrs. Flaherty who asked him how she could induce Bob to come back. It was Grierson who suggested to Lorentz that Flaherty was a man he should use. Flaherty accepted immediately. Here was a chance to leave Europe which was going to blow itself to smithereens; and the chance to make another picture.

The Land is the most controversial of Robert Flaherty's pictures.[1] It was begun in the summer of 1939 when the Roosevelt Administration was still trying to reconcile the old American *laissez faire* way of life with some degree of planning. U.S. Agriculture presented appalling contrasts. With the introduction of machines, great farms were thriving and producing more than ever before with fewer farm-hands. The migrant labour force produced by these redundant workers was swelled by the hands from smaller farms which had gone bankrupt because their methods were obsolete, under-capitalized. The fertility of these farms had run down from a variety of reasons; the cutting of forests had at the same time lowered the water-table and laid the great plains open to water- and wind-erosion. And the hordes of agricultural unemployed, called 'Okies' because many of them hailed from Oklahoma, struggled with one another in competition for the seasonal picking. Shack towns, or Hoovervilles, sprang up on the outskirts of cities; and in broken-down cars and trucks whole families roamed the continent like gipsies. But they were without the Romany philosophy; they were simple homesteaders who had been hit by something far more puzzling than famine. They were the victims of 'over-production', near to starving in a land where farmers were being paid by the Government not to raise hogs.

The plight of these people had been movingly portrayed in John Steinbeck's novel *The Grapes of Wrath*, 1939. Pare Lorentz's two films *The Plow that Broke the Plains* and *The River* had posed some of the problems on the screen. But both Steinbeck and Lorentz had shied

[1] Because the film has been seen by so few people, its narrative spoken by Flaherty himself and a description of the visuals are given in Appendix 4.

away from the stark horror, the former into romantic sentiment and the latter into an incantatory use of Indian names. The sordid suffering was covered in the aspic of Art.

It was this situation on which Flaherty was called to report; or rather he was to make a film to meet the needs of the U.S. Film Service under Pare Lorentz.

Things began to go wrong almost immediately. Pare Lorentz was supposed to be producer and co-director of the film. But he himself was so busy making a film about child-birth that he did not even have time to give evidence to the Congressional Committee investigating whether the U.S. Film Service should be given a regular appropriation.

As a result, Flaherty found that the Film Service for which he was to make the film ceased to exist before he started to shoot. His film would have to be made instead for the Agricultural Adjustment Administration, or Triple-A. His brief was to explain how the Triple-A was coping with this situation by a series of measures almost incomprehensible in print but surely intelligible in film. Russell Lord, an expert on soil-conservation and author of *Men of the Earth* (1930) was appointed script-adviser.[1]

Flaherty had to listen to interminable briefs by A.A.A. information officers, explaining the intricacies of something called 'PARITY'. To illustrate it, they would cover blackboards with diagrams which looked like play-by-play accounts of a football game. 'Alphabetical soup in the bureaucratic jungle,' Flaherty would mutter. 'What *is* Triple-A?'

Films were not made by information officers in government offices. They were made by going out and picking up what was there and feeling it and discovering what was in it.

But this assignment was not like the Eskimo fingering a piece of soapstone or a walrus tusk and releasing what lay within. It covered the continent; 20,000 miles, down south to the cotton fields, west to the irrigated and mechanized farms of Arizona, north through the dust-storm states of Iowa and Minnesota.

[1] He published accounts of working with Flaherty in *Forever the Land*, 1954, and the quarterly *The Land*, Vol. xii, No. 2, 1954, for quotations from which we make grateful acknowledgement.

In all, Flaherty made three big journeys to get his film. Mrs. Flaherty accompanied her husband for the shooting in the south and in the east, when Flaherty did his own camera-work. Russell Lord also went with them part of the time. He writes:

> The first field trip on the picture jumped on a straight drive to the heart of the country. Iowa in August enchanted Flaherty. 'The glory, the richness of this earth,' he said. He shot a sequence on corn, then some more on corn-machinery; then up to the lake country he rolled in his station-wagon, with a camera-platform atop it, to film granaries, boats and swarming railyards, bursting with the bounty of the great valley.
>
> Until this point the mood of the expedition was robust and cheerful. The weather favoured; clear sunshine fell day after day on the land. Flaherty was like a boy revisiting, rediscovering his homeland, marvelling at its beauty, friendliness and power. Everything was 'marvellous!' – the farms, the hotels in little places, the pinball games in the lobby, the apple-pie in dog-wagon restaurants, the prize-fights on the radio, the poker-games with matches for chips at night. Bob Flaherty had great gifts as a traveller. He was at home anywhere. He could eat anything. He could sleep in any bed, or in any car. And whenever there was no one else to sit up and talk with, there was always the telephone. His long-distance phone-bills – all 'personal' – startled many a hotel-keeper along the way. And a great, white-haired man with a ruddy face who would give small boys handfuls of nickels to play the pinball-machines is remembered from Muskogee, Oklahoma, to the Coast and back to Chillocothe, Ohio. 'He must be Santa Claus without the whiskers,' one wise child said.
>
> Southward, the mood and temper of the party were not so happy. The heat was terrific; the hotels were ovens; the food while occasionally 'marvellous' was not invariably so. England was at war, under bombardment. England to Flaherty was a second home. But the circumstance which most continually darkened his spirit was the condition of great stretches of cotton country. 'It is unbelievable!' he kept saying, 'unbelievable!' As the party worked westward, following the historic march of cotton, they came across homeless migrants in quantity. He started talking with them and taking their pictures. They told him their stories, and his anger and compassion knew no bounds.

Archibald MacLeish, the poet, has expressed the conviction that, simply as a moving-picture, *Man of Aran* is the greatest documentary or factual film ever made. 'And what,' MacLeish asked, when told of Flaherty's forthcoming American picture, 'what are you going to have that compares in effect with that woman wailing against the roar and beat of the sea?' Flaherty was feeling low in mind the day this question was put to him. He lifted his arms and replied with simple dignity, 'God knows. There is too much to this land. Our picture is no good now. It stinks!'

But later: 'It's coming to life! I distinctly feel that gentle thumping kick,' says Flaherty, jovial now, and expectant. Some of the pictures he took that summer in the cotton wasteland, and on the garden-ranches westward – 'American refugees wandering in a wasteland of their own making' – may be the answer to MacLeish's question.

Flaherty spent two years making *The Land*. Throughout it, he was harassed. It was the first time that he had really explored his native country. He had hitherto regarded his films of primitive life as an answer to the complex problems of the civilized world. Nanook with his perennial nearness to starvation was much worse off than the people of Europe exhausted by a war of their own making. *Man of Aran* had made the worries of the Wall Street tycoon ridiculous. But the Okies had a problem for which there was no primitive solution. They were starving in a land of plenty, homeless in a land of open spaces. This was industrial madness, and the enemy appeared to be the machine, the combine harvester and its robot relatives.

Flaherty was not a Luddite. He had a reverence and a delight in machines; a truly American joy in gadgets. But at this moment of anger, bitterness and sorrow, unable to disentangle what was ruining the people of his country, he became a Luddite in his hatred of the way machines were being used to push people into pauperdom.

'I never tackled a tougher or more confusing job,' he wrote a friend after the first year of shooting. 'There are times when I don't know whether I am standing on my head or not.'

Psychologically Flaherty's shooting of *The Land* was complicated by the war which had broken out in Europe. They were both part and parcel of the same mad thing.

Then there was the financial worry. Pare Lorentz was not an administrator, fixer or diplomat. Film stock and money weren't forthcoming when they were needed. Flaherty's cameraman Irving Lerner, an 'in-bred documentary man from New York', reported to his wife what must have been an emotional shock very similar to Flaherty's early in the shooting.

> . . . About 130 miles north-east of Memphis, we found a section of eroded land that made all of us shudder. We'd only up to then read about the rape of the land, but when you see it, the impact is so terrifying that your first impulse is to say, 'the hell with everything, I'm going to devote the rest of my life to planting trees and putting this land back into shape'.
>
> If the land itself is not terrifying enough, the people who still live on the land, who still try to sustain life on that land, are the most horrible sight of all. Human life, human standards of living, are obviously in direct ratio to the condition and the fertility of the soil. In this country there are very few Negroes; the 'poor whites' live in a fashion that is as bare as the poorest Negro share-cropper. We see them as we drive by; they have seldom seen an automobile. The children are without exception quite beautiful.

By mid-October 1939, Pare Lorentz and the Triple-A men announced there was no money left for shooting, while Flaherty insisted he needed another six weeks on location. Over the phone to Washington, Flaherty shouted: 'I won't stop shooting till I see the whites of all your eyes.'

If by some miracle Flaherty had been given John Grierson as producer on *The Land*, there is the possibility that a great and viable picture would have been made. With Grierson's understanding of government agencies and of economics on the one hand and Flaherty's visionary fury on the other something might have come which would have included the A.A.A. brief but so transcended it that it could have been shown all over the world today as the parable of man's abuse of the land from the Mesopotamian civilization onwards.

As it was, Flaherty struggled with an epic theme which he could not resolve.

Early on he called in an editor, Helen van Dongen, who was to develop the interpretative role of John Goldman.[1]

Helen van Dongen was used to directors obsessed with their films in hand. When she first met Flaherty, surrounded by friends in a small French restaurant in Washington, he talked the whole evening about the Eskimo and Polynesians.

Next morning she went to the Department of Agriculture for a 'work-session'. Flaherty was reading the papers. 'Hello,' he said, 'I find it too long to say Miss van Dongen, so I'll just call you Helen. O.K.?' He began to talk about the phoney war in Europe. He was committed to no side, but intently engaged all the time they were working together on the film.

She had no chance to discuss the idea, script or shape of the picture, before he switched from the war in Europe and said, 'Let's screen.' There was no script, just 70,000 feet of film (at that time: later there was a lot more). 'With every shot that appeared, I hoped he would tell me why he shot it, how he wanted it used, what it belonged with.' But all he did was groan and say, 'My God, what are we going to do with all this stuff?'

Back in the office, there would be more groaning, interrupted by things he'd seen on his shooting, fury about the plight of the Okies, ranting against civilization, Luddite fury at the slaughter of human skill by the introduction of machines, the unemployment caused, the horror of starvation in the midst of plenty and running through it all, the war, the war, the war.

'I was too inexperienced in Flaherty's method of working to make head or tail out of any possible connection between his remarks and his film. After three weeks, I was at an utter loss. We screened the same material over and over again, but he never came to the point at which he would outline his story.'

It was not of course a method of working, even at a deep unconscious level. Flaherty was a sort of film animal which cropped everything attractive in sight, but possessed no digestive juices to convert it into a moving picture.

[1] Helen van Dongen began work with Joris Ivens in Holland in 1929. She worked on *The Bridge*, *Rain*, *Zuiderzee*, *Borinage* and *The New Earth*. In 1926, she followed Ivens to the U.S.A. and edited *The Spanish Earth* and *The Four Hundred Million*. The quotes used are from an unpublished article written at the time.

Helen van Dongen wrote Joris Ivens, complaining that all Flaherty did was talk about the war, machines and civilization in the morning and screen the same old material in the afternoon. Joris Ivens answered: 'Observe, look and listen and you'll find out what he wants.'

To Helen this was cryptic, but when Flaherty was about to go out on his second shooting expedition, she said: 'And what shall *I* do?' 'Oh, *you* just go ahead!' he said in the most charming way.

Helen van Dongen had been overawed by Flaherty's reputation; she had felt that she had to serve his intentions. But now she began to think for him, to, if the neologism will be allowed, ciné-analyse him. 'It suddenly occurred to me that his worrying about the war, or his preoccupation with machines, were simply a different way of saying what he wanted to express in his film.

'Why did I not discover this before? Because it takes time to enter into an artist's mind; but when you do, you discover a rich field of interpretation. As Flaherty transposed his thoughts about the film, the "Okies", living and food in terms of war, destruction and machines, so could I later transpose and interpret them through his film material which, though not my own, had in each shot a special meaning that Flaherty wanted to put in it.

'It was worthwhile listening to all he said. There were certain inflexions, remarks, preoccupations, of which I was at once reminded when looking at his film material. Shots which had no meaning now looked different. I had to discover how to look at them through Flaherty's eyes.'

Helen van Dongen had a strong personal style of editing, which she deliberately suppressed in order to make *The Land* according to what she intuited was Flaherty's purpose. Some people have said that she 'ruined Flaherty's material because she did not understand his method of shooting'. This is nonsense. The truth is that Flaherty had never learnt to shoot a picture bearing in mind that it was going to have a sound-track. And even the most sympathetic editor had to translate him from silent to sound cutting.

There were agonies in the editing. In the sequence of the old coloured man in the rat-infested mansion, mumbling, 'Wheah they all gone?' Russell Lord says everyone was satisfied except Bob, who said it needed 'more fiddling with' before it was right.

'You and your fiddling!' said Frances and burst into tears.

'Ah, these women!' said Bob, beaming. 'I wear them all down.' Then he saw Helen van Dongen. 'Except *you*,' he added. 'You're a Dutch mule!'

The Land as it was shot was nothing more than a series of cries of pain. Europe and the United States, Flaherty had taken for granted, were civilized, needing perhaps to be recalled to simplicity by recollection of the epic virtues of primitive peoples, but threatened only by the decadence of luxury and affluence. The war in Europe and the hopeless vagabondage of the United States' unemployed shattered Flaherty's Café Royal and Coffee House Club concept of the civilized world.

This may seem a lesson which it had taken an American of fifty-four a long while to learn. But it must be remembered that since the age of nine, Flaherty had never had any contact with industrial strife. He had turned instinctively away to primitive people whose struggles were, at least in his view, exterior. Even in *Industrial Britain* his eyes had been turned to the skilled craftsmen at work and not to the workless and dispossessed.

Flaherty's shooting on *The Land* was brilliant. But he was conscious of the lack of centre. The family had always been his centre; but how make a film which spread across the United States centre on one family? A film producer might have guided him, suggesting a thematic treatment with the logic of music. But he had no such producer. He just went off shooting like mad and sending the stuff back to Helen van Dongen for her to sort it out.

It was impossible to sort out, because it did not make coherent sense. There were unforgettable moments, such as the boy moving uneasily in his sleep and his mother looking out from screen, explaining, 'He thinks he's shucking peas.' That moment, John Huston thought, was worth the whole of the film they made from *The Grapes of Wrath*. But the impact of the shot material as a whole was nothing more than the agonized despair of a man, certain of what was wrong, but unclear how it happened or could be put right.

Helen van Dongen made of it the only thing she possibly could. It was not a film in the sense that it had an argument or even a constructed pattern. It was a personal record of a journey, or series of journeys, across the United States. The only thing that would bind it together was the voice of the man who made it, who talked about it passionately as if it was a haunting nightmare. The visuals themselves were less striking than in any of Flaherty's other pictures; and this was to be expected. The aspects of indignity can be snatched by the camera; they cannot be rehearsed. The stark faces look out without any of the grace or glory characteristic of Flaherty's chosen people. Artistically this was the beginning of a phase of human suffering which would end with Belsen, the living corpses of the Burma Road and the monstrosities of Hiroshima.

Flaherty had the enormously irrelevant mind of a poet. While he was travelling across the United States, fully briefed by the Triple-A, with blackboard demonstrations of the logical justice and sweet sense of Parity, he was thinking equally of Britain, France and Germany, which he knew and loved. This was what had first confused Helen van Dongen, the way he kept on talking about the war all the morning and then screening *The Land* material all the afternoon.

Flaherty couldn't tell her that he was making a war picture. This was going on unconsciously; but *The Land* was Flaherty's unconscious reaction to the war in Europe and all the events which had built up to it and to what it would lead to in the same deep way that *Nanook* had been his unconscious reaction to the First World War and *Man of Aran* to the Wall Street slump and depression.

But there were several differences. Revillon Frères had wanted publicity, Gaumont-British had wanted entertainment, Triple-A wanted to further public support for their New Deal policies. Flaherty had entered the propagandist world in which John Grierson felt at home, but in which Flaherty was always a stranger. The sort of aims which Grierson might have held Flaherty to, if he had been in charge of *The Land* instead of Pare Lorentz, were utterly alien.

But even if Flaherty had in 1939 accepted the sort of governance which a Government agency felt it right to impose in the spending of public money, by the time that he had finished making his picture in 1941, the whole picture of U.S. agriculture had changed. By the

Lend-Lease agreements, U.S. farm production could be expanded. Spam took care of surpluses of pork. Farmers were encouraged to produce to maximum capacity. Arms factories and the increase in the armed forces reduced the numbers of the unemployed. As a picture, *The Land* was out of date, even before the 22-year-old English composer Richard Arnell wrote the score.

Russell Lord was assigned the credit for writing the commentary. He maintains that what he did was to listen to Flaherty's own comments as he watched the silent picture and write them down. This may be true of the personal passages in which Flaherty described what he saw on his journey. But it is not true of the incantatory passages, the idiom of which Russell Lord seems to have derived from Pare Lorentz.

Helen van Dongen had lured Flaherty into recording a wild-track commentary, as he thought for the guidance of the professional commentator. She didn't dare to tell him that she wanted to use his own voice. It would have completely inhibited him. Though one of the greatest private performers, with a superb variation of his voice, he was incapable of using it publicly. As it was only a guide-track ostensibly, he couldn't be forbidden to smoke while recording. He puffed and wheezed in the middle of sentences. They placed him far from the mike and turned the volume down between wheezings and covered themselves by a number of retakes. When they were satisfied, they announced to Flaherty that he was the commentator. He was furious. He submitted, all the same. The Dutch mule knew best.

At last the show-print was ready and shown to its sponsors. Triple-A was appalled. From their point of view the film was out of date. The labour situation was no longer true. Crop-limitation was no longer necessary. There were still useful things in the picture, such as the need for contour ploughing; but only a specialized audience could disentangle the wheat from the chaff. Instead of being given theatrical distribution, which it would have received uproariously in 1939, *The Land* was allowed limited showing non-theatrically to farmer audiences.

The State Department was called in to decide whether it was suitable for overseas exhibition and clamped down firmly. An internal battle was joined by Iris Barry of the Museum of Modern Art Film

Library trying to enlist support for general exhibition. And then came Pearl Harbor and the subject was blocked.

Until 1944, it was allowed limited circulation in the U.S.A. Then it was withdrawn, though a print was made available to the Robert Flaherty Foundation 'in recognition of the historic and artistic contributions made by Mr. Flaherty to the film medium'.

I find it hard to criticize *The Land* because I have not seen it since 1943, when by a caprice of Lend-Lease Paul Rotha managed to get a copy of it across to England. Both Rotha and Wright were able to view the film again in making their research. They were enormously impressed by it. Rotha considers it 'the first film in which Flaherty fully faced up to the sociological, technological and economic problems of our time'. John Grierson tells me that he thinks that it was the greatest picture that Flaherty ever made. Basil Wright says that it was the first time that Flaherty ever faced 'genuine' problems.

This is a formidable body of opinion and I regret that no copy of the picture has been given to the National Film Archive in London so that I, and others, can judge for ourselves. The film is historically important as much abroad as in the United States.

But I have a great sympathy with A.A.A. and with the State Department. No one would suggest that a newspaper should print an article which has become obsolete between the time of commissioning and its delivery. The story of the plundering of the United States by catch-crop farming had already been told in Fascist and Nazi propaganda for years before the war. If *The Land* had been circulated by the State Department, it could have caused incalculable damage to the Allies.[1]

Knowing the uses to which stock film material can be put, I am certain that the State Department is right to prevent the export of *The Land*. In the hands of communist editors it could be devastatingly used to prosecute the cold war not merely in the Iron Curtain countries but also among the Afro-Asian states.

I cannot agree with Rotha that Flaherty 'fully faced up to the sociological, technological and economic problems of our time' in *The*

[1]One has only to think of *Oom Kruger*, which justified the Nazi concentration camps in terms of the British conduct in the Boer War.

Land. This was something which Rotha himself tackled later in *World of Plenty* and *The World is Rich*, two films of argument adapting the technique of the Living Newspaper to the film. But *The Land* is of a different species. As an analysis of U.S. agricultural history, it avoided mention of greed and under-capitalization, which were even greater enemies of healthy agriculture than the villainous Machine. The American pioneer with his snatch-crop farming and his knowledge that to the west lay land as rich as that whose wealth he had plundered was the original villain; and in the United States, as elsewhere, the cause of this wasteful plunder was poverty. The pioneer could not afford to put back in the earth as much as he took out of it.

Richard Griffith tried to make a virtue out of the film's technical defects. 'The picture lacks that wholeness and gradual building towards a climax which have contributed to the pleasure of seeing a Flaherty film. This is a fractured film, its skeleton is awry, the bones stick out through the skin. But I think Flaherty meant it that way. . . . Flaherty forsakes the graceful smoothness of his "primitive" films for a form which suggests the horror of his broken journey. "Here we saw this," he says and passes on but not indifferently. If ever there was a personal film, this is it. It is a cry, a groan. . . . Flaherty cannot tell us what to do to help, can only shout at us at the end of the film to do *something*. To many people the tragic beauty of *The Land* will not be sufficient to compensate for the fact that it provides no blueprint. But I have been thinking a long time that films should pose the problem and leave it in the lap of the audience, for it is we who must answer for our lives, not our teachers, not our artists. . . .'[1]

Helen van Dongen has a different story. When she ran the print for Flaherty just before the première, 'groans were now and then audible, but not a word was said. When the lights went up, he slapped me hard in the back and said, "Now we know. We could go back to-morrow and really *make* this film." This view is endorsed by Olwen Vaughan, who begged a copy of the picture for the National Film Archive. Flaherty refused and when asked what he thought of the picture said, 'Oh, I suppose it's worth looking at, if it comes your way.' He was not a man to depreciate his own achievement.

[1] *Documentary News Letter*, Vol III, No. 2, 1942.

'It's amazing what the wash of rain can do!'

THE LAND — 1939-42
(all photographs enlarged from the film)

'Couldn't see how even a coyote could live in it'

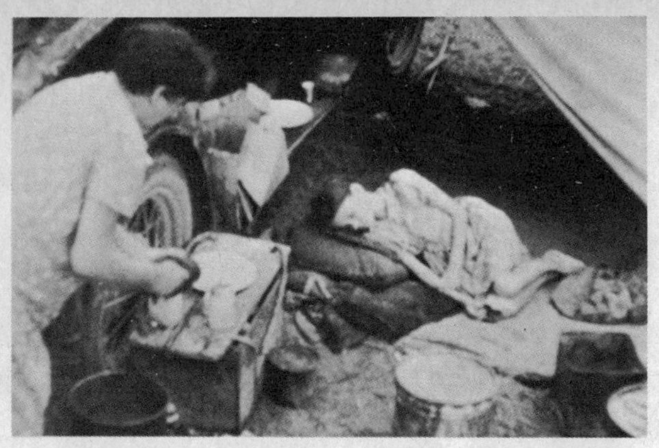

'Along our highways, there are more than a million people'

'A family of eight lives in this box of a trailer'

'We found this in Tennessee'

'Work is what they want — any kind of work'

'We came upon this family moving out'

'Heading West — that's where most of them go'

'Migrants — landless, homeless people'

'A hundred men for every job'

'Generation after generation — was beaten'

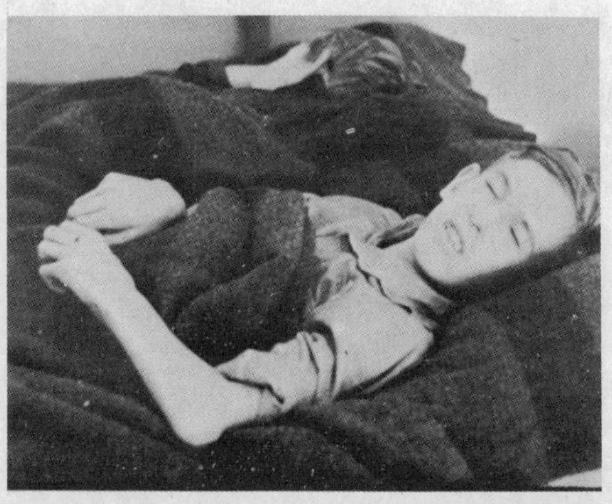

' "He thinks he's picking peas," she said'

'When soil fails, life fails'

'Good cattle, well fed. Good homes. Good farms'

'Most of the migrants are young people, with young children'

'A new world stands before him'

I think that Basil Wright is correct in seeing *The Land* as a 'watershed' in his development as an artist; in making it, 'he found a new certainty as a creative artist. Before *The Land* his conception of *Louisiana Story* could never have existed'.

This is true not merely of the alteration of his vision; it is true also of an alteration in his method. In Helen van Dongen he found an editor as sensitive as John Goldman, but with far greater experience of life and of films. He realized that the making of a film was a complex operation which he could not achieve with only the assistance of Frances and David Flaherty. *Louisiana Story* could never have been made if Helen van Dongen had not had the previous experience of working with him on *The Land.*

16 IN RETREAT

When Frances Flaherty signed the lease of the farm on the side of Black Mountain, Brattleboro, Vermont, she had the vision of a place of retirement. Why not, she thought, have the sentiment Wander No More translated into Erse (in memory of those happy days on Aran) and hand-lettered over the mantelpiece?

So when he returned to the United States and visited the farm, the first thing which struck Bob Flaherty as he entered the living-room were the cryptic words DUN ROVIN. That was in 1939.

In May, 1942, having wandered 20,000 miles across the States, many of them in the company of Frances, Bob Flaherty went back to Brattleboro. He was fifty-eight and his wife urged him that it was time for him to retire. 'I'm too old to lock horns with you young bucks any more,' he told Richard Griffith. 'I'll have to go off and graze by myself.'[1]

But this feeling came not from a sense that he had nothing more to give in film but from the unhappy conviction that he had tapped

[1] In a letter to Paul Rotha (12th August, 1959). In May 1942 Griffith was Assistant Curator at the Museum of Modern Art Film Library, New York.

all available sources of finance. At least while the war was on, nobody would want his sort of film.

Griffith himself went into the U.S. army, but in a few weeks was seconded to the newly-formed War Department Film Division, under the command of Col. Frank Capra, the director of *It Happened One Night* and *Mr. Deeds Goes to Town.*[1] One of the first members of Capra's staff he met was Flaherty, 'rovin' again.

'What in the name of God are you doing here?' Griffith asked.

'Me?' Bob said. 'I'm putting balls on the war effort.'

Nobody in fact knew what anyone was doing there at that moment. Capra, a master of story-pictures, knew nothing of documentary and was shopping for experience. When he took on a young man who had worked for Department of Agriculture films and who suggested that Flaherty should be called in, Capra agreed.

Eric Knight, who had also joined Capra, wrote Rotha, 27th June, 1942: 'Old Bob Flaherty is with us, and out on a job of work . . . a big job. We took him to a conference lunch and Bob shook his head like an innocent baby when a cocktail was suggested.'

Flaherty got on well with Capra, but nobody knew what to give Flaherty to do. Capra had no professional production unit in Washington and had to borrow one from U.S. Signal Corps, the personnel of which resented the new Capra unit. Col. W. B. Gillette of U.S. Signal Corps had been making military training films for years; and like any other military drill, these films had been made by numbers.

So when Eric Knight dreamed up a weekly newsreel, called *The State of the Nation*, to be shown to civilians in public theatres and soldiers in camps and overseas, Flaherty was sent off as director with a U.S. Signal Unit and found to his fury that he couldn't tell his corporal cameraman what to do except through his unit manager, a second lieutenant.

Through July, August and September 1942, Flaherty and his unit covered defence factories, parades and war-bond drives throughout the Eastern States, in the intervals between complaining to Capra and Gillette of mutual lack of co-operation. Flaherty and his unit provided

[1] For a full account of early wartime U.S. official film activities, see Griffith's appendix to Rotha's *Documentary Film* (1952).

the point of maximum contact, and therefore of maximum friction, between the rival organizations.

This initial conflict might have been smoothed over, if Flaherty had turned in the sort of material which could have been used easily in a newsreel. But editors, whether trained to newsreel or Hollywood techniques, were baffled by his rushes. 'Flaherty sent us a shot of a man throwing a ball at a pile of ninepins,' one moaned to Griffith, 'but he ain't sent us a reverse angle.'

Capra, despairing of Washington, moved his own unit to Hollywood; Flaherty was left the only member of his staff based on Washington. And the newsreel was not Capra's only headache. After nine months his unit hadn't produced a single film. The U.S. Signal Corps and the Pentagon pressed home their advantage. Something had to give. So Capra jettisoned the Newsreel[1] and with it Flaherty.

Capra delegated the task of sacking Flaherty to Major Leonard Spigelgass, an ex-Hollywood script-writer. Bob took it hard and when a year later he ran into Col. Capra in a New York bar, he said, 'You know, Frank, I don't know which I hate worse; you or the Japs.'

Griffith adds: 'To a degree Flaherty sabotaged himself . . . His heart was not in it. In spite of his jokes about adding to the virility of the war effort, he loathed all war propaganda, however innocuous, and hated being part of it. There was also the simple stupidity of putting a man of Flaherty's gifts and calibre to work on a newsreel.'

I think this should be taken further. Flaherty's gifts and calibre were not the reason why he failed as a newsreel director. The reason for that was that he had never learnt professionally to tell a story in film; in silent pictures, this deficiency was covered up by the use of sub-titles and in later pictures by the agony and bloody sweat of editors such as John Goldman and Helen van Dongen. He was not a good enough technician to shoot a newsreel story.

Then again though Griffith is right that his soul revolted against war propaganda, the use of words and films to build up hatred between one race of men and another, it is equally true that he hated all forms of propaganda, the use of art to produce the sort of social and political conditioning advocated by Grierson and his social-

[1] The Newsreel was later successfully revived by Major Spigelgass as the *Army-Navy Magazine*.

welfare group, by the Soviet directors or in a different way by Leni Riefenstal in the cult of Nazism.

The footage shot by Flaherty, despite Griffith's efforts, was never used. But it was no great loss. 'Most of the shooting was frankly as undistinguished as . . . well, newsreel,' said Griffith. But it was not as competent.

Flaherty returned to Vermont. On a conscious level he wanted to work for the Office of War Information or one of the other agencies. But at the same time he did not want to do any of the sort of jobs which they wanted done, the short-term, win-the-war jobs on which everyone else was concentrated.

There is a story told by John Huston about an evening with Bob Flaherty some years after the war. But since it is concerned with those personal roots of misery, violence and hatred which blossom in war, its place belongs here. It is needless to say that a story told about anyone by John Huston bears the stamp of its narrator.

'I have heard from men who have worked with him about Bob's wonderful ways with primitive people; how he would step into a critical, sometimes dangerous, situation and resolve the conflict through his powers of sympathy and understanding. I can well believe this, having been present at a demonstration of those powers.

'One night, Bob and I were coming away from a late party. I preceded him into the rainy street and stopped a cab. As I went to get in, somebody grabbed my arm. Turning, I beheld a dark little man, brandishing a toad-stabber. He was shouting something about the cab being his and my thinking I was better than he was because I was white. I stood very still and tried a rhythmic breathing exercise, while the toad-stabber described semi-circles near my throat.

'"I'm going to kill you," he said.

'Out of the corner of my eye I saw Bob approaching. When he got up to us he asked what was going on, and the little dark man replied that he was going to kill me because I thought I was better than he was.

'"Nothing of the sort," Bob said. "And put that knife away this instant, d'you hear?"

'The little man shifted his look from me to Bob and, taking the opportunity, I swung on him, knocking him down. The knife fell out of his hand and I picked it up. It was the kind where you touch a button to release a double-edged blade. It was for cutting throats . . . nothing else.

'Bob helped the little dark man to his feet. "You ought to be ashamed," Bob said. "Pulling a knife! What made you do such a thing?"

'"He called me a nigger."

'"No such thing," Bob said. "This gentleman," indicating me, "is without racial prejudice."

'The little man began to cry. "Call a policeman," he said. "Get me arrested. Have them send me to the Tombs. I want to go there, anyway, to be with my poor brother."

'"What's that?" Bob said.

'"My brother is in the Tombs. I must see him. That's where I wanted to go in the cab."

'"He says his brother is in the Tombs," Bob said, as though that threw an entirely different light on the matter.

'"Call a policeman," the little dark man sobbed.

'"Get into the cab, young man," Bob said. "We'll drop you off."

'"The hell we will," I said. "I'm tired and I want to go to bed and this little ape is coked to the eyeballs, can't you see?"

'"See what I mean? He thinks he is better than I am."

'"Have you been taking drugs?" Bob asked.

'The little man nodded.

'"Get into the cab," Bob said. "You too, John, We'll drop *you* off."

'He told the driver my address. His manner towards me was a little cold, as though I were the culprit . . . which, according to Bob's morality I was, for I was being ungenerous towards a human being in distress. I felt sure Bob was thinking that it had not been necessary for me to strike a blow; the little man would have put his knife away in due course, anyway. Bob was disappointed in me for having resorted to violence. He deplored violence among men. It was against the Divine will that we should do injury to one another. All his work bears this out; the conflicts in his pictures are those in which man engages his fundamental enemies . . . storm, hunger, cold. They are never between man and man.

'Naturally Bob was on the little dark man's side. He was the miserable one. He was wet from the rain, his brother was in jail, he was a victim of the drug habit, he was of an underprivileged race, and he had lost his knife.

'"Give his knife back to him, John," Bob said. It was his way of giving me the chance to redeem myself for having added to the little dark man's misfortunes . . . and perhaps for the sin of occupying a cab with him yet being so dry, so tearless.

'"He's all coked up," I said. "He might use it on you."

'"I want you to promise me," Bob said to the little man, "that if your knife is returned to you, you won't go about doing harm with it.'

'"Sure, I promise," he said.

'Bob took the toad-stabber out of my hand and gave it to him.

'"I don't think you should go down to the Tombs tonight, though," Bob said. "For one thing, they wouldn't let you see your brother at this hour, and for another, they'd probably arrest you on a narcotics charge. Have you got a place to sleep?"

'"I will get out on 15th Street, and go to the all-night picture show," said the little man.

'By this time we'd reached my door. As I was getting out, Bob said, "How about lunch tomorrow at the Coffee House Club?"

'"Sure," I said, "And if by chance you don't show up, I can tell Oliver and everybody just how it happened."

'Bob ignored this and leaning forward to the driver, said: "Down to 14th Street'."[1]

A favourite story of John Grierson's is how during the war he was about to leave New York City to return to Ottawa, when he received a telephone call from Flaherty asking him to break his journey at Brattleboro overnight, and bring some whisky with him.

Grierson is vivid in his description of how he filled a suitcase with quantities of various brands of whisky. When he was met at the station by Frances Flaherty, Frances picked up the suitcase and remarking on its heaviness asked him what it contained. 'Oh, it's just some equipment I'm taking back to Ottawa,' he said.

That evening he and Flaherty drank long after Frances retired to

[1] Sequence, No. 14, 1952.

bed. But at last Grierson turned in and as he did so, he heard heated voices coming from the Flahertys' bedroom.

There was silence; then footsteps along the passage and Grierson's door opened. 'John,' Bob said, 'you drink too much.' And the door closed.

The point of this story is supposed to be that Flaherty drank even more.

In fact, Flaherty, while being wildly generous with drinks for other people, seems to have been comparatively moderate himself. I have heard no story of Flaherty being drunk in the company of others, though many of others being drunk in his.

The years 1942–5 were the most frustrating in Flaherty's life. He could not reconcile himself to retirement on the farm. There were possibilities; he was sure there were possibilities. Orson Welles who had come to see him filming *Man of Aran*, suspicious at first but soon charmed, bought Flaherty's original story *Bonito the Bull* in 1942 for $12,000. He incorporated it in a documentary trilogy called *It's All True*. It was shot on 16 mm. Kodachrome (for later enlargement to 35 mm.), during a Latin-American tour made by Orson Welles and underwritten by the Office of the Co-ordinator of Inter-American Affairs to the tune of $300,000. Though RKO undertook the release, the film was never finished. But this didn't affect Flaherty's $12,000. It enabled him to go to New York, stay at the Concord Hotel on Lexington Avenue, renew his contacts at the Coffee House Club and Costello's Bar.

In 1943, the National Board of Review devoted the New Year number of its magazine to a Tribute to Flaherty.[1] It was flattering rather than encouraging, a memorial to the twentieth anniversary of *Nanook of the North* but not a salvo to the future, except in Richard Griffith's prophetic article, 'Flaherty and the Future', which reads like a prospectus for the floating of *Louisiana Story*.

'For a long time now he (Flaherty) has been looking forward to the future and what it will bring for ordinary men and women, turning over in his mind a film about the Machine, man's blessing and bane,

[1] Vol. XVIII, No. 1.

which was partly responsible for the wrecking of our recent past and which holds out so much hope for the future. But not alone do the movies need Flaherty today for this picture and the others he can make. What is needed more is a new respect for his quality and character as a film-maker. We might even forget for a while his brilliant way with cameras, and imitate instead the adventurer in him, the explorer who, like a child, finds newness and beauty in every ordinary thing, who sees the world and its creatures with a wondering and sentient eye, and finds in its exotic diversity one final unifying thing . . . our common need, our common hope.'

These tributes were gratifying, of course, but as Flaherty bitterly observed: 'Prestige never bought anyone a ham sandwich.'[1]

If we observe Flaherty's career dispassionately, I think that it is plain that he was not ready to make another film. There is a curious parallel between the two wars. In the latter part of the First World War he was ostensibly unemployed. But he was forced to do the thinking or meditation needed to turn the failure of the Belcher Islands assembly into the triumph of *Nanook*.

In the latter part of the Second World War, he was also recovering from a failure, *The Land*. It had failed as far as his sponsors were concerned, because it hadn't been shown. It had failed as far as he was concerned, because he had not made the picture about the machine as he wanted to make it.

Flaherty needed the period of fallowness in order in his slow digestive way to become prepared for his next major work. He may have fulminated against the sponsors for his frustration and his followers certainly accepted this blindly as a condemnation of the horrible commercial cinema. But if a sponsor had appeared in 1942 and told him to make the film that Griffith said he wanted to make about the Machine, he couldn't have made it.

There is a providence which looks after freelances, almost the only people who consider the lilies of the field. Flaherty did not starve. In 1944, he was commissioned by the Sugar Research Foundation to make a tour of the sugar-producing areas of the U.S. and report on

[1] True as this may have been with regard to ham sandwiches, prestige did in fact bring in all Flaherty's contracts, including, if we take the word in its widest sense, the contract for *Nanook*.

the use the Foundation might make of films. His report was accepted and he undertook to supervise three films to be made by his brother, David.

Another little assignment was the shooting in 1945 of footage at the Museum of the Rhode Island School of Design about the John Howard Benson technique of calligraphy. It never came to anything viewable as a completed film. Benson and Flaherty did not get on.

17 *LOUISIANA STORY*

Negotiations between Flaherty and the Standard Oil Company of New Jersey began in 1944 with the suggestion that he might make a film dramatizing to the public the risk and difficulties of getting oil from beneath the earth. From the point of view of Standard Oil, the important thing was to make the public aware of the work which went on, often fruitlessly, before oil was struck. An unimaginative board would have insisted on one of those vast, comprehensive and unviewable surveys of the risk capital which was sunk before the oil began to flow.

But Roy Stryker, the imaginative public relations officer of Standard Oil (N.J.) believed that given his head, Flaherty would produce an idea, not yet perceived, which would discover in the romance of oil-drilling a theme so compelling that it would play the commercial theatres. In so doing, it would create a general goodwill for the oil-industry as a whole; no acknowledgement would be given on the screen to Standard Oil, but the credit given in the Press and by word of mouth to Standard Oil for its sponsorship of a film which was a work of art would be worth hundreds of thousands of dollars in goodwill.

The terms proposed were by the standards of 'sponsored' film-making incredibly generous. The cost of production was to be underwritten by Standard Oil, but all receipts from the picture were to go to Flaherty. There had never been a contract like this; the conjunction of a firm as imaginative as Standard Oil and a director as implacably devoted to his art as Flaherty, and as extravagant.

At the outset of his career Revillon Frères had given him as free a hand and had produced his greatest masterpiece. That had followed the meditative idleness of the First World War. Now Standard Oil after the meditative idleness of the Second World War gave him a similar opportunity. In the first case, he went back to make once again the film of the primitive North which he had botched in the Belcher Islands. In the second, he was given the chance to make the film about the Machine, which he realized that he had failed to make in *The Land.* In *The Land* he had taken over *idées reçues* from Grierson, Lorentz, Russell Lord, Steinbeck and others and he hadn't digested them into a view of his own. It was filled with 'social significance', to use the cant term of the time; but artistically it was muddled and confused, in my opinion.

At the expense of Standard Oil, Flaherty and his wife set out to make a survey in order, for the first time in his career, to find a story, which could be submitted to a sponsor. They headed for the south-west, driving thousands of miles, looking at boom-towns and ghost-towns. There were limitless plains dotted with derricks, static structures above the earth connecting deposits of oil laid millions of years ago with the refineries which produced the gasoline to power their cars across the fields of Oklahoma and Texas. But nothing moved for a movie.

In the course of their travels, they reached the bayou country of Louisiana and were enchanted by the gentle, gay people of French descent living in this little-visited part of the United States. They preserved their individual culture and the Flahertys were delighted with their customs, folk-tales of werewolves and mermaids, still accepted from generations ago.

This was filmically exciting material, but there was no connection with oil, until one day, stopping the car for lunch near the edge of a bayou, they saw over the heads of the marsh grass, an oil-derrick being towed up the bayou by a launch. In motion, this familiar structure suddenly became poetry, its slim lines rising clean and taut above the unending flatness of the marshes.

'I looked at Frances. She looked at me. We knew then that we had our picture.

'Almost immediately a story began to take shape in our minds, built around that derrick which moved so majestically into the wilderness, probed for oil beneath the watery ooze and then moved on, leaving the land as untouched as before it came.

'But we had to translate our thesis – the impact of science on a simple, rural community – into terms of people. For our hero we dreamed up a half-wild Cajun boy of the woods and bayous. To personalize the impact of industry, we developed the character of a driller who would become a friend to the boy, eventually overcoming his shyness and reticence. . . .

'The story almost wrote itself. We shot it up to New York and got an okay from Jersey's board of directors. Only at that point did we make a definite deal to go ahead with the film.'

There are simplifications in this account, published originally as a publicity leaflet.[1] But it is no simplification that Flaherty immediately conceived his film as mirrored in the mind of the half-wild Cajun boy, Flaherty's innocent *alter ego*.

Flaherty set up unit headquarters in an old house in Abbeville, Louisiana. A large closet was turned into a dark-room, the front porch was made over to a cutting-room, a silent film projector was installed and for shooting he fitted a station-wagon with a camera-platform on top and acquired a cabin-cruiser in which to move around the bayous.

One of their most important locations was Avery Island, a preserve owned by Colonel Ned McIlhenny, teeming with wild life, including alligators. For oil-derrick and drilling sequences, the crew of Humble Rig Petite Anse No. 1 was made available by the Humble Oil and Refining Company, a Standard Oil Affiliate.

The unit was enlarged by the recruitment of Richard Leacock as cameraman and Helen van Dongen as editor and associate producer. Flaherty had learnt his technical weaknesses sufficiently to know that he needed, even when he resented, editorial surveillance.

[1] And reprinted in full in Griffith's *World of Robert Flaherty*.

The first task was to find characters. Frances and Ricky Leacock, going after a possible Cajun boy, stopped at a cabin to ask the way and then on a radio set they saw the photograph of a boy. It was the face they wanted, but the boy wasn't there. He had gone barefoot the twelve miles to the nearest town to buy an ice-cream cone. Frances and Ricky got in the car and drove off to find him, sitting on a curbstone. They took some tests and hurried back to Abbeville. They were superb. The boy was a natural and Joseph Boudreaux, as he was called, became thenceforward for the duration of the film Alexander Napoleon Ulysses Latour. From that moment onwards Flaherty demanded that no one should show any sign of affection to the boy except himself. This he had done with Mikeleen and with Sabu, but with Joseph Boudreaux one feels the *rapport* was more complete in both directions. It was not merely a question of Flaherty imposing his ideas on Joseph in the direction of the picture. It was perhaps even more Flaherty's entering the boy's world, a strange world in which there were werewolves and mermaids co-existing through group memory with racoons, alligators, catfish, parents and even oil-derricks.

Production began in May 1946, with the usual tests and background atmospheric material. But – perhaps the only legacy of *Elephant Boy* – there was an outline story down on paper; and on paper, it was a good story. A great deal of thought had gone into the symbolism of the story and the way the machine was to be equated with the primitive animism of mermaids and werewolves in the consciousness of the Cajun boy.

But when Helen van Dongen joined the unit in August, she discovered that this apparently logical story had not been broken down into a script and couldn't be, because Flaherty resisted any attempt to translate mood indicatives into photographic imperatives. When she tried to press Flaherty, he said: 'What is the longest distance between two points?'

His answer was 'A motion-picture.'

We are indebted to Helen van Dongen for access to the diary which she kept while working on the film. On 12th August she noted:

'Screened six reels of unassembled alligator material. . . . Very much involved in close-ups of ferocious-looking alligators, hissing and snapping at their as-yet unexisting victim. Suddenly an accompaniment of a Grieg Sonata! For piano and violin. Strangest combination – alligators and trembling violin. When I stole a look, the artistes were Frances and Bob, with Barbara sitting in a corner drawing a picture of the father playing the fiddle. The Sonata continued for at least half an hour, with the humidity so great that the fiddle was slightly out of tune. And I think the piano was too.'

This alligator sequence was the one which gave most trouble in the picture. On 20th August, Helen wrote: 'Shooting alligator going for bait. Alligator grabs bait, gets hook in his mouth, but refuses to put up a fight even though Sidney[1] admitted that he put a big plank on its tail and was dancing up and down on it to make him mad. Nothing doing. Lionel Le Blanc[2] puts a beam between the alligator's jaws and frees him from hook.'

Two days later, the Colonel himself arrived and forbade Flaherty's killing an alligator, though he had previously given permission for one to be killed provided it was replaced.

While this purely physical problem awaited solution Helen van Dongen tried to sort out what was supposed to be happening in all this alligator sequence.

From her diary one can see her bewilderment. There are too many variations on the same symbols. There is an alligator in the opening sequence of the completed picture; and that may be the same alligator which appears later. There is a wild racoon in the opening sequence – but that certainly isn't the same as the Cajun boy's tame racoon which disappears from the pirogue, or dug-out canoe (presumed eaten by the alligator) later on. She wrote:

'Puzzle: coon in pirogue – when introduced what does he do? When lost – if lost – how found? Possible introduction when surveyor comes to home of J.C. Coon with family in kitchen. J.C. takes it with him on first trip to oil-derrick. Shows it to Tom Smith, the driller. Does not always take it with him because animals are too lively and might distract attention from J.C., Coon in pirogue when

[1] Sidney Smith, just demobbed from the navy was hanging around as an assistant until he could get a place in college.

[2] Lionel Le Blanc, a hunter and trapper, who was overseer on Col. McIlhenny's estate also played the part of Joseph's father in the film. He looked Flaherty's double.

J.C. in pond looking for alligator. Disappears when J.C. disturbs alligator's nest. Did alligator eat it? Question unsolved. J.C. takes revenge on alligator for eating his coon? Or does J.C. only *think* so? Does J.C. tell his parents that coon has disappeared? Most probably since it is his pet and he broke down and cried in cypress forest. When does coon appear again? Does J.C. go on looking for him? As planned, J.C. gets coon back at end of film. It is Tom Smith who finds and returns him to J.C. But what causes Tom Smith to find coon? Coon got lost in pond or cypress swamp. Tom Smith is driller – has no reason to be in cypress forest, nor would coon think of going to vicinity of oil-derrick. Does J.C.'s persistence make him find coon himself....'

This entry is typical of many, illustrating the problems which arose from Flaherty's method of shooting off the cuff. The desperation of the newsreel editor presented with a shot of a man bowling ninepins with no reverse angle was multiplied a thousandfold for Helen van Dongen.

Frances Flaherty was equally worried about the waste of time. On 29th August, she discussed the problem with Helen van Dongen. It would take two years to make the film at this rate, because sequences were planned and thought out after shooting, instead of beforehand. Helen did not agree. They were also thought out before, but in no organized manner.

Two days later, Flaherty flung another spanner in the works. In place of J.C.'s actual pirogue, Flaherty had commissioned a beautiful new pirogue. J.C. would have to learn to paddle it and the shots of the new one wouldn't match the old, already photographed.

As if that wasn't enough, Flaherty wanted the craftsman to make another pirogue out of the other, and better, half of the cypress trunk and incorporate the making in the film as well. 'Are we going to make the same mistakes as Hollywood,' Helen asked, 'cramming six stories and three generations into one picture?'

She adds: 'Went out yesterday to location. Saw place where cypress swamps were filmed earlier, and alligators 1 and 2's nest. Was expecting to be dragged into Louisiana wilds. Instead to Avery Island, Colonel McIlhenny's home, branched off to tropical jungle – park with mown lawns and beautifully cultivated flowers and bushes.

SUSCHITZKY

London, 1949

The Latours' cabin

LOUISIANA STORY — 1946–48

The Latours — Mother, Father and son

Richard Leacock

'The Innocent Eye'

Son, Director and 'Father'

Flaherty and Helen van Dongen

'The Christmas Tree'

HENRI CARTIER-BRESSON

1946

RICHARD AVEDON

Just before the unrealized 'Cinerama' world tour in 1951

'I'm working now to destroy everything I've spent my life to build up'

So the camera never lies? Well, then the artistry of director and cameraman can darned well change location from an appealing jungle back to a foreboding, weird and eerie swamp. The cypress swamp, which looks so expansive and monumental on the screen in the rushes, is in reality nothing but a little pool with a few cypress trees!'

This was the first insight which Helen van Dongen had into Flaherty's imaginative translation of reality. In *The Land*, all the material apart from the sequence of the old Negro dusting off the old plantation-bell, had been shot unrehearsed. It was the nearest Flaherty ever came to 'true documentary'. It was plain from the start that *Louisiana Story* would develop in a completely different idiom, an idiom extremely difficult for an editor, however intuitive, to divine because of Flaherty's inarticulate Eskimo approach to the feel of his material.

Helen van Dongen knew that the film would be unique. But she hoped, since, unlike *The Land, Louisiana Story* was evolved by Flaherty himself that she would be able to discover through conversations what Flaherty was trying to do. 'The big problem,' she remarked on 3rd September, 'will be to begin a discussion with Flaherty. He has a tendency to take every point that is brought up as a criticism, even if presented in the mildest form of a question. It is hardly possible to have an exchange of ideas with him, merely in the interests of the film. This is one of the hardest parts of this job . . . a curious one-track mind. To get it to change to a slightly different idea is almost the slow process of an evolution.'

And so Helen van Dongen's diary goes on for month after month, a record of professional and intellectual exasperation at a man incapable of explaining what he was trying to do – despite his enormous anecdotal facility and gusto about the dead and mastered past. He seemed to fumble forward into any new artistic creation, like a half-blind man, relying upon a guide-dog, whom nevertheless he kept calling to heel.

The making of the picture consisted as much in obliterating in Helen van Dongen any of her preconceived ideas about editing as it did in actual shooting.

Here are some of the notes of the breakdown of Helen van Dongen's accepted ideas.

'October 5th. *Editor's note:* A hell of a way of trying to make a sequence when still so many shots are missing! No use shooting all facial expressions of J.C. either because we change the plan so often. Vicious circle: no use shooting until story of sequence is right; not possible to edit sequence properly until shots are made! Story won't be good until it runs so simply on the screen that it seems as if it never could have been written otherwise in the first place.'

This was followed on 23rd October, by a startling editorial discovery. 'Difficulty of keeping film authentic; sequences such as the catching of the alligator, or J.C. disturbing the alligator-nest, which are staged and planned by us, could be shot according to a preconceived shooting-script covering the action from every angle, with long-shots, medium-shots and close-ups, in order to have sufficient cutting material. When trying to do so however, it turned out that the sequence when edited told you that a camera had been ever present. No matter how naturally and beautifully played, the ever-present camera ruins the authenticity of the scene. Films like *Louisiana Story* should be shot in such way as if the camera were accidentally present to record the action while it happened without the subject being aware that a camera is present. This precludes automatically coverage from every angle or with more than two lenses. Obviously this makes the editing of such a sequence sometimes extremely difficult.'

This entry, made two months after Helen had started work on the picture, would have been made within the first week if Flaherty had been a self-conscious artist. As it was, Helen recorded it not as part of Flaherty's purpose – it was she who had made him try these other shots which didn't work – but as a discovery which she had made for herself and she went on to write an undelivered letter to Flaherty.

'Dear Mr. Director:

'Please invent some other way of shooting little boy and give him something *to do*. He is always wiggling his head from one side to another, and he is always "looking" – looking at alligators, looking at nests, looking at the coon, looking at trees, looking at birds . . . In one word – just looking all the time. I know we want to tell the story from the boy's point of view and we want to have the audience see things through his eyes. In each sequence separately he is fine. But if you string all the sequences together, I'm getting DAMNED tired of him! Will you please think of something – anything – to keep him busy in the film? I know I'm a nuisance, but please think up something. . . .

'Your Editor.'

Tension had mounted high between Flaherty and his editor, when in December Helen went into her cutting-room and found Frances Flaherty playing around with some material on which Helen was working. This was the last straw. Helen stormed off to Flaherty and demanded that her cutting-room should be ruled out of bounds to anybody except herself and him.

Flaherty tried to calm her down and persuade her that the whole thing was just a storm in a tea-cup. But to Helen this was not good enough. Either Mrs. Flaherty must be forbidden the cutting-room, or she quit the picture. Flaherty, who had never drawn any very firm distinctions about anybody's role except his own, wanted to temporize. But Helen, who had been out shopping for Mrs. Flaherty, was beyond temporizing. She packed her bags and left Abbeville immediately for New York.

Flaherty spent the next three weeks waiting for Helen van Dongen, that Dutch mule, to see reason. A series of long-distance telephone calls, however, failed to break down her resistance. It was only after Flaherty saw reason and gave his word that no one should enter her cutting-room that she returned to Abbeville on 14th January, 1947. The quarrel had its advantages. Flaherty realized that he could not make the picture without Helen van Dongen and Helen had had time to think how to turn Flaherty's weakness into fantastic strength. She had already gone some of the way in her recognition that the camera had to appear 'accidentally present' – as indeed it so often was. It needed only a twist to turn that lack of continuity into a dream-like logic. The very qualities which had troubled her orderly sense were to become advantages.

Now very slowly Flaherty and Helen began to evolve a common language. One finds in her diary phrases like 'phantasmagoria of oil-world, like dream-world where nothing is impossible'. Helen started attacking Flaherty's script not for its unreality, but for its falsity to dream. And gradually Flaherty, fighting all the way, began to admit her rightness.

By 19th March, the discussions began about the use of sound in the picture. Could commentary be dispensed with altogether? If not, what was the minimum necessary for clarity? Frances Flaherty had wanted sequences cut in certain ways to heighten suspense; but Helen had argued that unless the audience broadly understood what was happening suspense could not be built up. 'Not to know at all and revealing much too late throws an audience into confusion'. How much could be revealed?

In the completed picture, that argument remains unresolved. There is a great deal which Flaherty expected to come across in a first viewing, which doesn't come across, such as the twin magical objects kept beneath the boy's shirt, the bag of salt which blesses his fishing and the frog, to keep the werewolves away; and yet this very obscurity is something which makes *Louisiana Story* a film one wants to see over and over again. It has depth of style – in the way that books can have depths of style – which can only be plumbed through repeated study. If Helen van Dongen had prevailed, she would have made the film more widely popular, but shorter-lived.

The silent footage was shot with two Arriflex cameras and at the end a sound-crew with a Mitchell camera moved in for the synch-dialogue sequences. This posed a problem which Flaherty did not have time to solve.

He had taken enormous pains with the silent shooting, both in training his natural actors and in discovering the most dramatic way of presenting the material, such as drilling.

'We worked day after day shooting reams of stuff. But somehow we never could make that pesky derrick come alive. We could not recapture that exhilaration we had felt when we first saw it moving slowly up the bayou. Then we hit on it. At night! That's when it came alive! At night with the derrick's lights dancing and flickering on the dark surface of the water, the excitement that is the very essence of drilling for oil became visual. So we threw our daytime footage into the ash-can and started in all over again to shoot our drilling scenes against a night background.'

That sequence is one of the most magnificent in the film, even though one wonders 'Why the hell do they have to pay overtime working at night?' It is partly because of the superb shooting and editing, but it is also because of the wonderful sound-track. Weeks and months of thought and effort went into building up the night drilling sequence. But when Leonard Stark came down with the Mitchell sound camera, Flaherty faced for the first time in his career the shooting of dialogue on location. He had written specific speaking lines; but he hadn't rehearsed his actors beforehand; and he soon saw how hard it was to get his non-actors to get their lines by heart and speak them naturally. Either they forgot them; or they tried so hard to remember that they spoke them woodenly.

As Helen van Dongen explains:

'Flaherty solved this part of the problem by explaining to the group of "actors" (father, mother and son) the action to be "played" and the content of the dialogue to be spoken. One of the sequences in which this happened is the one "played" in the kitchen after the well has struck oil.

'Flaherty told the group of "actors" that, to celebrate the event, the father went on one of his rare visits to the nearest village to do some necessary shopping. He has now returned to the kitchen, starts unpacking the food and then remarks that he has also brought some presents. He asks the boy to hand one of the packages from the bix-box to his mother, who unpacks it and finds a new double-boiler. The boy gets a little impatient waiting for his own present, and asks the father what he has brought for him? The father scolds him at first for being unruly and then eventually hands him the present. (This is only a rough description and does no justice to Flaherty's subtle direction.)

'To make it easier for the "actors", Flaherty, after explaining to them the content of their dialogue, allowed them to use their own words. When "playing" this scene, they added a few unexpected twists and phrases. They also spoke in their own *patois* – French instead of using English. Not having to remember precise lines, their "acting" was excellent, but however beautifully this scene was played it could not be left all in one shot in the final film. Certain parts of the sequences had to be re-enacted for other camera-angles and lenses, so that, in the final sequence, we should get a more intimate response to some of the lines spoken. . . .

'It was only when starting to edit the "presents-in-the-kitchen" sequence that I became acutely aware that, although the dialogue in each retake was similar in content, not once did the "actors" use exactly the same words or sentence-formation. . . .'

Helen van Dongen managed to solve some of these problems in the cutting-room. They were problems which could have been avoided in some cases by the use of more than one camera. But there was the insuperable problem that the dialogue sequences were like blocks of concrete that had to be set in a structure as pliant as woven bamboo and they obtrude with their monolithic inflexibility.

In his accounts of making *Louisiana Story*, Flaherty told enthusiastically of recording wild-track sound effects on location. But Helen van Dongen says that when she and the sound-recordist, Benjamin Doniger, went out to get most of them, Flaherty didn't appear to be very interested. I think that this may well have been true, but that when it came to editing and mixing the sound-tracks, especially in the oil-derrick scenes, Flaherty became excited in the new dimension added to his film.

As was usual with a Flaherty film, shooting came to an end because he had spent all the money allocated for the completed picture. It can't be said that all this money went into the picture. From Abbeville Flaherty would ring up friends not only all over the United States but even in Europe, roaring down the telephone invitations to get on the next boat, train or plane and come out and see the location. Quite a number did. Edward Sammis of Standard Oil who went down several times writes: 'I don't think anyone ever counted the manifold rooms in the Flaherty's old house on the edge of Abbeville. Certainly no one ever counted the guests that inhabited them, a heterogeneous lot, drawn from all over the world by the warmth and compulsion of Bob's personality. One night there would be no one for dinner, all having vanished into the vastness of the bayous. The next, there might be seventeen, appearing as suddenly and mysteriously as the guests had disappeared the night before.' At any caution that the money was running out, Flaherty would roar, 'There's millions more where this came from.' He knew that Standard Oil, having sunk $175,000 in shooting the picture, wouldn't write the project off for the sake of a few grand.

His gamble was right, though the supplementary budget brought the total cost of the production up to $258,000.

The relation of music to natural sound was clearly going to be very important and Virgil Thomson, who had had previous experience of writing music for Pare Lorentz's two pictures, agreed to come in at an early stage and work not merely on the music but its relation to the whole track. He saw a version of the film in December 1947, and worked closely with Helen van Dongen up till the recording in April of the following year. His score was very subtle, with special themes written for each of the characters. Far from being the conventional 'musical background', the music grew with the film as it moved to its final form in the cutting-room and projection-theatre. Not merely musically but in its integration with the visuals and the immensely complicated natural sound-track, Thomson's score is one of the most interesting ever to be written for a film.[1]

Helen van Dongen had learnt during the making of *The Land* the importance of watching Flaherty during screenings of rushes or assemblies. 'During *Louisiana Story*, he hardly ever entered the cutting-room itself. His world was on the screen. Having edited a sequence, I would screen it to him, watching with one eye on the screen and the other on Flaherty. What he did not say in discussion was written all over his face during a screening. The way he put his hand through his hair, or smoked his eternal cigarette, or shuffled on his chair, spoke more than a torrent of words.'

Louisiana Story ran in to no sponsor trouble. Unlike A.A.A., Standard Oil was not selling policy. The prestige of being responsible for *Louisiana Story* was enough in itself; and surely no more perfect reconciliation of industrial progress with the natural order was ever conceived than the concluding shot of the boy climbing the 'Christmas tree' of the capped well with his coon in his arms, shouting farewell to his oil-men friends as the tugs tow their fabulous oil-derrick to new waters, and spitting into the lagoon to remind them that it was his magic not theirs which brought the oil. (See illustration.)

[1] In *The Technique of Film Editing*, ed. Karel Reisz (Farrar, Straus, 1953), there is a fascinating, detailed analysis of the editing of *Louisiana Story* by Helen van Dongen herself and in *The Technique of Film-music*, ed. Roger Manvell and John Huntley (Focal Press, 1957), pp. 99–109, there is an analysis of Virgil Thomson's score.

The film had its world première on 2nd August, 1948, at the Edinburgh Festival at the Caley Cinema to an audience of 2,000 people. Its reception was tremendous. Flaherty, on the line from New York, couldn't believe the reports of its ovation. At Venice, later the same year, it was awarded a prize for its 'lyrical valour'. And in 1949, Virgil Thomson was awarded the Pulitzer Prize for Music on the strength of his score, the first time that this prize had ever been awarded for music written to film. In New York City, it opened at the Sutton Theatre in September 1948, and in the United Kingdom, it was taken for distribution by the British Lion Corporation in a version slightly shorter than that shown at Edinburgh and Venice, but with Flaherty's approval.[1]

Financially it brought no returns proportionate to its cost. For world distribution rights, excluding North and South America, Canada, Denmark, Norway, Germany, Austria, Korea and Japan, for seven years, Korda's British Lion paid an advance of only £5,000 and no more money was forthcoming. In the U.S.A. it had a moderately successful distribution in art-houses through Lopert Films, before being more generally released in 1952 under the title *Cajun*, as a second feature to Armand Denis's *Watusi*. Only a few hundred dollars came from this last deal. But since then it has had a continuous non-theatrical distribution in many countries, besides being shown on television in the U.S.A., Canada and the United Kingdom.[2]

Considering that Standard Oil had paid for the film and assigned all profits to Flaherty, one may say that he did not do badly out of it, even though the share of the box-office returns was so small compared to the film's cost.

Critically *Louisiana Story* raised no storm of protest from the vociferous left. John Grierson, Flaherty's 'self appointed critical attorney',[3] was almost as silent. *Louisiana Story* was Flaherty's greatest

[1]The length given in the *Kinematograph Yearbook*, 1949, is 6,300 ft. (about 70 mins.). The copy in the National Film Archive (probably that shortened for U.K. distribution) is 5,854 (about 65 mins.), while the one held by the Flaherty Foundation is 7,000 ft. (about 77½ mins.).

[2]As a criticism of the Children's Film Foundation of Great Britain, it is worth noting that *Louisiana Story* was turned down as unsuitable for child audiences. Instead of laughing it off, Flaherty was deeply hurt. Information from John Goldman.

[3] *The Reporter*, New York, 16 October, 1951. In an obituary notice.

film achievement, but all Grierson had to say was 'Yet another brilliant evocation of the damn-fool sense of innocence this wonderful old character pursues: his eye keener than ever, sensibility softer and so on....'[1] Grierson's eye was less keen and his artistic sensibility toughened by years of socio-political propaganda.

Richard Griffith wrote that it was time to put an end to the 'perennial attempt to force Flaherty into the mould of social criticism, or alternatively to cast him into outer darkness as an irrelevant reactionary. Both alternatives are false. . . . Flaherty's role has been that of proclaiming to the world what a marvel the movie-camera can be when it is turned to real life.'[2]

Iaian Hamilton came nearer the truth.

'Flaherty has pitched away the last mechanics of prose, and the result is pure poetry. . . . This is elegy. Its theme is the wonder of childhood – Wordsworth's great theme; the setting, the swampland of Louisiana; the players, American oil-men and a family of French Canadians who have settled among the bayous. With the clear, true vision of a child, Flaherty contemplates place, people, animal and machine; and the lyrical intensity of his art evolves a slow statement of the marvel of life. How inadequate is the word "documentary" to describe such a work. It is like calling an ode "an article in verse".[3]

'There is no comment, no propaganda, no uplift. There is scarcely any dialogue. The actions of these people, as Virginia Woolf once wrote of Homeric characters, "seem laden with beauty because they do not know that they are beautiful". In every sequence where human beings are under the lens love is evoked. The floating derrick makes its stately arrival; oil is found and the well is capped; the derrick and its engineers depart; and Alexander Napoleon Ulysses Latour remains, a little enriched by the visitation.

'How sane is this, calm and sane and filled with meaning, like a deep pool in which now and then one glimpses the flicker and dart and fins. It is the very essence of romanticism. The Marxist critic, who

[1] *Documentary Film News*, Vol. 7, No. 68, August 1948.

[2] *Documentary Film* (ed. 1952), p. 311.

[3] This depends, comment Rotha and Wright, on the interpretation of the word, 'documentary'. I would agree, only adding that the public image of documentary in 1948 was not merely prosaic, but journalistic. A. C-M.

would have us glued body and soul to the hot hob of our political and economic existence, will rage at its "escapism". But he is concerned with the false world. Here, from a remote corner of a remote state, is Flaherty showing us the true world, the source – and it is bathed, like the work of any true poet, in "the master light of our seeing". The allusion is not extravagant. Works like this redeem the cinema and burn up like chaff the memory of its screaming vulgarities, its too solid mediocrities.'[1]

Of the contemporary views, Iaian Hamilton's came nearest to insight into the achievement of *Louisiana Story* as conceived by Flaherty and executed by himself and his fellow workers, especially Helen van Dongen, Ricky Leacock and Virgil Thomson.

Flaherty himself called *Louisiana Story* 'a fantasy', meaning that it exists in the world not of reality but of dream. It would also be true to describe it as a fable, in the sense that the people, the animals and the actions have a fabulous significance transcending the particular. Many people have observed that the film takes place within the consciousness of the Cajun Boy; but it is significant that the boy is not Joseph Boudreaux, but the mighty mytho-historical Alexander Napoleon Ulysses who in this incarnation is a Latour. He is not just a boy, but all boys who have dreamed of greatness; he is childhood. And he does not live in 'a remote corner of a remote state' in 1946–7, he lives in a place which compresses the history of the human race almost from the Garden of Eden to this very instant, and the history of the earth from long before the emergence of man.

His childhood is not just that of all children; it is also on another level, the childhood of the human race. The snakes and alligators which live in the swamp are the symbols of the predators which threaten the life of primitive man; and the mermaids and werewolves are the local spirits of good and evil which dwell in the minds, and rule the world, of stone-age people. It is a world of terror and magic and danger. But it is also a world of beauty and love and achievement; the beauty of a spider's web, of Spanish moss drooping from cypresses and mirrored in the water, the love of a wild racoon become a friend, the achievement of catching a catfish or killing a murderous alligator.

Hamilton was right to mention Wordsworth. Alexander Napoleon

[1] *Manchester Guardian*, 28th August, 1948.

Ulysses is free to wander and conquer; but on Jean Latour and his wife, the shades of the prison-house have closed. Jean is just a trapper, sceptical that the oil-men will find oil but careful to safeguard that he will not lose out, if they do. He and the oil-men live in a narrow adult world. But to the boy that world of launches, oil-derricks and machines is far easier to accept, because the boy's little world is already so much fuller than his father's.

Critics have tended to see the oil-derrick purely as the intrusion of the modern mechanical monster into a world of imagination peopled by such monsters as alligators and werewolves. What they have missed is that the oil-derrick with its clanking, roaring drills and pipes and chains is drilling down into a past, millions of years older than that which the boy inhabits, when before ever man emerged, the mineral oil deposits were trapped.

To the boy, this drilling is at first a terrifying thing; and the oil-men who jeer at his magic, his spit, the bag of salt within his shirt and the frog-familiar, seem to have no more understanding of what things are really like than any other adults.

But with time he becomes familiar both with the men and their strange machines; he accepts them as he accepts his parents.

Yet this does not mean that he accepts their narrow attitude to the world. Drilling is dangerous because it is a violation of the forces hidden beneath the earth, more dangerous, more powerful than those to be found on the surface.

When the blow-out comes, the boy sees it as a revenge, only to be expected when anyone ignores the need for propitiatory magic. And because he likes the men, he tries his own magic of salt and spit – almost but not quite offering his frog as well. And the oil begins to flow.

As soon as one begins to make explicit what is expressed in symbols, one begins to falsify. For me, part of the emotional impact of that magnificent final scene with Alexander Napoleon Ulysses Latour astride the 'Christmas tree' is that through the pipe up which the oil is welling, he is linked with pre-history. This is a fact and it doesn't matter whether or not Flaherty consciously planned this. The greatest symbolism is unconscious.

On the other hand, the film is resonant with deliberate symbols.

The boy begins with a rusty old rifle, he ends with a new one. The wild racoon is placed at the beginning to establish it as part of the wild before we find the boy with a pet one. What happens to the Latour family apart from a few presents from town does not matter; the boy is conqueror and hero of all the kingdoms of the world, Alexander, Napoleon and Ulysses rolled in one, waving to the friendly twentieth century while the riches of prehistoric time flow between his legs.[1]

There are of course criticisms to be made of *Louisiana Story*. The mother isn't even a sketch of a human being. The letter and newspaper inserts are film clichés to help the story on. The dialogue is stilted and halting and the catching of the alligator with the boy not using the tree to anchor his rope implausible. But these are minor flaws implicit in Flaherty's technique of shooting and from their very amateurishness give the film a sort of rough authenticity which might have been lost with smoother continuity.

[1] Whether Joseph Boudreaux retained (or for that matter ever possessed) the riches of childhood, with which Flaherty endowed him is not known. But he became, as one imagines Alexander Napoleon Ulysses would have done, an oil driller. Sabu, the elephant boy, *au contraire*, ended up a Cadillac-owning film-star; and Mikeleen, leaving Aran, grew up a mercenary soldier.

18 THE END

After the Hollywood première of *Louisiana Story*, Charles Chaplin, Jean Renoir and Dudley Nichols sent Flaherty what was intended as a congratulatory telegram. It read:

> DO THIS AGAIN AND YOU WILL BE IMMORTAL AND EXCOMMUNICATED FROM HOLLYWOOD WHICH IS A GOOD FATE.

It could scarcely have been more ironical, despite the goodwill which lay behind it. Flaherty had been excommunicated from Hollywood for twenty years and from British commercial film studios for ten. In the course of forty years, he had made five important films, had never been employed twice by the same people and had lost more people more money than any film director with the possible exception of Erich von Stroheim. The challenge 'Do this again' was doubly impossible. Firstly, a sponsor like Standard Oil comes once only in a lucky man's lifetime. And secondly, Flaherty had nothing from which to make another film. He was not a fertile film creator. Even *Louisiana Story* was the work of an amateur of genius; and what went to make it a brilliant success was the four years dialectical meditation, following the failure of *The Land*, upon the simplicities studied in the earlier films and the complexity of the machine.

Supposing Croesus had presented him with all the money in his treasury to make the greatest film of his life, Flaherty would have found it impossible to do so, because he had already made it.

About a lonely, limited genius such as Flaherty there congregates always a group of defenders, who find in his commercial failure, a justification for their own. But in fact, artistically Flaherty's life was remarkably free from failure. Apart from the farce of *Elephant Boy* and the misfiring of *Industrial Britain* and *The Land*, the only two pictures in which he was tied to government agencies, he had a wonderful run for other people's money.

Ah, but if only the cinema industry had been differently organized! say the self-appointed defenders of Flaherty. 'What would have happened then?'

What would probably have happened, if any Flaherty picture had made so much money that even he couldn't have squandered it, would have been that he would have ceased to be an inspired, but infuriating director and become a fuddled, but even more infuriating, producer.

As it was, he remained in director's harness. The tests he made for a film interpretation of Picasso's Guernica picture for the Museum of Modern Art in 1948 led to his presentation for the United States of *Michelangelo*, a *kulturfilm* directed in Italy by Dr. Curt Oertel in 1939, and captured by the American forces during the war. The film was offered to John Grierson during the war by the American O.S.S., but he refused to re-edit another film-maker's creative work, especially a film so devoid of social content. Helen van Dongen also turned down the offer.[1] But in 1950, Flaherty presented it under the title of *The Titan*. His adoption of it gave it wider publicity than if it had been edited for the American market by Grierson or van Dongen. But the confusion of the Oertel film prefaced by 'Flaherty Presents' made many people think that the *Louisiana Story* unit had shot the *Michelangelo* picture also.

The time had come for Flaherty to 'dun rovin' and retire to the seclusion of the farm at Brattleboro or if that was too great a sacrifice of the social life he loved among friends like Oliver St. John Gogarty,

[1] Grierson's and Helen van Dongen's information to Rotha and Wright.

John Huston and others at least to have cut down the financial part of his entertainment. To have done either would have been to deny the magnificent improvidence which was the weakness and glory of Robert Flaherty. Something had always turned up. It always would. He had never known the hardship of complete poverty.

In the spring of 1949, he was approached by the Vermont Historical Society and the Vermont Development Corporation to make a short 16-mm. colour film about the State of Vermont. As he was leaving for London and then Europe for the promotion of *Louisiana Story*, he delegated the direction of the picture to David Flaherty, who, with Leonard Stark as cameraman and Stefan Bodnariuk as editor, made *Green Mountain Land* covering the history, farming and industry of the state. It was issued in 1950 and was taken by the State Department for world-wide release in some thirty languages. But though Flaherty took a producer credit, he had little to do with the film.

During 1949, Bob and Frances Flaherty together visited London, Edinburgh, Paris and Cannes, the last named for the Film Festival. It was over ten years since they had been in Europe and in that time the continent had changed even more than they had. But it was a wonderful return for Flaherty, who had left England so broke and now brought his masterpiece. Flaherty alone went to its presentation in Stockholm and to Brussels, where its rapturous reception at the Film Festival moved him to tears.

In London, the Flahertys stayed at a private hotel in De Vere Gardens, Kensington.[1] Bob took one look at the Café Royal and beat a quick retreat. He found his new social headquarters in *Le Petit Club Francais*, which Olwen Vaughan had founded for the Free French during the war and which had (and still has) the atmosphere of shabby, comfortable bohemianism in which Flaherty loved to relax, upstairs in the restaurant on the first floor or in the ground-floor bar.

It was there in a party given to welcome Flaherty, as I understood, but probably really a party given by Flaherty himself to welcome old friends, that I met him for the first and only time.

As I have said, I had followed his films from the time I saw *Nanook of the North* as a schoolboy. I had also followed the course of British

[1] Where Wolfgang Suschitsky took a fine series of portraits of which two are reproduced in this book.

documentary from its inception as an outsider and from 1941 to 1946 had worked very closely with the movement as a member of the Ministry of Information Films Division. In 1949 my connection with the movement was sufficiently close for me to be invited to the Flaherty party. But as soon as I went inside, I knew that I didn't belong. There was this large Irishly handsome over-life-size man with the wonderful blue eyes and an outflow of human love which was almost insensitive because it gave out so much that it took very little in. And there, slightly in the background hovering, was Mrs. Flaherty, on whose face was recorded all the anxiety which was the history of being married to a genius profligately outgiving. It seemed to me that he was like a light and she was like a sensitive photographic plate; and for them, this was a totally different party.

Flaherty saw it as a reunion with old friends, a wonderful occasion for rejoicing because here were John Grierson's boys grown up to maturity. He was like a schoolmaster meeting old pupils who had made good in their own right.

It seemed to me that the shape of that party was a V. In 1949, Flaherty was in one camp and the British documentarians were in another. Their true meeting point was in the early thirties, when Flaherty had come over from Berlin as schoolmaster. The party was not to celebrate Flaherty's triumph in *Louisiana Story*. It was a sentimental reunion with a friend from the past. But Flaherty so irradiated that this was not the final or lasting impression of that meeting. I recall phrases from Oliver St. John Gogarty's word portrait: 'a big, expansive man with a face florid with enthusiasm and eyes clear as the Northern Ice . . . further removed from the mediocre than any man I've ever known.'

'I often regret that I never met Walt Whitman,' Gogarty wrote in that portrait, which had been published in *Tomorrow* a couple of years before.[1] 'But there is a lot of him reincarnated in Bob Flaherty. He, too, can take you into peace – "to behold the birth of stars, to learn one of the meanings, to launch off with absolute faith and never be quiet again", and the more faith we have the easier it will be for us, when our time comes, to glide down the slips.

'But absolute faith in what, you may ask? Absolute faith in the

[1]Reprinted in *Mourning became Mrs. Spendlove* (Creative Age Press, New York, 1948).

nature and the fate of man, a belief that there is a hero hidden in all men, and that when we are all in the same boat the hero will steer it. This is somewhat vague and abstract; but so is faith.'

And so is Oliver St. John Gogarty, vaguer and more abstract than the friend he was sketching.

'Flaherty is a phrase-maker and his generalities reveal deep thinking: "Every man is strong enough for the work on which his life depends."

'But it is not Flaherty's story-telling that makes him the most magnanimous man I've ever met. It is his power of making you forget the trivial things in life and look only at the elemental things that build up the dignity of man. "If only men were honest, there would be no wars." His face glows with the wonder of a child when he tells of the hidden paradises on the earth; or when he meets a friend. His finger never mutes the strings that vibrate in eternity. He has in him the expansiveness and generosity of the true American.

'The regions where his mind dwells few of us can commute, so the best we can do is to take care we do not miss him when he comes to town. . . .'

Clare Lawson Dick, Eileen Molony and Michael Bell of the B.B.C. took care not to miss him when he came to town. In 1949 he made a large number of recordings, some about his early travels and the making of *Nanook*, others of his favourite anecdotes, of which some were never broadcast because of his mike-shyness. 'If only we had our modern methods,' Michael Bell told me, 'I'd have had the French Club wired, and got all of the stories really as he told them.'

Bozo the Bear was not an original Flaherty story. He made it his own, because despite its slight impropriety it gave such scope to his gift for travellers story-telling, and the characteristic employment of suspense. I reproduce it here as the nearest to a verbatim example of the sort of magic with which he beguiled his listeners.

> Once I had a beautiful fight with a bear. Well, I was younger then than I am now, and a lot more active. It was in the twenties and I had been prospecting in the land north of Lake Superior, which was then quite unknown country and prospecting was a tough racket.
>
> I was going up a river with one Indian in a birch-bark canoe, and we had to carry our gear over a stretch of rapids in this river.

I had got a pack-sack on my back, and I was in the lead with the Indian behind me. Well, we followed the trail. . . it was awfully hot and there were lots of flies and mosquitoes bothering us . . . and at last I realized we had wandered off the trail. We were now in the bush, with this pack-sack on my back scratching the branches of the low-hanging trees and scrubs, and all that sort of thing.

I kept on floundering ahead, and finally I got out of the depth of the spruce trees in the forest. It was most gloomy, with very little light trickling through, and suddenly we came across a little glade, still very gloomy, but covered with grass and buttercups and so on. Now there were no more branches to impede us, and the grass looked very inviting, so I thought this was a very nice place to take a rest and get this pack-sack off my back for a while.

I was just going to take my pack-sack off when I looked across the glade . . . it was only 20 or 30 feet or so across . . . and I saw a shadow there. I looked again, and I began to realize what it was. My God! It was a bear!

There he stood up on end. He was nearly seven feet high . . . quite a big fellow. And while I was looking, he started to come towards me . . . slowly . . . on his hind legs with his paws weaving. I had just managed by this time to get my pack-sack off before there he was in front of me, weaving and sparring.

Well, I don't expect you to believe me, but I was getting desperate . . . there was only one thing to do. To hit him. And I did it. I hit him hard on the chin . . . and down he went. By God!

It was sickening to hear the thud as he fell to the ground. And as I looked down at him I never felt so sorry for anything in my life as I did when I saw that bear on the ground. He was looking up at me. He was an old bear . . . poor old fellow . . . and he had only one eye. One eye had gone, no doubt in some fight long ago; and he kept looking up at me with his one good eye in the most pitiful manner and a tear was glistening in the corner of his eye. I looked down, and I gulped, and instantly I bent over him and got him to his feet and straightened him up a little. And he looked at me in the most reproachful way . . . you can't imagine how I felt.

He was trying to talk . . . and he almost could. He almost called me Bob . . . I could swear he was mumbling, 'Bob'. And I called him Bozo. My Indian boy was rather frightened . . . he didn't know what to do; but I told him everything was all right. I said that instead of continuing on the trail, we would pitch camp and stay here and I'd do a little exploring.

Well, we got our tent up, and got a fire going, and, of course, just before, I had out a rope around Bozo's neck and tethered him to a stake. But we didn't need it; right from the start we were really pals. We got our fire going, and our bacon and beans fried, and we sat round the fire eating our supper . . . and, of course, we shared some with Bozo. Then we turned in for the night.

Next day we went through a cross-section of the area, to see what the country was like . . . what the rock formations were and all that sort of thing, you know. When we got back that evening, Bozo was still there all right. I had kept him tethered, though there was no need to really . . . it was more for appearance sake. And that sort of thing went on for several days . . . our friendship developing all the time. He would always grunt us a welcome when we came back into the camp.

On the fourth day we came back to camp a bit earlier than we had expected. And Bozo was not there. Then, by God, I heard something which makes any man fear God. There was an Indian reservation just across the river, and I heard someone shouting for blue murder. The Indian boy and I jumped up and rushed over just in time. By God! This Bozo had the Chief's daughter in his arms and was squeezing her to death! As I came up, the Indian Chief was white with anger. He told me, through my Indian boy, that they knew all about this bear. He had an evil name . . . he was the durndest bear in the country . . . and they weren't going to put up with him any more.

I could see the Chief was furious, and while he was caressing his daughter who was by now out of the bear's arms and examining her scratches, I slipped across to Bozo. Bozo looked at me again with that reproachful expression in his one eye. I could see the situation was going to be pretty serious unless something was done quickly; so I told Bozo I was very ashamed of him and he'd have to go without food for his bad behaviour unless he apologized. Well, I managed somehow to quieten all the others, but the Chief I could not quieten. He said, 'Look here, you've got to get that bear out of this country at once. We don't want him around here any more. We know all about him . . . everyone knows all about that bear. Get out!'

Well, I thought discretion was the better part of valour, too, and I decided anyway that it was as well if I finished my exploration pretty soon and got the next train, which started some hundreds of miles farther east. And I thought it would be a marvellous idea to take Bozo with me. I could tell the story of our friendship in these northern woods and of all that had happened. It would make a good story.

We got down to the railway, but we had to wait that night for the 'Overseas Limited' . . . the great train from the west which normally would not stop here. I got the station-master to flag the train. It came to a grumbling halt and finally pulled up . . . and there was I with a bear and an Indian and a lot of luggage ready to board this train.

There was the conductor looking down at us, and the brakeman behind him. I told him I wanted to take the bear with me. He said he wasn't going to take a bear on his train. But I thrust a twenty-dollar bill into his hand. He swallowed a bit and then said, 'Oh well, I'll fix a place in the baggage-car until we can figure out something better.'

So Bozo and I clambered aboard, and the Indian passed up our luggage, and I said 'Good-bye' to him. The conductor pulled the bell, and the train rolled on through the night. The conductor gave us a place of a sort . . . the train was packed absolutely full. It was a 'swank' train of the Canadian Pacific but the conductor gave us what he could, not a Pullman, of course, just a rough-and-ready place next to the baggage-car. Anyway, we were on the train; and I fixed my pack-sack in the corner and settled down into a seat, tethering Bozo to an iron leg of the seat. And I finally fell asleep, and Bozo did also. And the train went on roaring through the night.

Some time in the early hours of the morning I woke up and looked around. My God! Bozo was not there! I looked out of the coach, and called him . . . but there were no signs of him, not a sign anywhere. My heart began to race. What had happened? I knew the train hadn't stopped at any place. Where could he have gone? Was it possible that this bear with such a famous reputation among the Indians was clever enough to have got away from me and found himself a seat in a Pullman?

I didn't know what to think. . . . I daren't let myself think what might have happened. Well, I had to call the conductor, and as soon as he came, he was even more surprised than I was. There was only one thing to be done . . . we had to start looking for Bozo.

We came to the first Pullman, and the Negro porter asked what we wanted, and when we said we were looking for a bear, you can imagine his expression. We looked in the gentlemen's washroom, and I called out in the most wheedling tone I could muster, 'Bozo, are you there? Bozo, come on.' Not too loudly, of course, because we didn't want to wake the sleepers. But there was no answer.

We went through the Pullman, and peeped behind the green curtains into the upper and lower berths full of people snoring and whistling . . . all sound asleep. I kept calling Bozo's name, but the only sound to be heard was the roaring of the train through the night. Finally, we got to the ladies' room at the end of the car and we looked in there, but there was still no sign of Bozo. We had gone through Pullman after Pullman, the whole length of the train. And there was no sound to be heard of the bear.

And it was not until we got to the end of the very last Pullman, that we heard anything . . . a voice . . . a lady's voice . . . just a whisper from behind the curtains of a sleeping-berth:

'If you're a real gentleman, take off your fur coat!'

Flaherty was in Europe not merely to exploit *Louisiana Story*. He was hoping that by being around when his great film was exhibited someone would come forward with a proposal for some new film. There was a flicker of hope when his old friend Winifred Holmes introduced him to Sir Oliver Goonatilleke, then the High Commissioner for Ceylon in London (now Governor-General). The goodwill and desire for Flaherty to make a film in Ceylon was present on both sides, but not the funds and in the end of 1949, Flaherty went back to New York, while Frances went to India to visit her daughter Barbara.

Reports of the success of his European visit had reached Washington and a few weeks after his return, the State Department proposed to send him to the American zone of Germany as an unofficial ambassador of goodwill.

It was a statesmanlike decision. Flaherty was the symbol of the creative American, untouched by commercialism or big business, an antidote to the trade-representatives in uniform who swelled the ranks of the American army of occupation.

Taking with him *Nanook*, *Man of Aran* and *Louisiana Story*, he took up his headquarters at Frankfurt,[1] whence he visited Dusseldorf, Stuttgart, Munich, Augsberg, Mainz and Hamburg, showing his films and talking of his travels. In what Griffith calls 'the cold grey world of their defeat', the Germans found far more solace in the perennial hardships of the Arctic and the Western Isles and more refreshment in the magic of Alexander Napoleon Ulysses Latour's world than in the affluent ebullience of the American way of life. At Schluchsee, Flaherty was the guest of honour at a meeting of German film-clubs, the benign affirmation of human standards transcending frontiers.

While fulfilling his demanding schedule,[2] Flaherty still had one eye open for possible films. The most dramatic subject was obviously the line of demarcation between Western and Eastern Germany, commonly called the Iron Curtain. Flaherty's line of approach to the subject is indicated by his working title *The Green Border*.

But the project came to nothing. The tour was planned to conclude with a visit to Bremen, but in Hamburg Flaherty went down with bronchial pneumonia.

When he had recovered, the Flahertys returned to the United States. At the University of Michigan, Ann Arbor, Flaherty was presented with an honorary degree of Doctor of Fine Arts; and during the summer discussions went on about the possibility of Flaherty making a film in Hawaii about the peaceful co-existence of people of different races under the American flag for the Division of Motion Pictures, which is charged with making the American Way of Life known to the rest of the world.

[1]Where he was joined by Frances in March 1950.

[2]'The tour programme consisted of American *Haus* screenings of *Man of Aran*, Press and radio interviews, personal appearances at theatres, round-table discussions with professional people, film-club sessions, meetings with civic, religious and professional leaders and private as well as public screenings of *Louisiana Story* and *Man of Aran* ... The audience reaction to these films was extraordinary. In some places the applause lasted two minutes ... Mr. Flaherty's personal appearance in Germany plus the exhibition of his films exceeded in prestige value to the United States anything that had been done heretofore in this field.' State Dept. report, provided to authors by David Flaherty.

On 10th November, 1950, Flaherty submitted to the International Motion Picture Division, Department of State, a memorandum for a film, *East is West*, of which the purpose was:

> To show the successful amalgamation of races of the Far East (Japanese, Chinese, Filipinos, Koreans), with their different cultural backgrounds, in a progressive western democracy. The American territory of Hawaii, 'Crossroads of the Pacific', is the scene. Such a film would be an implicit refutation of the Communist line that Asiatic peoples are 'ruthlessly exploited by "American imperialists"'.
>
> Everyone born in the Islands, of whatever race, has the rights of citizenship. These citizens of Hawaii refer to our country not as the United States, but as 'the mainland'. Though the territory has not yet been granted statehood,[1] its people feel they are a part of the United States. The various racial groups and mixtures which comprise Hawaii's population of more than half a million respect each other, and rightly so, for their racial cultures are proud ones, not to be lost or discarded in the process of assimilation. A Buddhist temple is not at all incongruous among Christian churches, nor is a thatched Samoan village far from modern Honolulu. One does not apply the term 'Colonials' to the peoples of Hawaii, nor 'natives' to the indigenous Polynesians. . . . Democracy really works in Hawaii . . . and democracy does not breed condescension. . . .
>
> The pictorial and human resources for a film to express these important truths would seem to be limitless. The greatest task would be one of selection. From the handsome pure Hawaiians through the many fascinating mixtures of Polynesians with Japanese, Chinese and Caucasian blood, some wonderfully attractive types are surely to be found; and the more memorable the film's leading characters are, the better will a film achieve its purpose.
>
> The main target area must not be lost sight of. Peoples of the Far East must see their descendants portrayed with sympathy and dignity in their successful assimilation into the new life which democracy offers them. They will see the reality of a bridge between East and West.[2]

[1]Hawaii became the fiftieth state of the U.S.A. in 1959.

[2]We are indebted to the Robert Flaherty Foundation for access to this document.

The negotiations for the film foundered on the State Department's system of financing by payment in arrear. The Flahertys would have had to spend $20,000 or more on production, before they received any payment. They did not possess such a sum, nor could they induce any bank to advance the money on the strength of the State Department contract. Though a State Department contract might be 'legal tender at any bank', as they were assured, Flaherty had not the reputation of keeping within budget and at his age might very possibly have been prevented from fulfilling the contract by illness or death.

In an attempt to raise finance and also ensure continuity of any production he undertook, Flaherty announced late in 1950 the formation of a company consisting of a group of film workers 'to extend the Flaherty film traditions to short, institutional and public relations films for industry': Robert Flaherty Film Associates Incorporated, Vice-President, David Flaherty, offices West 52nd Street.

The Press-release might have been modelled upon any one of the British documentary hand-outs to sponsors from the thirties onwards, with the exception of the concluding paragraph:

'Heretofore, Flaherty has generally preferred to select his assistants particularly for each production; hence the organization of a permanent group to work under him represents something of an innovation.'

It was an innovation the necessity for which had been borne in on him by the attack of bronchial pneumonia earlier in the year. His health was failing and the attraction of the Hawaiian picture was the warmth of the climate.

But January 1951 found Flaherty in New York, where in the Museum of Modern Art Auditorium the Screen Directors Guild paid him honour with a festival, screening *Man of Aran* and *Louisiana Story* 9th January, *Industrial Britain, The Land* and *Moana* 10th January, and *Elephant Boy*[1] and *Nanook of the North* 11th January. There were cabled congratulations from friends all over the world.

[1] Extract from *The Screen Director*, Vol. VI, No. 1, January 1951. ELEPHANT BOYS' BOY. Burbank, Calif. – Sabu Dastagir, famed star of Robert Flaherty's *Elephant Boy* and other movies, celebrated the forthcoming Flaherty Film Festival by presenting his own 'production', 2nd January, at St. Joseph's Hospital here, where a son, Paul, was born to his wife, Marilyn Cooper, former stage actress.

Griffith describes a scene with Flaherty about this time in his suite at the Hotel Chelsea on 23rd St.

> The shabby old rooms were stacked with the loot of years of travel. Sunshine filtered in through dusty windows on cameras and tripods lined against the walls. Stills from the films were propped up on the mantelpiece for me to look at. On the coffee-stained work-table was a pile of messages from passers-by through New York who wanted to give him a hail. He had lived there six years, on and off, but it all looked like a camp that might be struck at dawn. As ever, he was poised for flight.
>
> Where to, this time? He paced the room as I quizzed him on future film plans about which he was vague. I was persistent; I wanted to know exactly what he saw ahead of him. Suddenly he sat down and looked at me and said, 'Well, say what you will, there's one thing they can't take away from us, the way we've lived these thirty years.'[1]

Flaherty was sixty-seven. He had lived hard and he had not really recovered from bronchial pneumonia. The Hawaiian film might have provided the refreshment he needed. Even some months at the farm might have set him up, if he could have endured that seclusion. As it was, he was approached by the late Mike Todd and the travel-film commentator Lowell Thomas, to make films all over the world, using Cinerama, a gigantic and complicated device, using a two-ton camera, designed to protect the movie industry from the inroads of television by making films to be projected on the wide screen by three projectors.

Grierson who was not with Flaherty at this time thinks that despite the fact that this method of film-making was contrary to all Flaherty's previous practice, Flaherty 'was as excited about "Cinerama" in itself as he was when he discovered a 17 in. lens'. Griffith says that Flaherty remarked to him, 'I'm working now to destroy everything I've spent my life to build up.' Frances Flaherty in an interview with Rotha, 17th August, 1957, went further still. 'Bob realized that Cinerama stood for everything against which he had fought all his movie-life. He went into it solely because he needed urgently to earn a living, for no other reason. He continually quarrelled with Mike Todd and Lowell Thomas,

[1] *The World of Robert Flaherty*, Richard Griffith.

who represented the exact opposite to all that Bob believed in and had worked for.'

The reader must reach his own conclusion. Perhaps the motivation was complex. He needed money. He didn't want to go to Brattleboro. 'Cinerama' was a challenge. Work was better than idleness. The lure of the box-office still called.

The first assignment was a sixty-minute newsreel of General MacArthur's triumphal return from Korea to Chicago. Apart from the fact that it was in 3-D, wide-screen colour, it was just like another newsreel. But while filming it, Flaherty caught a cold, which turned to virus-pneumonia.

He seemed to throw it off and according to Herman G. Weinberg he continued with his plans for the world tour. Weinberg recalls an evening in the Coffee House Club about a week before he was due to leave. 'Flaherty was in high spirits . . . the setting was the Coffee House Club. The talk was of the forthcoming journey. Everybody wanted to know about the new cameras – were they really three-dimensional? Flaherty did his best to explain, but his heart wasn't in it. . . .'

Griffith makes no mention of the projected world tour. According to him arthritis set suddenly in. For the first time in his life, he realized that he must rest and as the pains passed, he was getting ready to follow Frances up to the farm, when the pains suddenly recurred.

His doctor wouldn't let him leave New York, until he had 'done something' about the pains. Doing something consisted of doping Flaherty so heavily with morphine that he did not know what was going on half the time.

> He didn't let anyone know how bad he was, even Frances didn't take it in, and there he sat alone in his room at the Chelsea, day after day, and night after night. He couldn't lie in bed, the pain was so bad, and he had to sit out the night in an arm-chair. When finally we all caught on to what was happening, and Frances came down to New York from the farm, he rallied, fought off the arthritis – and then came down with shingles, equally painful and equally requiring constant drugs.
>
> I visited him every day. While he would welcome me and follow conversation with his eyes and occasionally say a pertinent

word or two, he had really withdrawn to some region of his own where none could follow him.

All this we attributed to the morphine, and when Frances told me one day, the tears of joy in her eyes, that a new 'miracle' drug had been found which had cleared up everything, I felt safe in taking a few days off, Frances's intention being to take Bob up to the farm at once.[1]

As Griffith told Flaherty about going away, Flaherty muttered: 'I'm through. I'm done for this time.' Griffith took no notice, because he had heard this sort of thing before in black moods. But when he got back, he found that Flaherty had been moved from the Chelsea – not to the farm but to the hospital. When Griffith telephoned to explain his absence, he heard Flaherty say: 'Tell Dick not to give me any of that stuff.' He seemed much better but did not want to see anyone.

Frances moved him to the farm. But though the specific diseases seemed to clear up, the ageing of his body of which these were merely symptoms could not be stopped. On 23rd July, 1951, he died of a cerebral thrombosis and his ashes were buried on the hill-side at Black Mountain under a slab of white stone.

[1] In a letter to Paul Rotha, 27th July, 1951.

19 EPILOGUE

Flaherty has been used by some people as a rod with which to castigate the film industry. He is portrayed as a martyr to film-art, rejected alike by commercial film moguls and sponsors from government and big business.

This is a disservice to an individual artist who, though he believed that the world owed him a living, never indulged in self-pity, however much he raged against commercialism and bureaucracy.

Film-making is the costliest of art-forms. Whoever puts up the money has a right to expect in return something tangible, such as more money, something useful such as a change in the political or social climate or something vaguely benevolent such as a bonus of goodwill.

However extravagant Flaherty may have been in his expenditure, he knew that he had to try to give value for money. Within the limits of his integrity, he tried to fulfil the requirements of his different backers. It was always a difficult equation; and in his lifetime it can only be said to have succeeded aesthetically twice, with his first major film and his last.

These were the only two occasions when he found sponsors who gave him a sum of money to make the sort of film that he wanted, relying on the goodwill which accrued from the financing of a work of art.

Flaherty's scant production is sometimes cited as a denunciation of our society. But G. W. Pabst, when himself complaining that if he had lowered his standards he could have made more than twenty films, replied to someone who cited Flaherty's six pictures in thirty years, 'Yet what films!' In terms of the celluloid medium Flaherty's production has lasted magnificently.

I began this biography in the belief that given a better type of film-sponsorship, Flaherty would have left a larger body of work. And perhaps in an ideal world this might have been true. But Flaherty was not an ideal film-maker. He consistently overspent his budgets, partly because he had never learnt to visualize his picture from beginning to end, but as much through sheer extravagance of entertainment and long-distance telephoning. No film-production of his could stand up to the inquisitorial eye of an accountant, demanding 'Was this necessary in terms of the film?' He was not an austere artist. He was a large profligate man, who made films which appealed to millions over years instead of to millions over months. His slow tempo was wrong for the big money.

Consequently he suffered.

I see nothing wrong in that. Man is a pleasure-loving creature and there is little worthwhile which he will do without the pressure of suffering. This was especially true of Flaherty who was a double artist. His easiest and most delightful form of expression was in telling stories. When he sat down in a restaurant, oozing over his chair, he would first command the menu and the wine-list, selecting what was best for the company according to his views. If there were ladies, it should be champagne and sweet champagne, because in his day the ladies liked their champagne sweet.

And then he would begin to hold forth with that wonderful command of eloquence, the bright blue eyes effulgent, the face like a sun and the hair like a halo. The dinner would be forgotten and the walls of the restaurant would fall away and his guests would be in Hudson Bay or the South Pacific or India. But not his own guests only. Conversation at tables within earshot would cease. Everybody would be listening, leaning nearer, those hard of hearing cupping their ears. Even the waiters stopped waiting. They hovered round listening, not wanting to miss the end of a story. And of course it was inevitable that several people would gravitate later to Flaherty's own table; and equally inevitable that Flaherty would insist on paying the final bill.

This sort of entertainment was meat and drink to Flaherty as a person, but it had only a postponing effect on his film work.[1] It eased the creative pressure, which in a film had to build almost to bursting point.

If Flaherty had been a film-producer, in the way that a battery-hen has to be an egg-producer, this tendency to evade producing films as long as possible, would have been very reprehensible. In any socially regimented society he would have been constantly in trouble. The Soviet Union which gave Eisenstein a fairly long break would have sent Flaherty to the salt-mines very soon.

Considering his temperament and the time at which he lived, I cannot imagine Flaherty producing many more films than he did. If he had made more films, they would have been less lasting.

I think that he was spiritually a very lazy man. He avoided feeling new things as long as he could. The various retreats which his wife found for him were unwilling, but necessary refuges. A more disciplined man would have drawn aside to think what his next steps should be. But while he had a dollar left of his own, he kept on hoping that something would turn up to postpone the need for thought.

Frances Flaherty, with her small private income and her inflexible puritan standards, played in his life an unenviable, but key, role. She had to get him back to her home, not merely to prevent financial disaster but also to build up the creative thought and energy for the next film. It was an invidious position because Flaherty was constantly trying to escape and to his drinking friends she appeared as a disapproving chatelaine.

But there is no doubt that her inflexibility gave Flaherty the polarity he needed. Without it, he would have talked himself out in the Coffee

[1] Charles Dickens had a similar duality. His acting and his readings produced an immediate effect which he found far more satisfying than his writing; and he killed himself through its over-indulgence.

House and Little French Club to become a legendary figure as fragile as Oliver St. John Gogarty.

John Grierson says that Flaherty had no knowledge of governance. In truth Frances Flaherty was his governance; the grim knowledge that when he was broke he had to go back to dependence, the wonderful certainty that when he was broke there was something to go back to. Those periods which some people lament as waste of creative time – especially the gap between the destruction of the Belcher Island footage and the making of *Nanook of the North* and the gap between *The Land* and the making of *Louisiana Story* – were probably the most creative periods of his life internally.

Mrs. Flaherty since her husband's death has become interested in Zen Buddhism. Flaherty, she says, is what Zen Buddhists would consider a Master.

I think she is right to the extent that Flaherty as a film-maker and as a story-teller belonged to those who are not concerned with the trivial things of Western civilization. But I don't think that his inspiration came from the mystics of the East. His story-telling belongs to the passage of the long nights in the winter arctic, when the same tale is told over and over again, but the content is less important than the manner. I have asked a number of people if they got bored at the repetition of the same story. I haven't found a person who did. It was like listening to the performance of a piece of music.

The recordings preserved in the archives of the B. B. C. capture little of the magic of his gift, which was in a literal sense a giving out to other people. Oliver St. John Gogarty observed that if you spent an hour in most people's company, you felt drained of life-blood; but with Flaherty, you felt as if you had had a transfusion. And Clare Lawson Dick, who with her family saw much of the Flahertys when they were in England after *Louisiana Story*, put it still more positively.

The Lawson Dicks and the Flahertys had arranged one afternoon to go to see *Bicycle Thieves*, but when they got to the cinema it was full and they had to kill three hours till the next performance. 'With anyone else that would have been sheer agony,' she said, 'but with Flaherty, it was sheer delight.'

She told me also that when he returned to the United States, Flaherty found that he had a few minutes at London Airport before the plane left and he tried to call her at the B.B.C. 'I shall never forgive myself,' she said. 'I wasn't in my office and I never heard his voice again.'

At that time Flaherty was in his sixties and Miss Lawson Dick was a young woman in her twenties; but she did not feel that he was an old man. The effulgence of his personality shone out, making other people seem dim.

Effulgence is the key-word. He was like a light shining, his power raised by the people he met. He did not have enemies, apart from the monstrous caricatures of the tycoons who had let him down. There were some people for whom he had little use, small, mean-minded men. But for most people, he just shone.

This is the reason why when one talks to people who knew him, very little emerges which is precise. There were the stories, the same stories snowballing over the years; there was the generosity, the thoughtfulness, the courtesy, the distaste of anything sexually shabby or psychologically perverse. What can one say of a light, except that it shines?

There must have been an intimate personality or rather personalities. Frances Flaherty, though less prominent, is a great person in her own right. Their private life with its quarrels and reconciliations, its conflicts and harmonies remained discreetly private. He never discussed his private affairs. At the same time the most voluble and the most reticent of men, he had the chivalry of a 'very parfit knight'. It is not within my scope to try to penetrate that reticence or to explore the complications of paternity. It must have been difficult for Flaherty to combine this wandering life with the duties of fatherhood; and equally difficult for his daughters to grow up under the shadow of a fabulous public figure. But it is the public figure which is important for this study, not the private man with his despairs and the lonely despondence which follows social elation.

The effect of Flaherty as a film-maker was as pronounced and vague as was his effect as a person. John Huston says that he and John Ford and William Wyler and Billy Wilder were all profoundly influenced by Flaherty. But how is a different matter. 'Flaherty was not the type of artist we can consider as the teacher,' said Jean Renoir. 'There will be no Flaherty School. Many people will try to imitate him, but they won't succeed; he had no system. His system was just to love the world, to love humanity, to love animals, and love is something you cannot teach.'

Love cannot be taught. But it can be experienced. Flaherty's films are not just moving pictures. They are experiences, similar in a geographical sense to visiting Paris or Rome or seeing the dawn rise over the Sinai desert. Flaherty is a country, which having once seen one never forgets.

But though one thinks of the places in which he filmed, Hudson Bay, Samoa, the Aran Islands, India, the United States, the Flaherty Country is of the mind, as charactertistic in its climate as the Kafka Continent, Graham Greeneland or Dostoevskigrad. The Flaherty Country is one where all conflict is externalized. Nature is so savage in its elemental force that men must work together if they are to survive; hunger, a blizzard, a break in the ice or shipwreck may any moment bring death, so we must live purely under the shadow of eternity.

The Flaherty world was distasteful to many people, because its symbols belonged not to the proud world of modern science in which Nature, licked, was on the run and Everyman was master of his fate and captain of his soul, with the assistance of a good psycho-analyst or a plentiful supply of tranquillisers. Flaherty showed an unfashionable sanity in a world nursing its neuroses and gastric ulcers as signs of sensitivity. He had the childish tactlessness of the little boy in Hans Andersen who pointed out that the King was wearing no clothes.

It is interesting that though documentary film technicians pay a direct tribute to what Flaherty taught them about how to look through a camera, the feature-film men think of him as a writer. Orson Welles said Flaherty reminded him of Nathaniel Hawthorne or Thoreau; a strange selection, when Herman Melville lay so much closer at hand. Like Melville, Flaherty had always the sense of the individual embodying some universal principle.

Why Flaherty succeeded but also failed as an artist was because he himself was the symbol of light, of goodness. He moved in a climate

[1] Huston's and Renoir's reminiscences were recorded for the B.B.C.'s *Portrait of Flaherty*, but not used in the programme broadcast. The full recordings are in the Museum of Modern Art, New York.

of love and he could not admit human evil into his world. There is no villain in his world except the natural elements. For him there was no Fall in the Garden of Eden. The expulsion would have been caused by a late frost and an attack of eel-worm and aphids. Subjective good and evil were evaded. His moral judgements stopped short at the end of the Creation. There was no Fall and no Redemption; no relentless Nemesis, no Hybris, no Furies. By some magical short cut, in a climate of elemental violence, the Garden of Eden could be found again – or reconstructed.

It is this which is his legacy to the world at large, a legacy not specifically filmic. In their different ways, both Giotto and Botticelli had this vision. So had Gaudier-Breszka almost always; and at their best D. H. Lawrence and Dylan Thomas. But it is not an entirely artistic vision. St. Francis of Assisi also had it.

I do not mean that there is any resemblance between all these and Flaherty on a superficial level; at that level they were as different from him as from one another. Yet they spring from the same soil; they exist, despite specific differences, in the same climate.

But there was also an indefinable film vision, which was transmitted not merely to Basil Wright and others who had had the benefit of working with Flaherty. Though Jean Renoir was quite right to say that Flaherty was not the sort of master to create a school (because he was technically always ill-equipped), he was the sort of cameraman-director to influence the vision of those who came after him as profoundly as Cézanne, Van Gogh and Picasso have influenced painters of today who are not conscious of any derivation. Bert Haanstra, Satyajit Ray, Rouquier and Sücksdorf, for example, are influenced by Robert Flaherty not directly as disciples but indirectly because their ways of using the camera are suggested by Flaherty's way.

This is the fashion in which an artistic tradition is made, in the Platonic metaphor of the relay race. 'Having torches, they pass them on to others.' The bearer possesses it as *his* torch the moment that he grasps it.

And this, I am sure, is the way that Flaherty would have wished it to be. He was the least pompous of men. The idea that anyone should sedulously imitate his methods would have filled him with horror.

But the thought that anything he had done might inspire, as it still does, someone else to go out and do something quite different would have delighted him. After all, that is in the true tradition; to tread for the first time a path never previously trodden, to discover a territory unknown or record a way of life about to sink into an oblivion.

APPENDICES

Appendices by Paul Rotha and Basil Wright

Appendix 1

NANOOK OF THE NORTH

It is a very simple picture. The sub-titles, written by Carl Stearns Clancy, inform the audience that the film was made at Hopewell Sound, Northern Ungava. Nanook, the hunter, and his family emerge from their kayak in surprising numbers. They use moss for fuel. They carry a large boat down to the water. (The launching is not shown.) They go to a trading post. Nanook kills a polar-bear with only his harpoon. He hangs out his fox- and bear-skins which are bartered for beads and knives. (The exterior of the trading-post is seen in the distance only.) In the post Nanook plays the old gramophone and tries to bite the record. One child is given castor oil and swallows it with relish.

Nanook then goes off on floating ice to catch fish, using two bits of ivory as bait on a seal-string line. He spears salmon with a trident and kills them with his teeth. News comes that walrus have been found. Nanook joins other hunters in a fleet of kayaks. They meet rough seas. The walrus are sighted. Nanook harpoons one and after a terrific struggle it is hauled ashore. The walrus weighs two tons. The hunters kill it and carve it up and begin eating it on the spot, using ivory knives. (The flesh is seen in close-up.)

Winter sets in. A blizzard envelops the trading-post. Nanook goes hunting with his family. The dog-team drags the sledge with difficulty over rough ice-crags. Nanook stalks and traps a white fox.

Nanook builds an igloo, carving it from blocks of frozen snow with his walrus-ivory knife, licking the blade so that it will freeze to make a cutting edge.

His children play slides. One has a miniature sledge. Everyone is gay and smiling.

With great care and skill Nanook makes the window for the igloo out of a block of ice and fixes a wedge of snow to reflect the light through the window. The family furnishes the igloo with their scanty treasures and then Nanook teaches his small son to use a bow and arrow to kill a small bear made from snow.

Morning. The family wakes. Nanook's wife, Nyla, chews his boots to soften the leather while Nanook rubs his bare toes. Then he eats his breakfast, smiling. Nyla washes the baby with her saliva. They prepare to set off for the seal-grounds, glazing the runners of the sledge with ice. Before they depart, there is savage scrapping among the dogs.

Nanook finds a breathing hole in the ice. Down it he thrusts his spear. There is a long struggle between Nanook hauling on his line and the seal under the ice. Nanook loses his balance and falls head over heels, but other members of the family come to the rescue and help Nanook haul the seal out. (The seal, as critics noticed, is very dead.) They cut it up and throw scraps to the dogs. In their fight over them, the dogs tangle their traces and so the departure for home is delayed.

They are forced to take refuge in a deserted igloo. The snow drifts up and the dogs, covered, become scarcely visible. But some small pups are given a little igloo kennel, specially made for them. Nanook and his family bed down naked inside their furs and hide sleeping-bags. Outside the blizzard rages but within Nanook is seen (in close-up) fast asleep.

Appendix 2

MOANA

Moana opens with a sequence reminiscent of *Nanook*, but shown in greater detail with many more individual shots. The camera tilts down from the sky through luxuriant foliage to reveal Fa'angase. A little boy, Pe'a (Flying Fox), is there too. Moana himself is pulling *taro* roots.

They move off to the village, carrying the food they have gathered. A trap is set for a wild boar. The village of Safune is introduced by a lovely vista shot. A boar has been caught in the trap and there is a struggle to catch and tie it up. Everyone returns to the village.

A fishing sequence follows, starting with the launching of a canoe. Fish are seen under crystal-clear water. Some are speared. Fa'angase finds a giant clam. Everyone is gay and carefree.

In the quiet of the village, the mother, Tu'ungaita, is making bark-cloth. The whole process is shown in great detail (with much use of close-ups). Finally the cloth is ready to be used as a *lava-lava*.

Pe'a twists a rope-ring, which he uses as a grip for his feet to climb a coconut tree. The camera slowly tilts up as he climbs higher and higher until he reaches the fruits in the soaring top. He twists them off and throws them down.

Sea breaks over the reef into the lagoon, white spume shooting up through blow-holes. Moana, his elder brother Leupenga and young Pe'a breast the waves in their out-rigger canoe. The canoe is swamped and the brothers swim in the sea. They go fishing along the rocky shore, the waves breaking over them.

Among the rocks the little boy is searching intently. He rubs two sticks together and makes a fire of coconut husks. A big mystery is created out of what he is trying to catch. It turns out to be a giant robber-crab.

There follows a turtle-hunt. A turtle is speared and after a hard struggle it is hauled into the canoe. When they reach shore Moana drills a hole in the turtle's shell and tethers it to a tree. Fa'angase strokes it like a pet.

Back in the village, Tu'ungaita is preparing a meal with great care, Coconuts are shredded, breadfruit made ready and strange foods. wrapped in palm leaves, are baked in an oven of hot stones. All is shown in detail (with big close-ups).

Moana is now anointed with oil in preparation for his ornate dressing for the *siva* dance. He and his betrothed, Fa'angase, perform their dance, the camera concentrating almost wholly on the boy, following his beautiful rhythmic movements.

The villagers gather for the ceremonial of the tattoo. The old *tufunga* (tattooer) makes ready. A long sequence shows the gradual tattooing of Moana, the tap-tapping of the needle points, the rubbing in of the dye, sweat being wiped away from the boy's brow, his mother fanning him with a palm-leaf while the *tufunga* works with grave, impassive face.

Meanwhile, the ritual of making the *kava* goes on. When made, the coconut shell from which it is drunk is passed by the chiefs from hand to hand in order of precedence. The people of Safune are now in full dance with their *siva*. The sun is sinking. The dancing gets faster and faster.

Inside their hut, the camera pans from Moana's parents across to Pe'a, who is asleep. Tu'ungaita covers him tenderly with a *tapa* cloth.

Outside Moana and Fa'angase dance their betrothal dance as the sun sinks behind the mountains.

Appendix 3

MAN OF ARAN

In form, *Man of Aran* follows closely the formula of *Nanook* and *Moana*. It opens as they did by establishing the family. The boy, Mikeleen, is discovered searching in a rock-pool. Maggie, his mother, is in their cottage at a cradle. The sea breaks in on the rocky shore. Maggie goes out on to the cliff-top and is joined by Mikeleen and they watch the curragh, with Tiger King and his crew, trying to make the run in to the shore. After a terrific struggle, the curragh is half-wrecked but the men get ashore. They all but lose their net but Maggie saves it. Thus right in the first sequence the ferocity of the sea and the islanders fight against it is made clear.

A title tells us how the people are dependent on what potatoes they can grow and how they scrape together the soil and seaweed for them to grow in. Tiger is seen breaking up rocks, while Maggie gathers seaweed. Tiger then patches and caulks his battered curragh. Mikeleen is up on the cliff-top fishing with a line which he holds between his toes. Suddenly he sees something down below and begins to scramble down the cliff. It turns out that he has spotted a basking-shark. A title tells us about the sharks – that they are the biggest fish found in the Atlantic. Then follows a sequence of the men in their curraghs harpooning the sharks in a comparatively calm sea. At the same time, we see Maggie and Mikeleen in the cottage. Night falls.

The struggle with the sharks goes on for two days. The oil from their livers is wanted for the lamps in the houses. The men put to sea again, which is now rougher. Maggie and Mikeleen watch from the cliffs. Other islanders appear on the shore. A big iron cauldron is rolled along the cliff. A peat fire is made beneath it. On shore a shark is cut up. Maggie stirs the cauldron. Night falls again. The boy and the animals – a lamb and a setter dog – are asleep.

Next day Maggie is carrying a heavy load of seaweed on her back along the cliffs. A ferocious sea has arisen. They catch sight of the curragh fighting its way back through giant waves towards a landing. As in the opening, there is a tremendous battle between the men and the sea before they finally get to shore. The curragh is lost but Tiger saves his harpoon and lines. The film ends with the family – Tiger, Maggie and Mikeleen – staring out at the wrath of the sea – their eternal enemy.

Appendix 4

THE LAND

The film begins with a title as stipulated and worded by the U.S. Department of Agriculture.

FOREWORD

> The strength that is America comes from the land. Our mighty war effort is the product of its land and people. Land: our soil, our minerals, our forests, our water-power. People: their skills, their inventiveness, their resourcefulness, their education, their health. Land and people, in war or in peace, this is our national wealth.
>
> This is the story of how rural America used machines to achieve an unbelievable production – but at a terrible cost to land and to people through the wastes of erosion and poverty; the story of the beginnings of reconstruction, and the hope of a world of freedom and abundance through the workings of a democracy and through man's mastery of his own machines.

From then on, and for the only time in all the films of Robert Flaherty, words matter a great deal to the film. Instead, therefore, of synopsizing the contents of *The Land* – as has been done with previous films – we believe that a fairer idea of the picture will be given if we alternate passages of the narration with brief descriptions of the pictures they accompany.[1]

The film opens with a farmer, his wife and child, strolling around their fine old stone farmhouse, built to last centuries, with roomy great barns and outhouses: rich country, rich grazing, rich crops.

It takes good land to raise a house like this.
It takes good farming
To have full bins.

Good people,
Of the solid old stock
That settled in this country
Three hundred years ago.
They built their houses to last forever.

In the same part of the country, beautiful but derelict farmhouses, desolate and discarded: crumbling old walls.

But even here,
In this rich state of Pennsylvania,
Which has some of the best farms and farmers in the country,
Trouble has crept in.

In the distance men walk across eroded land: the worn-out soil and farmers staring at it. Elsewhere, people wait in the shade, waiting for surplus food. Then to a meeting of farmers; they are discussing their many problems. Close-ups of their anxious, worried faces as they talk or listen.

All over the country there has been trouble.
Farmers meet and talk it over,
Talk over the deep problems of the land,
And the people —
Problems that no longer can any one man solve alone.

[1] The narration is the final version as supplied by the Robert Flaherty Foundation, by whose permission and that of the author, Russell Lord, it is printed. A first draft was published in Mr. Lord's book, *Forever the Land* (Harper & Bros. New York, 1950, pp. 29–36). Our descriptions of the visuals are made from our own screenings of the film checked against the final recording-script kindly loaned by Miss van Dongen.

Big storm clouds in a black sky, the countryside darkened by cloud shadows. Fields with furrows made by trickling water. Rushing water meeting more rushing water: together they make a torrential stream. The soil is washed away – and so erosion starts.

It is amazing what the wash of rain can do!

From Pennsylvania to Tennessee. Tremendous areas of eroded hill-sides, scarred and pitted by rushing water. Deep gullies and torn soil with the scabs of topsoil wearing off.

Tall trees grew here once,
And grass as high as a man.

A once lovely farm now surrounded by eroded land with patches of cotton. From the bare tree-roots, the soil has been washed away. Stranded fence-posts stick up from the desolate landscape. Negroes pick cotton. Then scenes of the dilapidated shacks of share-croppers. A sign reads: 'Prepare to Meet Thy God.' A Negro mother and her children stare at us from a field – hollow-eyed. And more vistas of barren, eroded land.

We found this in Tennessee,
But you can find it,
In greater or less degree,
In every state.
These devastated, sod-like patches of soil
Contain the vital elements
Upon which all life depends.

Old southern mansions, once so wealthy and so beautiful, are now only beautiful in their decay. Built to last for generations, now share-croppers live here. The sad, staring face of a share-cropper young girl haunts our memory; she looks half-witted standing idly beside a crumbling pillar. Another skull of an old mansion on the bleak hill-side.

It is here, in the old Cotton South,
Where our great Southern culture grew up,
Grew up on this land
Which was once so rich and beautiful,

Once so marvellous for its vigour;
But a culture that grew up on two great soil-wasting crops —
Tobacco, Cotton;
And the land, year after year,
And generation after generation,
Was beaten.
It is here that we see what erosion,
What the loss of the soil can do!
When soil fails, life fails.

The decayed ruins of what was once a fine old mansion. Spanish moss blows gently in the wind. Slowly the tall doors of the house are opened. An old, old Negro comes out. He walks across the hen-pecked forecourt and approaches an old plantation bell. He dusts the bell and slowly touches the clapper to its side. He looks around questioningly.

In one ruin of a house
We came upon an old Negro
Who lived there alone,
Along with the rats.
He didn't seem to know we were there.

No answer comes from the decayed, deserted mansion. Only the Spanish moss blows. Only a skinny chicken pecks on the pillared porch. The old Negro, murmuring to himself, climbs down from the bell. Slowly he retraces his steps to the mansion. He stops and looks round. The Spanish moss blows. The old Negro goes into the house, turns around and very slowly closes the doors.

'Where are they all gone?' he mutters.
'Where are they all gone?'

Oklahoma – flat, dry, barren land. The dust-bowl. Blowing dust and fine sand pile up against a tent and car. Tumbleweed capers away in a whirlwind of dust. A great vista spreads out—the Arkansas River.

A thousand miles west.
Here, spread over forty thousand square miles
Of our Great Plains

Is probably the most spectacular,
The most sudden, incredible erosion
This country ever had.

Millions of tons of topsoil
Blown away —
Three hundred million tons in a single storm!
Farm after farm blown into the sky.
And more farms,
More hundreds of thousands of tons,
Washed into our great rivers —
Washed, as here, into the fifteen-hundred-mile-long Arkansas,
Boats steamed up and down this river
Seventy years ago.
You can almost walk across it now.

Desert land with bashed wire-fences. Black naked land, streaked with erosion white. Cows scrubble for food in the far distance. And more dilapidated houses, on the verge of collapse, stand isolated in the barren landscape.

But the most sinister erosion,
Because it cannot be seen,
Is sheet erosion.
The gradual wasting, grain by grain,
Of nearly half of all our cultivated land.

Wasted land,
Wasted rivers.
Nowhere in the world
Has the drama of soil destruction
Been played so swiftly
And on so great a stage.

We enter along the main street into a deserted ghost-town. Shacks lean crazily sideways. Broken-down wagons and rusting machinery stand by derelict sheds. A starving cow, its bones sticking out of its hide, its eyes rimmed with black, crops at the stunted bush. It can hardly drag one leg after another.

We came to a town that cotton farmers founded
Not so many years ago.
'Go Forth,' they called it,
'Go Forth, Texas'
It died with the soil,
It died with the sort of farming
That kills the soil.

Three migrants, an old man, his wife and a young man, squat around a fire, trying to warm themselves in the early dawn. They are just passing through. Their car-trailer, looking like an old covered-wagon, has a chair tied on the back. The old woman's face is pitted with poverty. The starving cow stops to stare at us; then it hobbles away.

At the edge of the town
We came upon a scene
That is part and parcel of eroded land —
Migrants – landless, homeless people.

They had fire – but no food.

A recapitulation of the beginnings of erosion. A tiny trickling stream gradually gets bigger until it cuts through its banks. Gullies are formed and eventually the hill-sides are eroded. Billboards are erected on the useless dustbowl land – advertising this, selling that – but to whom? Migrants have no money. And over all, and all the time, the fine dust blows —

Once a soil begins to go, it is hard to stop it.
In three hundred years
We conquered a continent
And became the richest nation in the world.
But our soil we squandered,
Squandered at such a rate
That in less than a century,
If we go on as we have in the past,
The days of this nation's strength will be numbered.
'If my land cry out against me,
Or that the furrows thereof likewise complain,

Let thistles grow instead of wheat,
And cockle instead of barley.'
Job said this, more than two thousand years ago.

Encampment of migrants beside the road – with bleak tired faces and hollow eyes. Some of them look up at us, as if they are animals being stared at: and then they look away. A mother prepares food for a girl sleeping under a tent attached to a battered Model T Ford. A thin little girl moves her hand in her sleep. Families living on wheels – in broken-down cars and old trailers. The Wilder family of eight – seven of them children . . . live in this old trailer. Their Ford is completely collapsed. A little ragged boy stirs beans in a pot and upsets them. A little blonde girl chews gum. Another little boy has his arm in a sling. Their father sits on an upturned box absently smoking a cigarette. They have no mother. They have been living this way – 'on wheels' – for six years.

A family of eight lives in this box of a trailer.
Some of them were born in it,
Born on the road.
They make the best of it.
Work is what they want – *any kind of work.*

Along our highways
There are more than a million
Homeless people.

Outside a cabin, a man leads horses drawing a wagon. Another man crouches in the shade, watching. A third man leans against a tree, watching. The father begins to load the wagon with bits and pieces of furniture from the cabin. Their Ford has broken down for good. The mother nurses a baby. A little boy plays with a scooter. When the wagon is loaded and the family has clambered on to it, the father takes the reins. For a moment he looks back to what was their home, from which they have been evicted. They couldn't pay the rent any more. The wagon drives away. The cabin-door stands open. The Model T stands derelict. A broken chair and a doll are in a corner of one of the rooms. The wagon disappears into the distance. The man leaning against the tree stares after it.[1]

[1] Perhaps one of the most moving and beautiful sequences ever shot by Flaherty. – P.R.

We came to this family moving out:
The land has played out on him, he said.

Most of the migrants are gay young people,
With young children.

We had another name for these people once;
We called them pioneers.
Heading West —
That's where most of them go.

Great vistas of empty desert, with low hills on the horizon. A few stunted cactus. A solitary steer. A distant train sends out a plume of smoke across the sky. A big mountain stands across the valley. Twisted trees stand up from a plain.

America! The New World!
Three hundred years ago
This cry rang through Europe
To lift the hearts of the defeated,
The persecuted, the dispossessed.
A new world,
A new chance to live!

Migrants fill up their Ford roadster with water from a ditch. Three of them are packed in front. Two girls are in the rumble-seat. Their licence-plate says they are from Oklahoma. A mattress is on the car's roof, and a tractor behind. Another car with O.K. daubed on it drives away. The trees and fields pass by. Now they are big, rich, irrigated fields belonging to big Corporations. Many cars and trailers, most of them at breakdown point, jampack the dirt roads.

Arizona!
Forty-niners who passed through this country
Couldn't see how even a coyote could live in it —
No water.
But engineers came in not so long ago.
'We'll get more gold out of this country,' they said.
'Than the forty-niners ever dreamed of.'

They went into the mountains,
Built dams, and impounded it . . .
Great reservoirs of water!
Water, and sun that never fails —
Four crops a year!

A roadside fruit-stand, with prices showing how cheap is the fruit. Empty baskets and idle boys are at the edge of a vegetable-field. Groups of migrants on the roadside by the fields look for work, too. Men and women, young boys and girls. A bunch of men play dice. A man leans against an auto. A variety of licence-plates shows where they have come from. Not one State, but many.

Fruit – a box-full for the price of a dozen!
On they come
From almost every State.
A hundred men for every job.
They come to fields like these,
So rich, such is the magic of irrigation,
There is no end to the bounty they produce.

In a richly-irrigated lettuce field, Mexicans bend and swiftly cut lettuces, throwing them up into waiting trucks that move with them down the long rows.

But they go to the lettuce fields
And what do they find?
Filipinos and Mexicans do the work,
For the work is hard, and Filipinos and Mexicans are strong
And can do it better.

In the packing-sheds, lettuces go through the crating-machine. Hands pluck them off the ever-moving belt. The work is monotonous and hard.

In the sheds —
They might find a job there – packing.
But whether it's in the sheds or in the fields,
It's like a machine —
An endless belt.

Vast carrot-fields, with whole families of Mexicans picking at great speed. One man watches them: he wears a hip-pistol. He bootlegs them across the border. Children carry empty baskets back. More children stagger under baskets loaded with carrots and beans.

Down on the Rio Grande,
On the Mexican border,
Mexicans mostly do the work,
Many of them children.
Their pay is forty cents.
Good pay for a day
Down on the Rio Grande.

In the broccoli-fields, women and girls cut and tie broccoli at feverish speed. Men carry the full crates to a wagon drawn by horses. Hundreds of acres of broccoli and armies of pickers.

And here
Women get the work,
And glad they are to get it —
Lucky to get a day, two day's, work a week.
Women who had land and a roof to cover them once.

Thousands upon thousands on the move
From field to field —
One of the greatest migrations
In all the history of this restless country.

A migrant camp in the heart of a town. Children rummage in the garbage. Tents, trash and the inevitable broken-down autos. Inside one of the tents, an old woman is sewing. She looks down at her little son sleeping in a cot. He is emaciated. His hands move restlessly in his sleep. The woman leans over and strokes his forehead. Then she looks up at us.

'He thinks he's picking peas,' she said.
His hands keep moving
Even in his sleep.

Arizona cotton-fields. A tent-town at the edge of the fields. An empty truck is driven up. Men crowd together towards it. They clamber up over its sides. The fields are so huge that the pickers have to be transported to them. The men stand in the truck and stare at us. Indians, Negroes, Mexicans, Whites. . . . One Negro smiles at us. The loaded truck drives off.

But erosion alone
Is not the cause of all our driven people.
There are other forces at work,
And one, especially,
Much more powerful.
They come for the chopping,
Come for the picking,
Come by the thousands.
The cotton-pickers in our country
Number millions.
More migrants depend on cotton
Than on any other crop.

A new kind of cotton-picking machine noses its way through a cotton-field. It comes up close and passes us, the cotton dropping into the machine's basket. Sinister and robot-like, with only a single driver, one man.

But more powerful than all these millions
Is the machine.
It can pick more cotton in twenty minutes
Than a human hand can pick in two days.
It doesn't pick quite clean enough yet;
It is being perfected.
But who can tell?
One day it may be picking
Every boll of cotton in the world.

An angle-dozer uproots huge tree-stumps with effortless ease. A woman and two children come out of a house to watch the angle-dozer push aside two great boulders as if they were toys. Tree-tops shiver as the angle-dozer appears. The trees crash on to us and are pushed away by the giant-machine. Nothing can stand in its way it seems.

An acre cleared in an hour —
That's how fast it goes.
The man who drives it owns it.
He clears his neighbours' farms with it —
Charges five dollars an hour —
Clears anything you like.

Multiply this monster by ten thousand —
Take it to some new state in the world.
With such an army
You could clear the ground for a great new country
In no time at all!

A truck deposits empty boxes in a carrot-field. A carrot-picking machine pulls up the carrots like a zipper. Filipinos, Negroes, a young white girl, tie them into bundles.

Even for little things
There are now machines.
All they have to do is tie them up.

A grizzled old man – a farmer from Kentucky – stares at us with faraway eyes.

'I ain't had a piece of land for twenty years,' he said.
He told us he was a mountain man
From the Cumberland Mountains.

Scenes of the mountains: a hill-side with wheat-fields and the old man's farmhouse. Beautiful animals about the farm – shining horses and a donkey, a rooster and some fat chickens, a gleaming calf, a white horse rolling on the lush meadowland.

'Some of that country is just the same
As it was two hundred years ago.
The old farm's still there.
My great grandfather built the house;
Had everything a farm ought to have,
Everything a man needed.'

An old-time river steamboat, an old-time waterwheel. A man pressing sugar-cane and then boiling it for molasses. Finally, a lovely vista of a smiling and serene valley, a wheat-field with heads of wheat against the sky.

Stern-wheelers still runnin'
Up and down the river;
Grist mills still grindin'.
It's just an old-time country
With old-time ways.

The scene dissolves back to the carrot-field. A girl is listening, a Negro smokes a cigarette, the eyes of the old Kentucky farmer are dim with tears.

'I wake up nights sometimes
From dreamin' about it
And wishin' I was there.'

In rich Iowa, the fields are filled with crops and the barns are stacked with corn. There are fine fat cattle and hogs. A group of plump bulls turn their heads to look at us. A man ploughs with a team of horses. A hay-wagon draws up at a barn. The hay is hoisted in. A team of eight horses stands in a field. Other teams are ploughing. And then a small tractor skirts the edge of a field.

This is Iowa.
Nowhere is there better land.
Good cattle, well fed.
Good homes,
Good farms.

But even here in this rich state
There is trouble.
For years farmers have been struggling
With prices too low
To pay for the things they have to buy.
It's been hard for them
To make both ends meet,
To clothe and educate the children,
To pay taxes, to meet the notes at the bank.

Here and everywhere,
So many don't own their homes any more,
Nor the land either.
Almost fifty per cent now are tenants,
Living in other men's houses,
Working other men's land.

Horses were working all over the country
Not so long ago.
An area as large as England
Grew feed for them.

But that market is gone,
For today the feed is gasoline
For a machine.

A huge cornfield. Above the high corn in the distance is seen just the head of a corn-picker advancing towards us. It approaches like some monster through the corn until it is revealed in full as it passes close by us – a picker and husker combined – driven by one man. Its metal head is reared up like some pterodactyl as it goes relentlessly through the high corn-stalks.

And now this machine has come in —
The corn-picker.
You don't see many people in these fields any more,
Even at harvest time.

First, cascades of pouring grain. Then row upon row of advancing giant combine-harvesters. Great armies of wheat-machines.[1] Close-ups of grain streaming from a machine-spout into a truck. A glistening boy shovelling to keep the funnel clear for the flowing grain. The corn-picker again mowing through the corn-field: the giant harvesters on the vast plains – they vie with each other for speed and efficiency in the rich Middle-West.

Out in these wheat-fields farther west
You don't see many people either.

[1] These were stock shots, the only ones used in the film.

Thousands upon thousands
Only a few years ago
Harvested wheat.
Thousands more
Harvested corn.

People are waiting sullenly in the shade – waiting for surplus commidity food to be doled out to them at government relief-points. A woman drags away a bag of food. Others carry away bundles. They stand waiting in groups – with hangdog expressions. A girl has her arm round her brother. A starving woman squints at us – the sun in her resentful eyes: her hollow cheeks are black shadows, her expression is agonized, never to be forgotten. . . .

And here they are, some of them,
Crumbs of the machine.
A lame man who had walked in four miles on crutches
Said to us,
'I don't know what some of us would do
If it weren't for the food
The government gives us.'

Tall grain elevators reach up to the sky. A Great Lake wheat-barge, with its full belly, moves on the water. Cascades of grain are sprayed into a waiting ship. Men work in the grain up to their waists. Boats are tugged in the river. Grain-ships head into open water. The giant grain-elevators stand in ranks. Everywhere grain flows in abundance. Out in the fields the rows of wheat-machines advance towards us again. Locomotives puff past the elevators pulling wheat-laden trains. Grain pours down shutes into more grain-filled ships, boats and barges. Abundance is rife . . . until suddenly . . . a group of four ragged, emaciated children stare at us accusingly with black-rimmed eyes. Then two others . . . silent, accusing. . . .

The yield of fifteen thousand acres of wheat
In a single cargo —
The yield of armies of machines.
During the First World War

We started bringing these machines
Out of the wheat-fields;
And we fed the world.

They drown like rats in a vat, sometimes,
These men trimming the cargoes of wheat.
The farmers themselves
Have been drowned by this abundance.

More pouring wheat and then grain rising up moving elevators into an 'ever-normal' granary, its aluminum shining in the sun. Row upon row of these cylindrical granaries with grain being fed up into them.

To save themselves, our farmers
Have developed a nationwise system of granaries
To store the surplus of their important crops —
Their wheat, their corn, their cotton.
It was the only way
They could release their markets,
The only way they could carry on.
It is called the 'Ever-normal Granary' —
A vast reserve
Which now gives us tremendous strength;
For in the disrupted world we face,
It is vital as a weapon for our defence.

Here is the Ever-normal Granary
Of the Corn Belt —
In every township,
In every county,
Bins like these
Filled with corn.

A shepherd and his dog. The old man wipes his forehead and opens his collar. A flock of white sheep moves across a large valley. A great river of sheep flows over a hill-side. A cowhand on a beautiful horse watches a far-away moving herd of cattle. Snowcapped mountains are in the far distance. Other men on horses ride behind the cattle on the plain. Beef on the hoof. Then grain-boats on the river again. Trains shunting in the yards. Wheat-machines on the far horizon of the wheat-fields.

Abundance in the mountains —
Abundance on the ranges.
We have everything a nation ought to have,
Everything a nation needs.
We have the open strength,
We have the hidden strength,
Not only for today and for tomorrow,
But for the centuries of the nation.

A white horse is ploughing contours in a field. Two tractors are ploughing contours round a hill-side. A group of farmers discuss the contour-ploughing. The contours grow bigger and wider, eating into the fields. From the air, we can see the patterns made by different crops planted in the contours. A whole landscape is now streaked with curving bands.

A change has come over the land
In the last few years.
Farmers are turning to a new way
Of working it.
A new pattern —
New furrow lines,
New terrace lines,
To hold the rain where it falls
To prevent it from falling into torrents.
It is a pattern
That will always hold the soil,
No matter what the slash of wind
Or the wash of rain.
Fields enriched with clover turned under,
Enriched with lime,
With phosphate —
Enriched for the hearts and minds and bones
Of our children
And our children's children.
It is a new design.

We are now back at the farmers' meeting in Pennsylvania where we were near the opening. A farmer is talking about the new methods of contour-ploughing: others listen. Some nod their assent. Others join in the speaking. The farmer seen in the opening sequence listens. And finally there is a big vista of contour-ploughed land in Texas.

The farmers talk it over.
It looks practical,
It *is* practical.
Six million farmers,
Six million strong,
Are beginning to farm together,
To think together,
To act together.

We see again the stone farmhouse in Pennsylvania. Our farmer and his wife are looking over their land, talking with each other. We see a hill-side of black earth with young plants growing in contour formation. A white horse is busy at the spring planting. Young corn-plants are shooting up. Lastly, a close-up of the farmer and his wife.

Down in the Carolinas,
Up in Oregon,
In New Mexico,
Indiana,
Maine,
In the high North-west,
The Texas plains —
The face of the land made over,
Made strong again.
Made strong for ever.
We are saving the soil.
With our fabulous machines
We can make every last acre of this country strong again.
With machines we can produce food enough
To feed the world.

At the farmers' meeting, our farmer is now speaking. Others listen in thought. Then we see once more the people waiting for the surplus food to be doled out – the hungry, the poor, the displaced. Waiting for food – for work – for help of any and every kind —

> But what about the people?
> These homeless thousands
> Our machines have dispossessed,
> And the thousands more
> Who will struggle on the land.
> When will we find the way,
> Learn to live with the incredible power we have won —
> These miraculous machines?

And now we are back with the great wheat-machines, their blades rotating in the sunlight. Row upon row of them advance across the wide plains, as if nothing can ever halt them. Far up in the summer sky, the pale moon hangs like a ghostly silver disc.

> The strength of man is not great.
> He has not in his arms and back
> The strength of a great machine.
> But man has a mind.
> He can think,
> He can govern,
> He can plan.
> A new world stands before him,
> An abundance beyond his dreams.
> The great fact is the land,
> The land itself,
> And the people,
> And the spirit of the people.

Appendix 5

LOUISIANA STORY

The film opens in a dark, eerie swamp, with strange birds, alligators and many, many fantastic growths. Huge water-lily leaves float on the surface of the *bayous*. Giant cypress trees drape their beard-like streamers of Spanish moss. Everywhere there is dark water, with mysterious bubbles rising to the surface. An alligator glides by smoothly and dangerously. (A narrator's voice spoken by Flaherty himself tells us where we are.)

But there is something else gliding by, too, half-hidden among the hanging Spanish moss and creepers. A *pirogue* – a little slender dug-out canoe – and in it, standing up as he paddles, a boy – skilfully guiding his boat among the giant trees and large floating leaves. He is Alexander Napoleon Ulysses Latour, a Cajun boy of twelve or so, who lives and hunts and roams the Petite Anse *bayou* country in Louisiana. He believes in werewolves with long noses and red eyes; and in mermaids with green hair who swim into these lagoons from the sea. And to protect himself from their evils, he carries a little bag of salt tied to his waist and a mysterious something which he keeps inside his shirt.

A huge water-snake zigzags through the water. An alligator rears its snout. The boy hears something, is worried, and looks around him furtively. Then he smiles. It is only a false alarm. Presently he sees a wild raccoon in the branches of a cypress tree. He calls to it, imitating the noise it makes. Then he leaves the swamp, tying up his canoe. He takes his rusty rifle with him and sets out on a hunting expedition among the tall reeds. He sees something and raises his rifle to take aim. Just as he is about to fire, there is an explosion. Before he has time to think what it can be, he hears another sound and sees a strange amphibious monster, a 'swamp-buggy', on caterpillar treads, climbing up the bank out of the water. It crashes into the reeds close to where he is hiding. The boy is scared. He races back to his *pirogue* and paddles swiftly home.

In a cabin at the edge of the *bayou*, the boy's father, Jean Latour, is talking with a visitor, a stranger. A tale is told and an old Irish song is sung – 'I eat when I'm hungry, I drink when I'm dry —'[1] The boy reaches his home, with its coon skins and enormous alligator-hide hung on the outside wall of the cabin. He stares in wonderment at the stranger's beautiful motor-launch moored to the bank. He goes up to the door of the cabin and listens.

Jean Latour is signing a document the stranger has brought. The stranger is an oil-scout. The paper is an agreement to give the oil company permission to drill for oil on Latour's property. Latour is sceptical about there being any oil but the agreement is signed.

Soon the oil-men arrive and start their operations. Surveys are made. The oil-scout's fast launch sends waves skimming across the water. There are more explosions. Latour hangs out his raccoon-skins, taking little notice of it all. One day the boy is climbing around in the cypress trees, playing with Jo-Jo, his new pet raccoon. Suddenly he looks up. He sees something towering high above the tallest trees. A graceful, slender structure has appeared, its metal girders glinting like silver in the sun. It moves slowly and majestically up the *bayou* towards him. He races to the cabin to tell his father. Finally, the oil derrick comes to rest in the *bayou* not far from Latour's cabin. It's going to probe deep through the water into the earth – two, maybe three miles down.

For some time the boy is too shy to go near the derrick but one day he approaches cautiously in his canoe. Two of the oil-men call out to

[1] The same song, curiously enough, the tinkers sing in *No Resting Place*, although I did not know it at the time. P. R.

him to 'Come aboard'. But he is too scared. After some banter between the boy and the oil-driller and his boiler-man on the derrick, the boy shows them a big catfish he has caught. One of the men says, 'You must have used *some* bait to catch that fellow.' The boy replies, 'It's not the bait. Watch! I show you how to catch a *big* catfish.' He spits on his hook, drops the line and in a moment pulls up a fish, but only a tiny one. The men have a good laugh. The boy refuses their invitation to come aboard and paddles away in his *pirogue*.

One evening, however, he plucks up enough courage to approach the brilliantly lit-up, strange monster, and as he grows close, the reflections of the shining steel derrick flicker and dance on the surface of the lagoon. He hears the strangest sounds he has ever heard in his life coming from within it. Ninety-foot lengths of pipes are being joined end-to-end and driven through the water down into the earth. The boy stealthily climbs aboard. Tom Smith, the driller, calls out. 'Come on over!'

In the deafening noise, the boy goes over fearfully and apprehensively watches the long pipes, one after another, plunging down into the earth. He is struck with wonder at the magic of this monster, but he wants Tom to know that he, too, has some magic. He shows his bag of salt to the driller. But the boy's father has been searching for him and appears on the derrick to scold him. Tom, however, cries out that he's glad to have the boy aboard.

Then we are back again in the cypress swamp. The boy is paddling his *pirogue*; with him is Jo-Jo, his pet coon. The boy is obviously on some errand – something which might be dangerous. And he is keeping an eye and an ear open for his enemies the werewolves, and their accomplices, the alligators. Presently he lands the canoe, ties it up and ties up Jo-Jo too. He goes off into the deep forest, leaving the coon chattering away and fearful, trying to break loose.

An alligator slithers into the water. The boy clutches his bag of salt. He watches the creature disappear, then he stealthily approaches a mound of earth in a clearing. Down on his knees, he scrapes away the earth and reveals some alligator's eggs. He picks one of them up. A baby alligator is breaking out of its shell. He holds it in his hand and is so fascinated by it that he does not see the mother alligator slowly coming out of the water and up the bank towards him. As the alligator lunges at him the boy jumps clear just in time and runs for his life.

When he gets back to his *pirogue*, he finds it empty. Jo-Jo has broken away. The boy goes back into the forest searching everywhere for the coon and calling to him. But all he hears are the birds mocking back at him. With tears in his eyes for the loss of his pet, the boy returns to the *pirogue*. Suddenly, he sees an alligator rushing through the water like a speed-boat towards a large bird standing on a branch in the water. The alligator's jaws snap and the egret is between them. As the boy watched this act of sudden death, he realizes what must have happened to his coon. He makes up his mind to have his revenge.

Out in the water, the boy sets a trap – a hook baited with beef-steak – and then waits half-hidden by leaves at the end of a fifty-foot line attached to the trap. The alligator sees the bait and moves slowly and sinisterly towards it. At last it snatches the bait, the line pulls tight and the fight is on. A fierce tug-of-war takes place between the boy and the alligator. The boy begins to get dragged into the water. He slides farther and farther in through the slime. But his father has heard his cries and the noise of the battle and comes to the rescue just in time to prevent the boy from being pulled under the water. As he leads him away, the boy says, 'He killed my coon.' 'Never mind,' says his father, 'we'll get him', and he points in the direction of the escaped alligator.

All this while, the oil-crew have been drilling deeper and deeper. In their launch Latour and the boy go by. The boy displays the alligator's hide. 'The boy here got him,' calls the father. 'All by himself, too.' Then one day the boy, who is quite at home now aboard this machine which once terrified him, is out on the derrick fishing. The boiler-man grins at him as the boy spits on his bait and throws the hook into the water. Out on the marshes, Latour is setting his traps.

Tom Smith, the driller, has been telling the boy stories of the mishaps that sometimes occur with oil-drilling. To the boy this is all magic: everything about the whole huge device is magic. But he knows what really makes the trouble at the bottom of the deep hole – it is the werewolves. The boy is still fishing from the derrick and the boiler-man still watching him. Suddenly the boy looks up. The boiler-man looks up too. He begins to run. Other men run. Is it possible? It's happening here. A blow-up. The boy flies for his life.

Newspaper headlines tell of the wildcat blow-out.

The derrick is now lying idle, with the crew standing by waiting to hear whether or not it is going to be abandoned. The boy is wandering about on the slippery derrick. He's very sad. His father calls out to him from the bank to come along home and goes off himself. But the boy creeps down on to the deserted floor of the derrick. He walks slowly across to the abandoned bore-hole down which they were drilling. He looks round to see that he is not being watched. Then he takes out his little bag of salt and lets it stream down into the bore-hole. Then he puts his hand into his shirt-front and takes out the 'something' we have been wondering about for a long time. It is a live frog – his extra protection against the werewolves. For one moment he thinks he will drop this precious charm down the bore-hole as well. But he can't bring himself to do it, and he puts the tiny creature back into his shirt. He starts to go away when another thought strikes him. He takes a furtive glance round and then, for good measure, spits down the hole.

The boy now goes down to the deck where the idle crew are hanging around. The boiler-man sees him. 'Well, look who's here! What have you been up to? Lost your salt? Have those things been after you again?' The boy is hurt by the way they laugh at him, particularly his friend Tom. In all his life he had never felt so hurt. The men joke, saying that they could use some of that magic salt of his for the well. Tom snaps his fingers. 'I've got it! Why don't we get him to do what he did to his bait?' The boy shyly says, 'I did.' They laugh raucously and the boy, deeply hurt, goes away.

The next day, the boy is at home in the cabin, peeling potatoes for his mother. His father is making ready some traps. The boy is sad. The derrick will be going away any time now. Suddenly, they all hear the sound. It's the derrick pump working again. The boy is overjoyed. He knew all along that his magic would work. Now at last the derrick-crew will strike oil. It will come gushing up. And it does.

This means, of course, that the Latour family can now afford some more much-needed things for their home. Jean Latour returns from town to the cabin with stocks of food and some presents. A shining new boiling-pan for the mother. The boy asks if there is anything for him? His father says that he's been too naughty to have a present and starts unwrapping a parcel which he says is a new pump. But it turns out to be a new rifle – the one thing the boy has been longing for. He goes outside on the porch and sits down to examine it. While he is sitting there, he hears a familiar sound. It's the cry of Jo-Jo, the coon. He was not killed by the alligator after all. He has been wandering about in the forest and the swamp but has now found his way home.

The oil-derrick, this fabulous structure which once amazed the boy so much, has now done its work. The tugs are towing it away down the lagoon. It moves slowly, imperiously, out of sight. Taking his coon with him, the boy goes to wave good-bye to his friends. The bore has been capped with a 'Christmas tree'. The boy clambers up on to it, with his coon in his arms. He calls out and waves to Tom Smith for the last time. He spits into the water to remind the oil-men that it was *his* magic, not theirs which brought the oil.

Appendix 6

THE FILMS OF ROBERT J. FLAHERTY

Note: Screen-credits which appear on a film can often be a matter of company policy and/or contractual obligation. The following credits are not in every case those which appeared on the screen but rather a selection made by the authors after careful and considered investigation.

NANOOK OF THE NORTH (1920–21)

Produced for: Revillon Frères, New York.
Script, Direction and Photography: Robert J. Flaherty.
Assistant-Editor: Charles Gelb.
Titles written by: Carl Stearns Clancy and Robert J. Flaherty.
Distribution: Pathé (U.S.A.); Jury (United Kingdom).
Length: 5 reels (approx. 70 mins.). 5,036 feet.

New York premiere: 11th June, 1922. London premiere: early September, 1922.

The Museum of Modern Art Film Library, New York, holds a duplicate negative, a fine-grain master-print, 2 35-mm. prints and 2 16-mm. prints.

The National Film Archive, London, holds 1 35 mm. print for preservation, 1 35-mm. print and 1 16-mm. print for circulation.

Re-issued in July, 1947, in a sound-film version.
Narration written by: Ralph Schoolman.
Spoken by: Berry Kroger.

Music by: Rudolph Schramm.
Produced from the original by: Herbert Edwards.
Distribution: United Artists.
Length: 50 mins. 4,500 feet.

Note: Until 1st November, 1960, distribution was controlled by Northern Productions Inc., New York, under an agreement made by Revillon Frères, but by virtue of the latter company having assigned to the Robert Flaherty Foundation in 1956 its controlling interest in the film, control of distribution passed to the Foundation on the expiration of the agreement with Northern Productions. The Foundation is free to distribute the original silent version.[1]

MOANA (A Romance of the Golden Age) (1923–5)
Production: Famous-Players-Lasky, U.S.A.
Script, Direction and Photography: Robert J. Flaherty and Frances Hubbard Flaherty.
Production Assistant: David Flaherty.
Technical Assistant: Lancelot H. Clark.
Titles written by: Robert J. Flaherty and Julian Johnson.
Distribution: Paramount Pictures Corporation.
Length: 7 reels (approx. 90 mins.). 6,055 feet.
with: Ta'avale, Fa'angase, Tu'ungaita, *et al.*

New York premiere: 7th February, 1926. London premiere: late May, 1926.

Note: Paramount still holds the copyright.
The Museum of Modern Art Film Library, New York, holds a duplicate negative, a fine-grain master-print, 2 35-mm. prints and 5 16-mm. prints for distribution non-theatrically under certain conditions to non-paying audiences.
The National Film Archive, London, holds 1 35 mm. print for preservation and 1 35-mm. print for circulation.

THE POTTERY-MAKER (1925)
Produced for: the Metropolitan Museum of Art, New York (Arts and Crafts Department).
Script, Direction and Photography: Robert J. Flaherty.
Length: 1 reel (approx. 14 mins.).

[1] The Robert J. Flaherty Foundation has now been superseded by International Film Seminars Inc.

Note: Copyright is held by the Metropolitan Museum of Art.
The Museum of Modern Art Film Library, New York, holds 2 negatives (1 of cuts) and 6 35-mm. prints (3 of cuts).

THE TWENTY-FOUR DOLLAR ISLAND (1926–7)

Production: Pictorial Clubs, New York.
Script, Direction and Photography: Robert J. Flaherty.
Length: 2 reels (approx. 20 mins.).

A 1-reel copy, 16 mm., was held by the Museum of Modern Art Film Library, New York, up till 10th February, 1959, when it was returned by request to its owner, Mr. Joseph Cornell.

INDUSTRIAL BRITAIN (1931)

Production: Empire Marketing Board Film Unit, London.
Produced by: John Grierson.
Direction of Photography: Robert J. Flaherty.
Additional Direction: John Grierson, Basil Wright, Arthur Elton.
Production Manager: J. P. R. Golightly.
Assistant: John Taylor.
Editing: John Grierson and Edgar Anstey.
Narration spoken by: Donald Calthrop.
Distribution: Gaumont-British Distributors Ltd.
Length: 2 reels (approx. 21½ mins.). 1,913 feet.

First British screening, November, 1933, as first of 'Imperial Six' Series.

Note: Copyright, original negative and all distribution rights held by the Central Office of Information on behalf of Her Majesty's Government.
The National Film Archive, London, holds 1 35-mm. fine-grain print for preservation and 2 35-mm. prints for circulation.
The Museum of Modern Art Film Library, New York, holds 1 35-mm. print and 1 16-mm. print on loan from British Information Services.

MAN OF ARAN (1932–4)

Production: Gainsborough Pictures Ltd. (associate of the Gaumont-British Picture Corporation Ltd.), London.
Script, Direction and Photography: Robert J. Flaherty in association with Frances Hubbard Flaherty.
Assistant and Additional Photography: David Flaherty.
Laboratory Work and Additional Photography: John Taylor.

Editor: John Goldman.
Music: John Greenwood.
Distribution: Gaumont-British Distributors Ltd.
Length: 7 reels (approx. 76 mins.). 6,832 feet.
with: Tiger King, Maggie Dirrane, Mikeleen Dillane.

London premiere: 25th April, 1934. New York premiere: 18th October, 1934.

Note: The copyright is held by the J. Arthur Rank Organization. The Robert Flaherty Foundation has acquired by purchase the 16-mm. distribution rights in the U.S.A. only until 1st January, 1963.
The National Film Archive, London, holds 1 35-mm. preservation print.
The Museum of Modern Art Film Library, New York, holds 2 35-mm. prints for circulation.

ELEPHANT BOY (1935–7)

Production: London Film Productions Ltd, England.
Producer: Alexander Korda.
Screenplay: John Collier, based on Kipling's *Toomai of the Elephants.*
Screenplay Collaboration: Akos Tolnay and Marcia de Silva.
Location Direction: Robert J. Flaherty.
Studio Direction: Zoltan Korda.
Assistant Director: David Flaherty.
Photography: Osmond H. Borradaile.
Production Manager: Teddy Baird.
Sound Recording: W. S. Bland, H. G. Cape.
Editor: Charles Crichton.
Distribution: United Artists Corporation.
Length: 8 reels (approx. 81 mins.). 7,300 feet.
with: Sabu, Walter Hudd, Alan Jeayes, Wilfred Hyde-White.

London premiere: 7th April, 1937. New York premiere: 5th April, 1937.

Note: Copyright and original negative held by London Film Productions, but has been sold for television in the United Kingdom and abroad.
The National Film Archive, London, holds 1 35-mm. preservation print.
The Museum of Modern Art Film Library, New York, holds 1 35-mm. print for circulation.

THE LAND (1939–42)

Produced for: The Agricultural Adjustment Administration of the United States Department of Agriculture.
Script, Direction and Photography: Robert J. Flaherty.
Additional Photography: Irving Lerner, Floyd Crosby.
Production Manager: Douglas Baker.
Editor: Helen van Dongen.
Music: Richard Arnell.
Played by: The National Youth Administration Symphony under the direction of Fritz Mahler.
Narration written by: Russell Lord and Robert J. Flaherty.
spoken by: Robert J. Flaherty.
Distribution: Non-theatrical only (see below).
Length: 4 reels (approx. 43 mins.). 3,900 feet.

First shown at the Museum of Modern Art, New York, to a private audience, April, 1942.
The Museum of Modern Art Film Library holds the original negative on behalf of the U.S. Department of Agriculture, 2 35-mm. prints and 1 16-mm. print for limited circulation. A copy is also held by the Robert Flaherty Foundation for limited circulation. The film was withdrawn from all other circulation in 1944.

LOUISIANA STORY (1946–8)

Produced for: The Standard Oil Company of New Jersey, U.S.A.
Story: Frances and Robert J. Flaherty.
Produced and Directed by: Robert J. Flaherty.
Associate-Producers: Richard Leacock, Helen van Dongen.
Photography: Richard Leacock.
Editor: Helen van Dongen.
Editorial Assistant: Ralph Rosenblum.
Music: Virgil Thomson.
Technical Assistant for Music: Harry Brant.
Music played by: Members of the Philadelphia Orchestra, under the direction of Eugene Ormandy.
Sound Recording: Benjamin Doniger.
Sound Assistant: Leonard Stark.
Music Recording: Bob Fine.
Re-recordist: Dick Vorisek.
Distribution: Lopert Films (U.S.A.). British Lion Films Corp. (United Kingdom).

Length: 7 reels (approx. 77 mins.), 7,000 feet.[1]
with: Joseph Boudreaux, Lionel LeBlanc, Frank Hardy.

British premiere: Edinburgh Film Festival, 22nd August, 1948.
New York premiere: September, 1948.
The Museum of Modern Art Film Library, New York, holds 2 35-mm. prints.
The National Film Archive, London, holds 1 35-mm. print for preservation and 1 35-mm. print for circulation.
Note: The copyright is held by the stockholders of Robert Flaherty Productions Inc., a liquidated corporation, of which Mrs. Frances Flaherty is trustee. Mrs. Flaherty and David Flaherty hold the controlling interest.

The above filmography has been approved by the Robert Flaherty Foundation.

SOME BOOKS CONSULTED

The World of Robert Flaherty, Richard Griffith (Duell, Sloan & Pearce, 1953).
My Eskimo Friends, Robert J. Flaherty (Doubleday, 1924).
On Documentary, John Grierson, ed. by H. Forsyth Hardy (Harcourt, Brace, 1947).
The Captain's Chair, Robert J. Flaherty (Scribner, 1938).
White Master, Robert J. Flaherty (Routledge, 1939).
Eskimo, Edmund Carpenter (U. of Toronto Press and Oxford, 1959).
Samoa under the Sailing Gods, Newton A. Rowe (Putnam, 1930).
Voyage to the Amorous Islands, Newton A. Rowe (Essential Books, 1956).
White Shadows in the South Seas, Frederick O'Brien (Grosset & Dunlap, 1928).
The Vagrant Viking, Peter Freuchen (Julian Messner, 1953).
The Aran Islands, J. M. Synge (Luce, 1911).
Man of Aran, Pat Mullen (E. P. Dutton, 1935).
Elephant Dance, Frances H. Flaherty (Scribner, 1937).
Forever the Land, Russell Lord (Harper, 1950).
History of the British Film, Vol. II, Rachel Low (Allen & Unwin, 1949).

[1] For note on the divergent lengths of the British and American versions, see p. 224.

Life against Death, Norman O. Brown (Wesleyan University Press, 1959).

and:

The Film Till Now, Paul Rotha (Funk & Wagnalls, 1950; Vision, 1960).

Documentary Film, Paul Rotha, Richard Griffith and Sinclair Road (Faber & Faber, London, 1952 edition).

also:

Geographical Review (American Geographical Society, New York, 1918).

among journals, etc., which have been of value:

British: *Sight and Sound*, *Films and Filming*, *World Film News* (defunct), *Close Up* (defunct), *Cinema Quarterly* (defunct), *Sequence* (defunct).

North American: *Film News*, *Motion Picture Herald*, *New York Times*, *New Movies*, *Canadian Newsreel*, *Variety*.

Note: In 1934, the *Sunday Referee* (defunct), London, published in seven parts (29th July–9th September) what it called an autobiography of Robert Flaherty but it was in the main reminiscences of the years in the North which appeared again in his two novels. The series was geared to the current publicity for *Man of Aran*: Isidore Ostrer, who headed the Gaumont-British Film Corporation, also owned the *Sunday Referee*.

ACKNOWLEDGEMENTS

Note: The following list was drawn up in January, 1960, when the first MS was completed. Some of the persons and sources named may not, however, have found appropriate inclusion in Arthur Calder-Marshall's preceding text. We have retained them nevertheless because of the help so kindly given at the time.

P.R. B.W.

First thanks, of course, go to Mrs. Frances Flaherty and Mr. David Flaherty for their invaluable help in supplying information and checking the original MS of this book, as well as their giving permission to quote so generously from their published works and those by Flaherty himself.

From the first interview at Black Mountain Farm, Brattleboro, in August, 1957, up till the last moment, David Flaherty has been to endless trouble to assist us which, in view of his many other commitments, is greatly appreciated. We are also much indebted to the Robert Flaherty Foundation[1] for making so much material available in the way of documents, copyrights, photographs, etc.

All the way through the advice, anecdotes and information supplied by Dr. John Grierson have been of immense value. We thank him for allowing us to reproduce some of his published work. Of equal help all through the preparation of our book, both in long first-hand talks and in correspondence, has been Richard Griffith, Curator of the Museum of Modern Art Film Library, whose own book *The World of Robert Flaherty* we have plundered so deeply. We thank him for his permission for so doing.

Both Griffith and Grierson knew Flaherty intimately and we are indebted to the fact that they have read our original MS and set their seal of approval on it. Without it, we should have been unhappy.

We are also grateful to many others who knew Flaherty as a friend or who worked with him, which was often the same thing. Some of them sent us ample notes or appreciations specially written for the purpose and most of those listed now have read our original MS either in part or in whole:

> Richard Arnell, Osmond H. Borradaile, J. N. G. Davidson, Helen Durant (van Dongen), J. P. R. Golightly, Irving Lerner, John Monck (Goldman), Newton A. Rowe and John Taylor.

Of these, we specially acknowledge our debt to Helen van Dongen for putting at our disposal her production-diary kept during the making of *Louisiana Story* and for various unpublished notes she made for a book at the time she worked on *The Land*. Mr. John Monck, who as John Goldman edited *Man of Aran*, sent us an admirable series of specially-written notes of which unfortunately there has been only space for a short extract.

Many others have supplied us with memories and anecdotes, either in personal talks or by letter, of this remarkable artist who is the subject of this biography. They are:

> Edgar Anstey, Teddy Baird, Sir Michael Balcon, Cedric Belfrage, Hans Beller, Sir David Cunnynghame, T. H. Curtis, Ernestine Evans, Hugh Findlay, H. Forsyth Hardy, Winifred Holmes, the Earl of Huntingdon, Augustus John, Denis Johnston, Boris

[1] Now called International Film Seminars Inc.

Kaufman, Richard Leacock, Albert Lewin, Margery Lockett, Russell Lord, Evelyn Lyon-Fellowes, E. Hayter Preston, Adi K. Sett, Olwen Vaughan, Harry Watt and Herman G. Weinberg.

Others who have helped in many smaller ways include:

Ralph Bond, Hopie Burnup, Prof. Edmund Carpenter, D. R. C. Coats, John Collier, Alicia Coulter, Campbell Dixon, Edward M. Foote, Willi Haas, Frank Horrabin, R. V. H. Keating, Arthur Knight, Lord Killanin, C. A. Lejeune, Carl Lochnan, Jonas Mekas, Hans Nieter, 'Pem', W. R. Rodgers, Col. H. A. Ruttan, David Schrire and J. R. F. Thompson.

We also acknowledge the following:

Miss Eileen Molony and Mr. Michael Bell for the loan of B.B.C. scripts and telediphone recordings of talks made by Mr. and Mrs. Flaherty in London.

Mr. Oliver Lawson Dick for scripts and tape-recordings of the B.B.C. programme *Portrait of Robert Flaherty*, produced by W. R. Rodgers on 2nd September, 1952.

Sir Arthur Elton for access to an unpublished MS left to him by the late Sir Stephen Tallents relating to the history of the Empire Marketing Board Film Unit.

Mr. W. E. Greening for permitting us to read parts of his unpublished MS of the life of Sir William McKenzie.

Among various organizations and the like to which we are indebted for their co-operation are:

The Museum of Modern Art Film Library, New York, and the National Film Archive, London, for their screenings of the Flaherty films; the British Film Institute for the help of its Information Department; and the National Board of Review of Motion Pictures, New York, the Royal Geographic Society, London; and the Central Office of Information, London.

We make acknowledgement to the following publishers, other than those mentioned above, for permission to quote from their books:

My Eskimo Friends (Heinemann), *Samoa Under the Sailing Gods* (Putnam), *White Shadows in the South Seas* (T. Werner Laurie), *Mourning Became Mrs. Spendlove* (Creative Age Press), *Footnotes to the Film* (Lovat Dickson), *Grierson on Documentary* (Collins), *Elephant Boy* and *Man of Aran* (Faber & Faber), *Eskimo* (Toronto

University Press), *Best Moving Pictures of 1922–23* (Small, Maynard), *Forever the Land* (Harper & Brothers), *Cinema* (Pelican).

Among newspapers and journals from which we have quoted we are obliged to:

The Guardian, *The Observer*, *The Spectator*, *The New Yorker*, *Sight and Sound*, *National Board of Review Journal*, *World Film News*, *Close Up*, *Sequence* and *Cinema Quarterly*.

For photographs, we thank the following:

Mrs. Frances Flaherty, Wolfgang Suschitzky, Henri Cartier-Bresson, Prof. Edmund Carpenter, Arnold Eagle, John Monck, Richard Avedon, Hayter Preston, Osmond H. Borradaile, and the Standard Oil Co. (N.J.), Cosmo-Siteo Co., the National Film Archive, London, the Royal Ontario Museum, and especially the Museum of Modern Art Film Library for making available to us for selection such a magnificent number of prints.

We also remember with gratitude the generous help given in the United States during the summer of 1957 in the early days of research by the late Mrs. Irma Bernay.

Finally we thank those of Flaherty's old friends in England who helped make possible the completion of the original MS and its many weeks of revision in 1959.

Addendum by Arthur Calder-Marshall:

Apart from sundry of those mentioned above, especially Edgar Anstey, Michael Bell, Oliver Lawson Dick, John Grierson, Newton Rowe, and John Taylor, I would like to record my thanks to Clare Lawson Dick, Lady Elton and Oliver Vaughan. March, 1963.

INDEX

Note: The Appendices are not included.